CW00551770

Berengaria:
In Search of Richard the Lionheart's Queen

Berengaria

In Search of
Richard the Lionheart's
Queen

Ann Trindade

FOUR COURTS PRESS

Set in 9.5 on 13 point Sabon
with Delphin One display headings
by Sheila Stephenson
and published by
FOUR COURTS PRESS LTD
Fumbally Lane, Dublin 8, Ireland
e-mail: info@four-courts-press.ie
and in North America by
FOUR COURTS PRESS
c/o ISBS, 5804 N.E. Hassalo Street, Portland, OR 97213.

© Ann Trindade 1999

A catalogue record for this title
is available from the British Library.

ISBN 1-85182-434-0

All rights reserved. No part of this publication may be
reproduced, stored in or introduced into a retrieval system,
or transmitted, in any form or by any means (electronic,
mechanical, photocopying, recording or otherwise),
without the prior written permission of the copyright owner.

ACKNOWLEDGMENT
Publication of this work was assisted
by a special grant from
the University of Melbourne.

Printed in Great Britain
by MPG Books Ltd, Bodmin, Cornwall

Contents

9
PREFACE

13
Chapter One
WHY BERENGARIA?

29
Chapter Two
DAUGHTER

57
Chapter Three
BRIDE

107
Chapter Four
QUEEN

137
Chapter Five
WIDOW

183
Chapter Six
SHALL THESE STONES SPEAK?

199
NOTES

222
BIBLIOGRAPHY

234
INDEX

En soledad vivía
y en soledad ha puesto ya su nido,
y en soledad la guía
a solas su querido,
también en soledad de amor herido.

San Juan de la Cruz

Preface

The abbey of Fontevraud lies in a green valley some fifteen minutes by road from the old town of Saumur in western France. The tourist trade is brisk, particularly in spring and summer, and a large part of it comes from across the Channel. The English, the locals tell you knowledgeably, come to see 'les gisants des Plantagenêts', because, as you know, the English were here once, a long time ago! The *gisants,* or reclining effigies, lie side by side in the restored chapter house. The abbey itself, carefully restored and immaculately maintained, like most public monuments in France, has a long and extremely colourful history, from its foundation in 1101 by Robert d'Arbrissel, the eccentric Breton preacher, to its temporary (mis)use as a military prison in the earlier part of the twentieth century. For the English-speaking tourist with even a fleeting sense of history, its most important associations are with the Angevin monarchs of the late twelfth century and their families, many of whom spent long periods of residence here, sought refuge here in old age and chose the abbey for their final resting place.

The *gisants* are four in number: Henry II, king of England from 1154 to 1189, Eleanor of Aquitaine, his wife, Richard the Lionheart, the most famous of their sons, and Isabelle of Angoulême, second wife of their youngest son, John 'Lackland', who was ultimately to surrender most of his father's possessions in this part of France to the hated Philip Augustus in an ignominious prelude to the loss of Normandy itself.

Despite the imposing dimensions and solid construction of the restored abbey and its outbuildings, the interior is both cool and light, without that sinister and gloomy clutter characteristic of so many ancient monuments. Sunlight streams through upper windows onto the mellow stonework and throws the effigies into sharp relief. Conventional though such sculptures may be, it takes only a very small exercise of the imagination to clothe the cold features with living flesh, with the help of the physical descriptions and general impressions left by contemporary chroniclers. Here is Henry, stocky, muscular, red-faced, choleric and impulsive; Eleanor, universally acknowledged even in middle age as an outstanding beauty, with the close-set eyes and sharp features admired by medieval poets. But it is on Richard that the eye lingers longest: taller than his father, finer of features, with his red-gold hair, flinty blue eyes and thin-lipped mouth. Lion Heart: well-named, a legend in his own time and still, in ours, surrounded by an aura of glamour and romance which neither the solemn strictures of nineteenth-century historians nor any amount of fashionable revisionism can ever quite dispel. Here lies one of England's most famous kings, immortalised on stage and screen as an English hero, who spent no more than six months in total as king on English soil, spoke no English and would cheerfully have sold the lot to finance his escapades if someone had made him the right offer!

About forty kilometres north of Fontevraud, on the outskirts of Le Mans, surrounded by copses of lime, poplar and beech, stands the abbey of l'Epau, or to give it its full name, Notre Dame de la Piété Dieu de l'Epau, the last of the Cistercian foundations in the medieval diocese of Maine. Like Fontevraud, it has been painstakingly restored and maintained since its conversion from private ownership to the status of a national monument. Smaller and more homely than Fontevraud, it attracts few foreign tourists, though local people – couples, families, pensioners – come at weekends or on holidays to stroll in the deer park or along the leafy banks of the swift-moving Huisne. On my last visit a bridal party had driven out to be photographed in the abbey grounds: it seemed a pleasantly appropriate use for a building which still has a local feel to it and which belongs to the people of Le Mans as much as it did at the time of its foundation in 1230. The chapter house, adjacent to the chapel, conveys a similar impression of intimacy, almost of domesticity. Its bleached stone floor is bare except for a single handsome tomb with a recumbent effigy upon it. The effigy is that of a woman, a crowned queen, with strong solemn features and loose flowing hair, like a bride. She holds on her breast a book with her own image in relief on its cover, while her feet rest on a watchful lion and beneath him, a small hound, the traditional emblem of faithfulness and loyalty. An inscription on the side of the tomb reads:

> This mausoleum dedicated to Berengaria, most serene Queen of the English and foundress of this monastery, was restored and relocated in this most solemn place and in it were placed the bones which were found in the ancient grave AD 27 May 1672. It was taken from the abbey of Pietas Dei and replaced in the Cathedral Church 2nd December 1821.

It is Richard's queen who lies here in the abbey she founded barely a year before her death. Although this identification was initially disputed by a few local historians, most scholars believe that the remains of a woman discovered in 1960 and brought to rest in this spot are those of the queen. Separated from her famous husband in death as she was for most of her life, Berengaria remains a mystery, the most elusive of England's queens. A seventeenth-century description of the seal originally attached to the foundation charter of the abbey and now lost, speaks of a lady in a long cloak, holding in one hand a *fleur de lis* and, in the other, a dove. On the reverse side, she is holding a flower and a cross surmounted by a dove and *fleur de lis*.

These images, from both the tomb and the seal, suggest seclusion, piety, passivity, fidelity, endurance – qualities traditionally associated with women. They provide an immediate contrast with the attributes ascribed to Richard: mobility, physical strength, courage, ferocity, bravado and excess. In Richard's case, historians have succeeded in looking beyond the stereotypes, and reexamining the testimony of past sources, exposing editorial bias and the distorting effect of literary convention. From their research has emerged a much more complex picture of Richard's career and a better appreciation of his context and significance.

It is more difficult to do the same for Berengaria. None the less, it is the aim of this study to attempt this: to look again at the texts and the context, to acknowledge the effect of neglect, prejudice and gender bias in an attempt to come closer to the real person. We shall see her as an individual woman in the context of a culture represented to us today as dominated by chivalric and courtly influences and as a widowed queen at a crucial turning point in the long struggle between England and France.

I should like to acknowledge with gratitude the assistance of a number of institutions, friends and colleagues in the United Kingdom, Ireland, France, Spain and Australia. As this book is intended not only for medievalists but for the general interested reader, I have tried to keep the documentation to a minimum and to confine it where possible to works available in English. This has not, unfortunately, been possible in the case of many of the older sources, which have not been translated into English, and where the most appropriate secondary sources are in Spanish or French. All quotations have been given in English, however, and the translations, unless acknowledged, are my own.

CHAPTER ONE

Why Berengaria?

Medieval studies have a long and distinguished history in Europe and North America, but in more recent times a welcome and somewhat overdue interest in women's history has contributed considerably to our knowledge of an important aspect of medieval life. As a result, not only has the institution of queenship received closer attention, but the lives of individual queens have been studied in some detail. Many of these women, whether queens in their own right or queens consort, are known to us from a variety of substantial and reliable sources.[1]

Berengaria is a notable exception. She has been described as 'shadowy', 'enigmatic', '*un peu fade*' (rather colourless) and 'moving silently in the background of events'. These comments are based in part on the sparse details available in the contemporary chronicles where the accounts of the policies, achievements, character and even physical appearance of her famous husband are, by contrast, extensive and full of interest. Berengaria only engages the attention of these chroniclers for a brief spell at the time of her marriage, in rather unusual circumstances, to Richard, but they have little to say about her in any other context, and the additional evidence concerning her life both before and after marriage – by far the greater part of her sixty-odd years – has to be quarried from rather unyielding sources. Few of these are in continuous narrative form, but comprise a variety of documents of an administrative, legal or ecclesiastical nature. Berengaria might well be seen as an unpromising subject for a conventional biography.

If the Church historians and chroniclers of the twelfth and thirteenth centuries have little to say about Berengaria, nineteenth- and twentieth-century historians, both academic and popular, have interpreted the existing material in ways which are almost entirely dismissive. Anthony Bridge[2] pronounces her, on the evidence, to be 'dull, plain and worthy', while M. Meade[3] in her eulogistic portrait of Eleanor of Aquitaine, describes her as 'unlike Eleanor ... a passive female who allowed herself to be buffeted around by the winds of circumstance and never raise a finger on her own behalf', a surprising comment which stands at odds with the historical record or suggests a licence more appropriate to a popular novelist than to a serious historian. But no one has, as yet, bothered to correct this view.

While Richard and his immediate family have provided inspiration for a good many historical novels, the novelists have, for the most part, neglected Berengaria in favour of the more colourful members of the 'devil's brood': where she does appear in romantic fiction, it is often as a marginal figure, such as the frivolous, immature consort of Sir Walter Scott's novels or the unresponsive spouse, cold, unloved and unloving, of Maurice Hewlett's early twentieth-century novel, *The Life and Death of Richard Yea and Nay*.[4] For Hewlett, as for other more recent writers, Berengaria's supposed inadequacies provide a convenient starting point for Richard's extra-marital activities. Three best-selling women writers of the recent past have painted a more sympathetic portrait: in Margaret Campbell Barnes' novel *Like Us They Lived*, Richard is a Mr Rochester figure, brutal, impulsive and tormented, who is redeemed by the enduring love of Berengaria, while in Nora Lofts' *The Lute Player*, it is Richard's homosexual love for Blondel with which the faithful wife must compete. Jean Plaidy, in *The Heart of the Lion*, suggests a similar conflict.

What is acceptable in a work of fiction is less admissible in writing which aspires to some kind of historical accuracy. Even the inspired conjecture to which all historians occasionally resort, needs to be supported at least by circumstantial evidence. Some of the writers cited above have not bothered to offer any evidence in support of their generalisations. They have been content to settle for the traditional stereotyping of women which has remained remarkably constant over the centuries. Thus we have, across the spectrum of 'history' and 'fiction', Berengaria as the beautiful virgin bride, the neglected wife, the helpless widow and, in more misogynistic mode, the 'barren' woman, the frigid, unattractive kill-joy and the pathetic victim who is largely to blame for her own misfortunes.

Berengaria's case is by no means unique. It merely highlights a wider pattern, to which feminist historians have successfully drawn attention in a range of important studies over the last thirty years or so: the 'writing out' of women in representations of the past. 'Winners', says Joel Rosenthal in a lively introduction to a recent collection of essays entitled *Medieval Women and the Sources of Medieval History*,[5] 'write history'. And where there are winners, there are also, unfortunately, losers. Who are the losers here? We may give a variety of answers to this question but Rosenthal goes on to ask another question, and to suggest an answer: 'What material was ignored, buried and falsified in the sources that the winners were so careful to edit in their own favour and to whom did it belong? One response to this alternative question, today, is women.'

There are obvious problems inherent in this approach. In some cases the process of 'writing out' has been all too successful and the activities of women in particular cultures, together with those of religious and ethnic minorities and other marginalised groups, are no longer retrievable. No one thought to ask a shepherd in Wales or a rush-cutter on Sedgemoor what they were doing when King Harold was shot in the eye at Hastings, and it is unlikely that the answer would have been particularly illuminating. Nor would it be other than naive to suggest that there was ever an abundance of authentic, comprehensive, objective, bias-free sources which some benighted male conspiracy contrived in each successive generation to doctor and distort. But everyone is now aware of the problem.

In other cases, fortunately, the long and laborious process of writing women back in again has achieved real gains, and the women students who outnumber their male counterparts in Arts faculties and Humanities departments the world over need no longer look in vain for their reflection in the looking glass of history. It would be unfair, too, to deny the contribution of earlier scholars, men and women, with no special theoretical orientation, whose studies of individual women's lives and female social groups have helped to lay the foundations of the discipline on which a new generation, more eclectic in its use of both technology and theory but less well-grounded in such traditional skills as palaeography, codicology and philology, has been able to build.

These concessions made, due recognition must be given to the central achievements of the women's history movement, which has been able to focus much more explicitly on the question of cultural bias, to challenge established concepts of the past and to expose the fragility of many perspectives and positions which had hitherto been regarded as non-negotiable. As a result of these endeavours, 'History', as Judith Anderson and Bonnie Zinsser observe, 'can never be the same again.'[6]

The first of such traditional positions to be challenged was the convention whereby women were defined in historical writing primarily in terms of their gender, that is, in contradistinction to men. Perhaps this was understandable: women have always been the 'other'. There is no documented culture, past or present, in which women have not been defined in terms of their gender, a cultural construct based on the assumption that biology is destiny. It is inevitable then that, in each society or culture, the custodians of accepted values should have followed the same pattern in their attempts to record, codify and prescribe.

From earliest recorded times women have had to come to terms with this and in many cases to accept their own marginalisation. A few have succeeded in turning this to their own advantage; far more have learned to 'master the strategies of those in subordinate positions: pleasing, manipulating, enduring, surviving'. The textual records of the high Middle Ages (the so-called 'courtly' age), both fiction and non-fiction, afford numerous examples of women who 'chose' one or other of these strategies. Each of them, while offering a solution for the individual, is isolating and divisive. The importance of women as a group is downplayed and their shared concerns denied. Women's participation in the written record becomes incidental, anecdotal, or they are reduced to an anonymous collectivity.

Even the mystic or devotional literature which reflects a potentially more liberating theology than the writings of some of the

early Church fathers and their medieval exegetes, tends to concep-
tualise male and female spirituality differently.[7] Physical virginity is
far less prominent in the counsels offered to men generally and male
religious in particular. Much of the literature addressed to female
religious, on the other hand, treats virginity as a mystical, almost a
magical property, and the language used in such texts is rich in nuptial imagery, drawing on the Song of Songs and other biblical texts
and representing Christ as the Bridegroom and the individual religious as the *Sponsa* or Bride. While much of this imagery is inherited from the Hebrew scriptures, Judaism never made the leap from
the poetic – and prophetic – theme of Israel as God's Chosen Bride
to the obsessive Christian concern with physical virginity, which
accorded to celibacy a higher degree of merit than to a fruitful and
faithful conjugality, the norm in Judaism.[8]

Misogynistic and demeaning representations of women are as
common in pagan antiquity as they are in Judaeo-Christian cultures
where their reappearance in the writings of medieval churchmen
merely adds a spurious gloss of pseudo-theological authority to the
old prejudices and fears. In other ways the medieval Church did
attempt to alleviate the worst excesses of secular society, particularly its marriage practices. Duby's well-known theory of the 'two
models' – the secular and the ecclesiastical – has been seen at times
as over-simplistic but it has served a useful purpose in highlighting
the development of marriage by consent, marital affection and the
indissolubility of the sacrament in a milieu in which women had,
for several centuries, been traded as commodities, repudiated and
abandoned at will. Although some scholars have seen this as limit-
ing women's opportunities for advancement, it is the institution of
agnatic lineage and primogeniture, rather than the doctrine of indissolubility itself, which marginalised women and made their situation more precarious, as David Herlihy has frequently argued.[9]

For a few aristocratic women, entry into the religious life and
particularly a career as an abbess or prioress could offer a kind of
independence difficult if not impossible to achieve without property
and/or marriage. Women could, and some did, aspire to positions
of intellectual and spiritual eminence by this path, though not
always without incurring hostility and suspicion.

A few theologians could even write of the motherhood of God and the strain of mysticism later embodied in the incandescent verses of St John of the Cross, would even lift the notion of the individual soul as bride of Christ onto a plane which transcends the limitation of gender, in a manner closer to the ambivalence of the 'cosmic' religions than to the formulaic propositions of Semitic monotheism. But this was rare: Christ himself may have said that in heaven there was neither marrying nor giving in marriage (i.e., that sexual differences would be transcended) but institutional religion could hardly have been expected to show enthusiasm for such a potentially dangerous idea and, like many of Christianity's more revolutionary tenets, it became neutralised into a pious hope for the future rather than a blueprint for the here and now.

Small wonder then that these powerful and enduring archetypes, reinforced by ecclesiastical sanction or political pragmatism, should dictate the conventions by which medieval women's lives were circumscribed. To retrieve, reassess and realign the material is doubly difficult because other biases intervene, such as nationalism or ethnocentricity. Historical overviews of Richard the Lionheart and his rival and one-time intimate, Philip Augustus of France, are an obvious instance.

Because Berengaria's role has been consistently defined by her relationship with Richard, French historians of the nineteenth and twentieth centuries were happy to exaggerate her status as victim, in order to emphasise Richard's moral turpitude.[10] For English historians, Richard's reputation as national hero has inevitably cast her in a different but equally demeaning role. These perspectives have, inevitably, influenced the reader's perception of Richard and his queen.

It is not difficult to summarise the brief accounts of Berengaria's appearances in the earliest accounts of the third crusade and the life and times of Richard the Lionheart. We first read of her on her arrival in Sicily with Richard's mother Eleanor, shortly before her marriage on 12 May 1191 at Limassol in Cyprus to the recently crowned king of England. The circumstances of the marriage negotiations are nowhere described, and historians have been left to make informed guesses as to their nature. Almost immediately after

the wedding Richard and Berengaria left Cyprus separately for
Palestine, where they spent one and a half years before returning,
separately again, Berengaria in company with her sister-in-law,
Joanna, the widowed queen of Sicily, and Richard, after a series of
adventures in disguise, falling captive to his enemies in Austria. On
the evidence of later events, it is assumed that they became
estranged in Palestine, but, whether or not this was the case, on
Richard's release and return to Normandy and Anjou, they were
not often together, partly because of Richard's frequent military
excursions. Around 1195 they were reconciled by the good offices
of an unnamed hermit and/or Hugh of Avalon, bishop of Lincoln,
who reproached the king for improper sexual conduct. Richard
died shortly after this, of a gangrenous wound incurred in the siege
of the castle of Chalus-Chabrol, leaving Berengaria childless.
Berengaria did not remarry but lived in Le Mans for thirty years
until her death in the abbey she founded on the outskirts of the
city. She is remembered as a benefactor of several other religious
congregations and institutions and was regarded as a model of
piety.

Even this bare summary provokes our curiosity and prompts as
yet unanswered questions. Was it true, as two of the earliest crusade
narratives claim, that Richard had fallen in love with Berengaria in
his youth, before coming to the throne? When and how did they
meet? What were Berengaria's experiences on the crusade? Why is
it said that Richard and his bride became estranged? What were the
sins with which Richard was reproached by churchmen, and which
had caused him to neglect his wife? Was this why they had no children? If, as some claim, Berengaria was 'barren', why did Richard
not repudiate her, as so many others did when their wives were no
longer of use to them? Was Berengaria summoned to Richard's
death-bed? What was the role of Eleanor, the possessive mother, in
all this? Why did Berengaria not remarry or return to Spain? What
happened to her during the thirty years of widowhood? And finally,
the inevitable speculation, can we ever know what sort of a person
she was?

Those who see history as essentially political, dynastic or economic will, no doubt, dismiss these questions as trivial or naive.

Once more the perspective of the 'winners' asserts itself: fighting wars, subduing territories, massacring prisoners, laying waste towns and villages, outsmarting political opponents, buying and selling, making pacts, deals and appointments to high office, these are *serious* activities. They are also activities almost exclusively controlled by men, in which women seldom figure more than marginally and intermittently. When we try to turn the picture inside out, however, and, moving these events into the background, focus more closely on some of the detail, the episodes at the margins, the significant gaps and spaces, a different picture begins to emerge.

This leads to new questions: what do we know or what can we infer about Berengaria's background, her childhood and upbringing in the medieval Spanish kingdom of Navarre, whose strategic position on the Pyrenees and control of some of the cities along the pilgrimage route to Compostella gave it a certain political importance for the Angevin and Capetian monarchies to the North?

Her date of birth is not known – not uncommon in the case of women – and the problem is compounded by the paucity of early Navarrese sources, but working back from the date of her death and the general agreement that the female remains found in the abbey of l'Epau in 1960 are hers, we may assume that she was between 21 and 26 when she married Richard in 1191. This is late by medieval standards and there are no records of earlier betrothals or discontinued marriage negotiations which might explain it. We may need to look for an alternative explanation.

What is known about Berengaria's family and the social, political and cultural context to which it belonged? How helpful are medieval Spanish sources and how have they been traditionally interpreted by Spanish historiography? The Hispanic peninsula at this turning point in the history of the reconquest was a complex cultural mosaic quite different from the lands north of the Loire or even just across the mountains: Jewish and Muslim influences formed part of this legacy, though these have been partly obscured by the bias of some nationalist Spanish historians of the nineteenth and twentieth centuries.[11]

How would such a background have influenced a woman marrying into a different culture? Berengaria, of course, was not the only Spanish princess of the time to leave her homeland and marry into a powerful dynasty of northern Europe: her sister Blanca, whose son, Thibault IV, was ultimately to succeed his uncle Sancho El Fuerte on the throne of Navarre, married Eleanor of Aquitaine's grandson Thibault III of Champagne and spent twenty years as regent during her son's infancy at a crucial time in the struggle between England and France. Blanca's life in some ways paralleled that of her sister though hers was of necessity a more public role. Something can be inferred about their common background and perhaps similar personalities, from the history of Blanca's regency. The movement was not all one-way either: Plantagenet princesses too, were married to Spanish, Sicilian and Occitanian kings, and counts, for similar dynastic reasons.

Nor was Berengaria the only crowned queen to have taken part in a crusade. Her reactions and experiences have not been recorded but, again, the extraordinary circumstances in which she found herself must arouse curiosity and interest. A royal marriage which begins on the eve of an active military campaign, in physical and climatic conditions of great rigour, in an atmosphere of heightened religious and nationalistic fervour, must be subject to considerable stress.

Were these unusual conditions and the stresses to which they would have given rise, factors in the apparent failure of Berengaria to conceive – or at least to bear – a child? The common assumption is that she was infertile – I eschew the demeaning term 'barren', which the dictionary lists as referring to land, plants and women, *in that order* – and one extreme view is that the marriage was never even consummated. Given Richard's intense involvement in military matters, his intermittent bouts of sickness and his questionable sexual preferences, we might wonder why it is assumed that the inadequacy was Berengaria's. Male infertility and impotence have always been treated with greater sensitivity than infertility in women, and the fact that Richard fathered *one* ex-nuptial child in his youth (in contrast to the numerous 'bastards' acknowledged by most of his peers)[12] is not a decisive argument.

After Richard's return from captivity in 1194, Berengaria's movements are much less well-documented than those of her husband. Some historians insist that she went, more or less voluntarily, into semi-retirement in her dower lands in Maine and Anjou. But what was the alternative? Richard was constantly on the move in the escalating conflict with his old rival Philip Augustus of France, his principal companions were no longer the Norman churchmen and administrators of his early reign but military advisors, including a large number of mercenaries, some of ill-repute.

The circumstances of Richard's death, too, have not always been clearly explained. French propaganda from the last century has represented this accidental death from a cross-bow shot as the consequence not only of Richard's well-known arrogance and risk-taking but of his greed and lust for treasure. John Gillingham[13] has demolished this and other embellishments, but the accounts are still somewhat terse and lacking in detail, giving rise to such apocryphal elaborations as that of Walter of Guiseborough, which depicts Richard on his deathbed warned by doctors not to indulge in sexual activities.[14] Accounts of the last days are coloured by partisan views of one kind or another. The absence of Berengaria from these accounts cannot be taken as evidence that she was deliberately excluded. Richard's mother Eleanor, whose devotion to her son is well-attested, played an important role in the last rites and would no doubt have wished to exercise some control over their recording. The proprieties of the day would have made it unlikely for a spouse not to have been present at some part of the obsequies, but a bitter and disappointed mother-in-law, blaming her daughter-in-law for the lack of an heir, might well have attempted, and succeeded in, removing her from the official record.

Be that as it may, Berengaria's thirty years of widowhood in Le Mans are no longer of any interest to the English chroniclers. They become instead part of the history of the city and diocese of Le Mans, a region of considerable antiquity and interest for an impressive number of local historians. Significantly, scholars working in this area have taken a very different view of Berengaria's personality and achievements from the views of Richard's biographers, ancient and modern. The great Pope Innocent III, himself one of the outstanding figures of his day, was among her best-known champions. His letters show that he found her a doughty and enthusiastic emulator of the importunate widow of the parable. What happened in the interim? How did the *mal mariée*, the passive, colourless victim become a strong decisive survivor?

In reality, those long years of widowhood reveal, on the basis of the record, a strong, courageous woman, independent, solitary, battling against difficult political and economic circumstances, with little interest in the trappings of a courtly existence, sustained by her faith in Christ and her loyalty to the See of St Peter, not afraid to assert her rights against powerful enemies, both lay and clerical. All this was with no sons to champion her cause, no father to protect her interests, with only the support of her sister and perhaps of her reclusive brother several hundred miles away whose steadily deteriorating health made him an unlikely source of assistance. Even now, the reputation of the dead husband cast a long shadow over his widow: as an innocent relict of Angevin power she was an embarrassment to the French and their local clients, including the many opportunists who had changed sides, and a potential financial liability to her brother-in-law, King John, and his successor.

Berengaria's life illustrates very clearly the constraints under which medieval women, even aristocratic ones, were obliged to live. She left the obscurity of a tranquil childhood, to enjoy a brief moment of celebrity as a bride, followed by the vicissitudes of a stressful marriage into a difficult family and a long, childless widowhood in a foreign land.

Like the majority of women in her day, Berengaria was all the time at the mercy of political events whose course was dictated by others; only at the very end of her life did she succeed in carrying to fruition a project of her own. It is perhaps less easy today than in the past to see the foundation of an abbey as an exciting achievement. It was, admittedly, a common practice among the pious nobility of both sexes to endow religious houses often with a view to retiring or dying there in old age. The regular donations of prominent men and women to religious foundations have sometimes been compared in a general way with the sponsorship of good causes by wealthy philanthropists and shrewd entrepreneurs today. There was, however, a genuinely spiritual dimension involved which still survives in part at least, today, in Catholic countries, in memorial masses for the dead and other practices. Part reparation for the past, part insurance for the future, these practices also signal official recognition that in the last resort, old wrongs can be righted, human imperfections healed and hope triumph over adversity. The foundation of the abbey of l'Epau, the culmination of a quarter of a century of generous donations to the religious foundations, makes a fitting conclusion to the story of Berengaria.

Our search for Richard's queen leads us through a variety of historical documents, chronicles, charters, records, letters, treaties and so on. Most historians also supplement their descriptions of institutions and practices with reference to contemporary fiction. Our knowledge of the training of young noblemen, knightly ideals, the conduct of tournaments, feasting and other entertainments, costume and accepted canons of beauty is often extended and enriched by the use of literary texts. The distinction between 'literary' and 'non-literary' texts is itself often hard to maintain: the chronicles of a writer like the twelfth-century Jerseyman Wace,[15] for instance, or biographies such as that of William the Marshal[16] are part history, part fiction.

Literary sources must be used with particular caution, however, because it is difficult to draw firm conclusions about women's lives and conditions from those texts which have been characterised as 'courtly' and which were produced prolifically in the latter part of the twelfth century under Anglo-Norman or Continental patronage. It is something of a paradox that this literature above all – romances, lyrics, lais – has been seen as a response to female tastes and the growing importance of women in an increasingly leisured aristocracy when its actual representation of women is so clearly shaped by a male perspective. Georges Duby has made this point on more than one occasion, in the light of his own interest in the history of marriage, sexual relationships and the condition of women in what he has labelled, the Male Middle Ages (Mâle Moyen Age).[17]

The debates over the origins of the troubadour lyric in the south, the meaning of the frequently used expression 'fin'amors' and the notion of 'courtly' love in the narrative and lyric poetry of northern France and Anglo-Norman England cannot be summarised here. Although these literary genres are clearly related, there are significant differences between the fin'amors of the troubadours and the courtly code of the north. Moreover, it is doubtful whether 'courtliness' in the literary sense ever existed as a distinct ideology.

Much of this literature is highly conventional, even artificial: few would be bold enough to claim that 'courts of love' ever existed as real institutions or that the values conveyed by the vocabulary of courtly love ever reflected contemporary social reality. Literature is always related to 'real' life, but often in ways much more complex than mere imitation. Escapism, fantasy, protest, subversion, irony are also present, even if, at times, expressed with caution and subtlety.

There may well have been a considerable body of lyric poetry composed by women in the earliest European vernacular tradition.[18] Yet the troubadour poetry which seems to have originated with William IX of Aquitaine[19] is masculinist in its orientation, despite the existence of a few poems composed by women. These women, for whom modern critics have resuscitated the old and rare term *trobairitz*,[20] expressed themselves differently from their male counterparts and in ways which merit study and attention, but the weight of their contribution has been overstressed. The poetry of the troubadours, for the most part, offers a perverse and unreal image of women, in language which is artificial and often obscure. With its *senhals* (mysterious pseudonyms) the bizarre masculine *midons* (literally 'my lord') for the lady and its camp little 'in-jokes', this poetry is frequently self-indulgent and narcissistic.

In the romances of Chrétien de Troyes and the Tristan poems, as well as in the minor verse romances, all of which were so influential in courtly societies across Europe, the theme of love and its place in the chivalric code, while probably appealing to better educated women patrons and audiences, in no way reflects the totality of women's experiences. The range of female characters presented in this narrative fiction is a narrow one: the beautiful maiden, the object of a quest, the seductive enchantress, the treacherous deceiver, however delicately and decoratively presented, are essentially a male creation. This is woman as framed by the male imagination.

Some categories of women are not represented in this literature, perhaps because they represent unwelcome realities: where do we find the repudiated spouse or the neglected fiancée? Where in courtly literature is there a heroine comparable to poor Ingeborg of Denmark, queen of France, repudiated by her husband on the day after her wedding, slandered, banished, humiliated, imprisoned and only grudgingly reinstated after long years of suffering and repeated pressure from the Pope? Occasionally a woman is depicted as suffering a slight at the hands of her lover or her spouse, but she is not usually portrayed as a heroine, and such incidents are usually minor ones. In this respect, aristocratic literature contrasts notably with popular tradition, where the folklore type known as the 'Calumniated Wife' is extremely common. Occasionally this theme does appear in 'courtly' literature, though not usually in French.[21]

Although courtly texts, and particularly the lays and romances, are useful for the details they provide about background, settings, architecture, food, clothing, hunting, archery etc., it would be unwise to see in them a comprehensive and accurate reflection of the position of women in medieval society. In essence these romances are concerned with chivalry: any serious messages they convey are directed towards men, while female audiences and readers had to content themselves with the decorative, diversionary elements. It would not have been surprising if many of them were willing to accept this, and even to toy with the amusing illusion that women like a Guinevere, an Isolt, could, at least in the escapist world of fiction, exercise such apparent power over the sex which in daily reality controlled every aspect of their lives.[22] Courtly literature, then, must be used with caution.

There are very few biographical accounts of Berengaria available in English. Agnes Strickland devoted one chapter to her in her classic *Lives of the Queens of England*,[23] and Mary Anne Everett Green mentions her in another nineteenth-century work on royal princesses.[24] These early works are not without interest but their authors did not have access to the full range of information which we have today. Much more recently, Mairin Mitchell published a book-length 'biography' entitled *Berengaria: Enigmatic Queen of England* but it is unsatisfactory for a number of reasons.[25]

Strickland's account is characterised by a Victorian sentimentality which glosses over the harsher aspects of Richard's character and leaves us with an inappropriate picture of a pair of star-crossed pre-Raphaelite lovers. Mitchell's work is superficial and makes many claims for which no evidence at all is forthcoming. It displays a credulous and uncritical attitude to secondary sources and is unlikely to dispel the 'enigma' of its title. The best account is still the short mid nineteenth-century biography by Henri Chardon,[26] which, as the author freely acknowledges, concentrates almost exclusively on Berengaria's life as a widow in Le Mans and has very little to say about her background or her relations with Richard. In recent years a brief article by Elizabeth Hallam, delivered on the occasion of a congress to celebrate the transfer of Berengaria's bones to the abbey of l'Epau,[27] supplies a useful overview but is of necessity limited in scope and relies heavily in places on recent biographies of Richard.

Richard's life and times have been more than adequately explored from the contemporary accounts of Roger of Howden, Richard of Devizes and others[28] to the prolific output of John Gillingham[29] and other modern historians.[30] As all the modern biographers cover the same ground and call upon the same range of primary sources, the reader who wishes to know something about Richard has an enviable array of choices. The figure of Richard in folklore and popular tradition including stage, screen and comic strip represents another area rich in possibilities for research.[31] Berengaria is almost entirely absent from this tradition.

There is, in the final resort, insufficient source material to provide a detailed narrative account of Berengaria's life in the conventional manner, to set against the numerous nineteenth- and twentieth-century biographies of her famous husband. But the insights afforded, first by 'histories of women' and subsequently by feminist history, have provided a key to understanding and evaluating the few precious references we do have. The first category includes many fine studies of individual women's lives and times and overviews based on these pioneering works, while feminist and gender-based studies have attempted, often with considerable success, to deconstruct the texts themselves, showing how their various contextual influences and cultural biases shape the construction of both masculinity and femininity.

In recent years too, there have been a number of useful and important studies of medieval queenship as an institution.[32] These, too, help to throw light on the meagre details afforded by the chronicles and records. Berengaria's life, her background and the choices which were made for her by others, can be compared and contrasted with those of other medieval princesses and her achievements can be assessed against these constraints.

CHAPTER TWO

Daughter

'Mountains bring us nearer to God' (*La montaña nos acerca a Dios*), says a modern Navarrese writer,[1] and the history of this northernmost Spanish province, to the present day, illustrates the importance of its geographical position. There is a cohesion and a self-awareness about the place, and its people are proud of their distinctive culture and identity. One modern scholar[2] has referred to the 'durability' of the region, and that durability is in part derived from a combination of history, geography and a consciousness of difference. But within the province too, there is contrast and diversity, from the bilingual street signs in Basque and Castilian to the neat Pyrenean villages with their Swiss-looking villas contrasting with the grander vistas of the broad plains and river valleys to the south. Navarre is and always has been a region with a proudly independent outlook and a strong sense of its own identity. This was Berengaria's homeland, where she spent the first twenty or so years of her life. It is here in the most distinctive of Spanish provinces, that the search for Richard's queen begins.

When not referred to by name in the early sources – Spanish, French, Occitan or Latin – Berengaria, or Berenguela, is often simply called 'the daughter of the king of Navarre.' Contemporary readers or audiences must presumably have recognised the reference. But how much is generally known outside Spain about medieval Navarre? If we are to flesh out the bare details of Berengaria's background supplied by the French and Anglo-Norman chroniclers, we must look more closely at the history and culture of her homeland.

The small kingdom of Navarre, roughly coterminous with the modern Spanish province of the same name, presents itself in the twelfth century as a microcosm of the cultural, religious and linguistic complexity of the peninsula generally.[3] Its position on the Pyrenean frontier was of crucial importance, as was its effective control over the two principal passes of Somport and Roncesvalles, through which merchants, envoys and pilgrims passed en route for northern Spain. At various points in its history, including the reign of the last monarch of the Jiménez dynasty, Berengaria's brother, Sancho El Fuerte (The Strong), it also controlled territory north of the mountains, the region known to the Spanish as Ultrapuertos – 'beyond the passes'.[4] Sancho El Fuerte once exercised sovereignty over the now French town of St Jean Pied de Port, where a steep and narrow cobbled street still leads to the Gate of Spain, through which the pilgrims passed, and the modern castle from the ramparts of which a visitor may look across to the spot where Roland fell, replaces one which was part of Berengaria's disputed dowry in 1198. One hundred and fifty years earlier, Navarrese influence had even extended as far north as Bayonne and Bordeaux. In the last decades of his reign, Sancho El Fuerte once again appeared to exercise some sort of authority over these areas, with the apparent consent of the king of England.

The main pilgrimage routes from northern Europe began to converge on Spanish soil and passed through such Navarrese towns as Pamplona, Puente la Reina and Estella. Not only did this mean a steady stream of visitors, perhaps upwards of two hundred thousand a year, passing through these towns, but substantial populations of foreigners, mainly French-speaking, grew up in a number of them, with royal or ecclesiastical approval and encouragement. This added further to the cosmopolitan flavour of a society which already included Basques, Navarrese, Jews, *mudejares* (Muslims) often in significant numbers, as well as *muladíes*, or 'renegade' former Christians, and the descendants of slaves.[5]

This small Spanish kingdom, linked in each generation by ties of blood and marriage to its Christian neighbours, Aragon, Castile and Leon – ties which did not prevent the outbreak of frequent hostilities punctuated by uneasy truces – proclaimed its independence

in 1134 in the reign of Berengaria's grandfather García Ramirez El
Restaurador (The Restorer), a descendant of the Jiménez dynasty
and thus sprung from the same epic lineage as Rodrigo Diaz, the
great Cid Campeador. The *Fuero General de Navarra* describes the
distinctive ceremony by which the Navarrese rulers were inaugu-
rated: after such preliminaries as a vigil, a mass, an enrobing, the
issuing of currency and a celebratory meal, the king was raised
(*alzado*) on his shield by the *ricoshombres*, the leading nobles, who
all shouted three times '*Real! Real! Real!*' (royal).[6]

It is not strictly accurate to describe the early monarchs as kings.
At first known only as *dux*, then as kings of Pamplona, the
Navarrese monarchs began to use the title 'rey de Navarra' in the
reign of Sancho VI El Sabio (The Wise), Berengaria's father, around
1153. It was not until 1195 that they were granted official recognition by papal proclamation, during the reign of Sancho El Fuerte,
Berengaria's brother, who played a decisive role in the famous battle
of Las Navas de Tolosa in 1212. This date commemorates the decisive assertion of Christian supremacy over the Muslims in Spain,
though Muslim rule continued in the extreme south for a hundred
or so years. Sancho El Fuerte died in 1234, without legitimate issue,
and the crown passed to his nephew Thibaut of Champagne,
known to historians as the 'posthumous' and to literary scholars as
'*le chansonnier*' (the minstrel). For the next few centuries, Navarre
was to be ruled by French kings.

Apart from non-narrative sources such as legal documents,
records, charters, accounts etc., which are in any case not abundant
for the early period,[7] there are a dozen or so early Spanish chronicles which touch upon the reigns of the Jiménez kings of Navarre.[8]
These interlinked sources often supply a great deal of information
about reigning monarchs but have less to say about other less
prominent family members, particularly the women. Almost all of
them mention Berengaria's marriage in 1191 to King Richard of
England, and these accounts vary from a very brief entry to a
slightly more elaborate but not necessarily more informative
account. Many of these sources are not in any real sense independent and some of them clearly rely on French or Anglo-Norman
sources, such as Roger of Howden or the Continuation of William

of Tyre. Despite their limitations, their witness is useful, suggesting how posterity would view the children of King Sancho.

The chronicles generally begin by listing the children of King Sancho El Sabio of Navarre. One of the earliest, the *Liber Regum*, probably composed between 1194 and 1211,[9] says:

> ... the king, Don Sancho of Navarre, took as wife the daughter of the Emperor of Castile and had children by her, the king, Don Sancho, the Infante Don Ferrando and the queen of England and the countess of Champagne and the Infanta Dona Costanza who died at Daroca.

The later thirteenth-century *Primera Crónica General de España*, also called the *Estoria de España*,[10] compiled under the patronage of Alfonso X of Castile, states that

> ... the first was called dona Berenguela and she was married to King Richard of England, then he died without offspring and she lived a long time in the city of Cenomania and was buried there.

The sixteenth-century *Libro de las generaciones*,[11] compiled by the scribe M. Larraya of Tudela, includes material transcribed from a much earlier source – probably *c*.1258-70 – and is thought to be in part an amplification of the earlier *Liber Regum*. This text states:

> The King Don Sancho of Navarre took as wife the daughter of the Emperor of Spain and had with her two sons and three daughters: one the Infante don Sancho, the other the Infante don Ferrando and daughters, dona Belenguera, dona Costanca and dona Blanca. Dona Belenguera married the king of England, dona Blanca married the count of Champagne. The Infante don Ferrando died in Tudela in the month of December in MCCXLV and is buried in Pamplona and the Infanta dona Costanca died at Pradillas.

The late thirteenth- to early fourteenth-century crusade chronicle entitled *La Gran Conquista de Ultramar*[12] describes Richard's marriage to Berengaria at Limassol in Cyprus en route for the crusade and attributes the arrangement to Eleanor the queen mother 'because she had ill-will towards the lineage of the king of France'. As this version is clearly influenced by the inaccurate work of the continuator of William of Tyre, its value is limited.

Two influential fifteenth-century chronicles, the *Crónica* of Garci Lopez de Roncesvalles,[13] and the *Crónica de los reyes de Navarra*, of Carlos, principe de Viana,[14] also give details of Berengaria and her siblings. The former gives an extremely compressed account of the marriages of Berengaria and Blanca but omits the death of Costanza and has no mention at all of Fernando. The latter represents a much more systematic attempt to compile an official history of the kings of Navarre, using a variety of sources, including the *Crónica* of Garci Lopez itself. It is unusual in that, of the children of King Sancho VI, it gives the greatest space to the Infante Fernando, describing the great strength and bravery which he displayed in feats of arms including the tournament in the square of Tudela, where he met his untimely death at the age of thirty years during the celebration of the feast of Saint Nicolas.[15]

Carlos also mentions another brother named Sancho – not the future king – who became bishop of Pamplona. The existence of this brother is not attested anywhere else, and may be an error, although it could just possibly refer to an illegitimate son of the king. It was this error which gave rise to the later identification of this person with Remiro, illegitimate son of King Sancho VII, El Fuerte, who became bishop of Pamplona after serving as chancellor of the court of Champagne. It is perhaps surprising that the prince, who was writing not long after the events in question, should have made this error, but confusion over the number of offspring of kings is not uncommon, suggesting that the distinction between legitimate and illegitimate children, while of obvious importance for the succession, was not absolute and that the 'nuclear' family was not a significant category.[16]

The references to Berengaria and her sister Blanca are brief and differ very little from those in the *Cronica*. Another early source, the *Llibre dels Feyts*[17] of Jaume, prince of Aragon, contains valuable first-hand reminiscences of Jaume's dealings with Sancho El

Fuerte but has nothing to say about Sancho's sisters. The most important of these early sources and one which was used by several other writers of both vernacular and Latin histories, is the chronicle entitled *De Rebus Hispaniae*, written around 1240 by the gifted and prolific Archbishop Rodrigo Jiménez de Rada of Toledo,[18] who was himself Navarrese, born at Puente la Reina in 1170 or 1180. He travelled extensively in Italy and France and was an admirer and supporter of King Sancho VII El Fuerte, Berengaria's brother, about whose reign he writes with obvious first hand knowledge. Unlike Prince Jaume, however, the archbishop does comment on the king's sisters.

The archbishop's reference to Berengaria is lengthier than the other sources cited and, given his own close connection with the family, we may consider his testimony particularly valuable. The entry reads as follows:

> Sancho, however, king of Navarre, took as his wife Beata daughter of the Emperor, who bore him two sons, Sancho who succeeded to the throne, who was known as the 'Shut Away' (*Encerrado*) because he hid himself away from all but a few servants and lived in the fort of Tudela. He also had another son, Fernando, who was beloved in the eyes of all on account of his rectitude, but by an unhappy chance, he died at Tudela from injuries received when he fell from his horse. He also had three daughters. Berenguela was the wife of King Richard of England. When he died without issue, she lived on as a most praiseworthy widow and stayed for the most part in the city of Le Mans, which she held as part of her marriage dower, devoting herself to almsgiving, prayer and good works, witnessing as an example to all women of chastity and religion and in the same city she came to the end of her days with a happy death. The second daughter of the king of Navarre was Constanza who died not yet married. The third daughter was Blanca who married Theobald, count of Champagne, and gave birth to his posthumous son Theobald.

In all these various chronicles the entries in question are succinct and rather uninformative. They are written in a kind of code. Because Berengaria and the other women are marginal to the main narrative, their inclusion follows a predictable pattern based on familial relationships, daughter of, spouse of, mother of particular men. This pattern is best illustrated in the case of Blanca in the last extract: daughter of Sancho the king, wife of the count of Champagne, mother of Thibaut, who became in turn the first of a succession of 'French' kings of Navarre. Blanca's death is not mentioned, although it would have been known to the author – she died in March 1229, shortly before the death of her sister Berengaria – because her status is conclusively defined by maternity. What happened to her after this is not significant. Constanza, probably the eldest girl, may have been the Infanta for whom a marriage was projected by Sancho El Fuerte with the king of Aragon around 1198. Pope Innocent III vetoed it on the grounds of consanguinity.[19] We do not know when she died because her death is not recorded in the late thirteenth-century Obituary of the Cathedral of Pamplona, but she was still alive in 1202 when King John issued a safe conduct for her envoy to travel to his territory.[20] It is possible that hers are the remains of a woman interred with those of Sancho El Fuerte in the Colegio Real at Roncesvalles, since his two lawful marriages both ended in divorce, though others think that the remains are those of his last consort, Clemencia of Toulouse.[21]

Costanza (referred to as Teresa in a later annalistic source) is the daughter of a king, and her inclusion in the record is thus appropriate but, as her death preempts the possibility of marriage and maternity, her status is defined as *nondum nupta* (not yet married). Her case contrasts with that of her brother Fernando, who also died unmarried but whose marital status is not mentioned in this or other accounts. In some of them, including the last example, a strong sense of loss is suggested in the words *casu miserabile* (by an unfortunate accident): in other texts the word used to describe his unmarried state is *joven* (young), a term with far wider and more positive connotations than *soltero*, the vernacular (masculine) equivalent of *nondum nupta*. Moreover, Fernando, like his brother, is depicted in at least two of these extracts as an individual with distinctive personal characteristics, upon which the author feels moved to comment.

Jiménez de Rada's reference to Berengaria is particularly interesting because it suggests something of her personality and can be compared with his other references to prominent women, such as the English-born Queen Eleanor of Castile, whom he praises for her shrewd judgements.[22] Although the reference reflects to some extent conventional Christian expectations concerning pious widowhood, Don Rodrigo, who probably knew Berengaria and her siblings personally, does not dismiss her in one line as a queen who failed to deliver the required son. Interestingly, the archbishop, unlike some modern commentators, does not attribute the infertility to Berengaria but merely states the correct legal position, that Richard died without issue (*sine prole*). In the absence of sons, however, Berengaria is credited with a substitute spiritual maternity: her *viduitas laudabilis* (praiseworthy widowhood) brings forth the fruits of the spirit: alms, prayer, good works, continence, religious devotion and a happy death. The warmth of the archbishop's feeling was obviously noticed by the later annalist Moret, who comments on it as follows: 'The Archbishop Don Rodrigo, who recorded her living for many years, praised her holy widowhood, completely devoted to prayer, almsgiving and outstanding examples of sanctity.'[23]

On the other hand, Bishop Gonzalo de la Hinojosa, who translated and adapted Don Rodrigo's chronicle into Castilian – and to whom Berengaria would have been a more remote figure – reverts to the normal pattern and omits the personal detail: 'She married King Richard of England and died without children and was buried in the monastery in the city of Le Mans.'[24]

Many of these earlier sources were used by the author of the seventeenth-century *Anales del Reino de Navarra*, the Jesuit José Moret y Mendi.[25] Moret's important work provides a long, detailed and continuous account of the reigns of the last two Jiménez kings of Navarre, Berengaria's father and brother. In addition to the Spanish sources, Moret used the twelfth-century Anglo-Norman chronicler, Roger of Howden, for matters concerning the English connection. He also adds a number of conjectures of his own. He occasionally refers to probable or possible communications between

Navarre and the Angevin world during Berengaria's lifetime, but it is not possible to say whether these references are based on any lost written record, on hearsay or on his own guesswork.

It is possible, however, to a limited extent, to fill in the gaps in the information provided by these brief early references. Some of the details are unfortunately irretrievable. As we have noted, Berengaria's date of birth is nowhere recorded, nor are those of her sisters, because it was not common practice to do so, especially in the case of girls. Nor do we know where Berengaria or her sisters were born. It is unlikely to have been Pamplona, which was above all an episcopal city where successive bishops exercised a virtually exclusive sovereignty, although its status as a royal capital did come to be recognised eventually and its monarchs were buried there and the details of their activities recorded in its cathedral archives.[26]

The kings of Navarre were, like many of their royal contemporaries, essentially peripatetic and Berengaria may have been born at Tudela, which was the preferred place of residence of both her father and her brother and from 1194 the city most closely connected with the royal family.[27] Other possibilities include Olite or Estella, which housed the royal treasury.

Something of the milieu in which Berengaria and her siblings grew up can be glimpsed from studies of the life and times of her father King Sancho El Sabio,[28] who reigned from 1150 to 1194. This long reign was spent in almost continuous hostilities with his immediate neighbours, the kings of Castile, Leon and Aragon, all of whom at various times, singly or collectively, challenged his sovereignty over disputed territories.

The ultimate origins of this family and its immediate ancestor, García Ramirez El Restaurador go back at least to the ninth century. One modern writer has described Berengaria as a Basque. It is difficult to say exactly what this means. If the primary reference of words like Basque, Navarrese, Castilian, is linguistic (though such terms do often come to acquire a politico-geographical meaning, as in the case of the twelfth- and thirteenth-century use of *Angli* and *Engleis* to denote both English and Anglo-Norman speakers hailing from England), we have no evidence that Berengaria or any other member of her family spoke Basque.

The Basque language was not written down before the sixteenth century and I have been unable to find any early reference to royal Basque-speakers. On the other hand, people described as Basques and Navarrese are constantly spoken of in association, even in early sources, and evidence suggests that, before the mid twelfth century at least, Basque-speakers were in the majority in the rural areas, especially in the Saltus Vasconum, while the speakers of Romance (Aragonese-Navarese) increased their political influence along the river plains and in the cities. The Navarrese language was finally ensured a permanent status by its adoption as the official language of the royal chancellery in 1180. Given the family ties with Castile, Aragon, Barcelona etc., it seems more likely that Berengaria and her family were Romance-speakers.[29]

But at least one strand in the ancestry of the kings of Navarre goes back to a dynasty with Basque antecedents as well as Muslim connections. The ancestor of this dynasty was Iñigo Arista (*c.*820 AD), a remote and mysterious figure whose reputation in the eyes of Spanish nationalist historians of the old school was clouded by his alliances with an influential Muslim confederacy of the ninth century, the Bani Qasi, *muladíes* or *renegados* (i.e., of Christian origin), centred on the Ebro valley.[30] Other early records show a network of such connections, whether with indigenous *muladíes* or immigrants of Arab or Berber stock. The important city of Tudela was founded by Muslims in 800, and in 852 Muza ibn Muza, wali of Tudela, broke his alliance with the emir and established relations with the local Christians, many of whom would have been of mixed Romano-Visigothic ancestry. Around 951 a 'queen' of Navarre is recorded as acknowledging the overlordship of Abd-ar-Rahman, Muslim governor of Tudela, while Muslim names appear occasionally in early dynastic records. Jose María Lacarra points out that 'mixed' marriage alliances were frequent in this period and that such unions had the effect of increasing the influence of the Romance language at the expense of Basque. Even after Tudela fell into the hands of Alfonso El Batallador, Berengaria's ancestor, Muslims were allowed to live safely in an area known as the Morería, today the *barrio* de San Juan, to the west of the city. The city itself was surrounded by Muslim settlements within a radius of twenty kilometres for much of the twelfth and thirteenth centuries.

Berengaria's own immediate family was linked to a number of the most powerful ruling houses in medieval Europe. Her mother was the daughter of the 'emperor' of Castile, and her maternal grandmother, after whom she was named, was a daughter of the count of Barcelona. Her father's family was in part of French descent. Her background was thus as exogamous as that of her famous husband to be, whose ancestry was Norman, Angevin and Occitan, in both the geographical and the linguistic sense, none of which precluded him from becoming one of England's enduring folk-heroes. This mixed ancestry was only a reflection of the diversity of the kingdom of Navarre itself and of the Hispanic peninsula in general, and proof of the political importance of dynastic marriages.

From what is known about social organisation during the reign of the Jiménez dynasty, Navarre was a feudal aristocracy, with the important class of nobles known as the *ricoshombres* commanding the allegiance of the lower *hidalguía* (*hidalgo* originally meaning something like 'man of substance'), which was divided into two categories, the *caballeros*, or military men, and the *infanzones*, or descendants of noble families later known as the *nobleza de sangre*. The king's relations with these classes of the aristocracy were not always easy. But Navarre was unusual in one respect: its citizens, of whatever rank or persuasion, were from relatively early times, protected by a series of *fueros*, those characteristically Spanish legal promulgations, which have been likened to the English Magna Carta.

Between approximately 1076 and 1180 virtually every town in the kingdom was covered by one or other of these charters, beginning with the town of Jaca, technically outside the kingdom, in 1076 and that of Estella in 1090. Individual *fueros* were sometimes granted to minorities such as Jews or 'Francos'. Many of these earlier promulgations were subsumed in the important *Fuero General de Navarra*, drafted in 1237 or thereabouts, during the reign of Thibaut, Berengaria's nephew, but drawing on much older materials, including local ones like those mentioned above. This 'foral' protection, as it has been labelled, was an important factor in the protection of both Jews and Muslims, who were numerous in parts of the kingdom during the reign of both Sancho El Sabio and his son Sancho El Fuerte.

The relation between Christians and Muslims was still, in the mid-twelfth century, a complex one. At the time of Berengaria's infancy, the whole territory south of a line running from Lisbon in the west to Tortosa in the east was ruled by Muslims. Two centuries earlier the two communities had been even more closely enmeshed, with local groups of Christians and Muslims in constantly shifting coalitions as far north as Pamplona and Saragossa. There was, as Robert Burns puts it, no real northern border between Muslim and Christian.[31]

The Anglo-Norman *Song of Roland*, probably the most famous medieval epic in a Romance language, celebrates the triumphs of Christian France over the terrifying pagan hordes of Spanish Islam in a battle which took place over three hundred years before the poem itself, in the form in which it is now familiar, took shape. It represents a later North European perspective which combines ignorance of the enemy with a dogmatic insistence that 'Pagans are wrong and Christians are right'. This is very different from the situation prevailing in Spain, even in the mid-twelfth century (ironically, the 'original ' enemy at the battle of Roncesvalles in 778 were the nominally Christian *vascones*, who have been identified as either Gascons or Basques).

It would be naive, of course, to see Christian-Muslim relations in medieval Spain as being entirely amicable. The ferocious triumphalism which characterises accounts of the battle of Las Navas de Tolosa in 1212 gives the lie to that. On the other hand, the proximity in which the two faiths had lived for several centuries resulted in a pragmatism which often expressed itself in tolerance and occasionally friendship.

The existence of 'transitional' communities and minority enclaves is a recurrent feature of Spanish history until the expulsion of the Jews and Muslims in 1492. *Mozárabes* were Christians living under Moorish rule; *mudéjares*, their Muslim counterparts in Christian societies. *Muwallads* were ethnic Spanish Muslims, while, later, *moriscos* were the covert Muslims forcibly converted to Christianity who preserved their secret identity in the face of great danger. The Jewish equivalent of the *moriscos* are properly called *conversos* rather than the insulting and inappropriate term *marranos*.

The brilliant artistic and intellectual achievements of Muslim Spain were obviously attractive to their less cultured Christian neighbours, and conversion was by no means a one-way process: the great poet and aesthete Ibn Hazm of Cordoba was the son of a convert from Christianity. Although there were, during the last centuries of Muslim rule, intermittent movements towards puritanism and fundamentalism, the general legacy of Spanish Islam is one of considerable cultural achievement. Even at moments of intense conflict there was often a grudging mutual respect: one of the most famous families of *ricoshombres* – the ruling elite – in medieval Navarre bore the name Almoravid in memory of an ancestral victory over the dynasty of the same name.

Jews, too, lived in relative peace under both Christian and Muslim rule, in what has been described as a symbiotic relationship with one or the other of the majority communities. Their contribution to science and letters, medicine and philosophy, was an outstanding one.[32] They were particularly prominent in Navarre, where Alfonso El Batallador extended to them in 1121 the protection of the *fuero* of Nájera, first promulgated in 1119 and renewed in 1170. Sancho El Sabio extended the protection offered under this law to Jews in other cities, and his son continued to protect the Jews and defend them until his death. The *Fuero General de Navarra*[33] contains extensive recommendations for the protection of Jews, stating, for instance, that anyone who kills a Jew or a Moor in the market place or any other public place must pay a fine of 500 *sueldos*, while any Christian who 'draws blood' will be fined 200 *sueldos*. Above all, they were guaranteed religious freedom. Tudela had the largest Jewish community, followed by Pamplona, Estella and Sanguesa. The occupations they favoured were many; not only commercial ones – butchers, furriers, cloth merchants, goldsmiths – but professions such as ambassadors, couriers, physicians. Berengaria's father himself had a trusted Jewish physician, Salomón

Alfaquí (an Arabic honorific) of Tudela and frequently employed Jews as counsellors and negotiators. There were also many famous Jewish intellectuals whose names are known to us today, such as the famous Benjamin of Tudela (1127-73) and the logician Abraham ibn Ezra. Jews also held land, cultivated vines and pioneered irrigation methods.[34]

The values which prevailed at the court of King Sancho VI must in some way have influenced the children who grew up there, but the attitude in northern France was very different, as became clear when Sancho El Fuerte was succeeded by his nephew Thibaut of Champagne. In 1247 the Jews of Navarre complained to Pope Innocent IV of harassment and persecution by the French-born king.[35] Although Jews everywhere in the Christian world were dependent on the goodwill of their Christian overlords and were on many occasions bought and sold or used as bargaining chips in commercial deals, in the royal domain of France especially and in the powerful ducal territories which owed it allegiance, they were also liable to have their property confiscated, to be subjected to sudden attacks of persecution or summary deportation.

While some Church leaders warned against excessive displays of anti-Semitism, others indulged in it themselves and encouraged it in others. Ultimately there was no escape from the appalling and unjust charge of deicide, which might be invoked at any time with horrendous consequences.[36] Berengaria's later dealings with the Jews of Le Mans suggest that she did not follow the example of her father and brother: on the one hand, she had occasional recourse to Jewish financiers for advice and loans; on the other, she encouraged attempts to convert them and permitted and perhaps even initiated the confiscation of their property in order that it might be donated to religious orders. Many such donations are recorded in France generally, under both Angevin and Capetian rule, with the laconic addition: *quod Judaeis fuit/fuerat* (formerly belonging to Jews); but there does not seem to be any record of compensation for such seizures.

In addition to Muslims and Jews, Navarrese cities had substantial enclaves of *francigeni*, French, or more accurately, Occitan speakers, living under official protection, enjoying on occasion a status akin to that of the *ricoshombres* but exempt from military obligations.[37] They were particularly valued for their commercial activities. In Pamplona, where they were settled from 1070, they were associated with the area around San Cernin. 'Franci' were present in the other major Navarrese cities too as part of the general repopulation of areas captured from the Muslims.

French influence was most marked in the Church and particularly in the encouragement of first Cluniac (*c.*1032) and then Cistercian (*c.*1131) orders to come into the country. French influence was less marked in the development of the literary arts. Surprisingly, perhaps, it appears that troubadour activity did not flourish at the court of Navarre, as it did to varying degrees, in Aragon and Castile, although some troubadours did pass through the territory, and the '*bos reis Navars*' and his daughter are mentioned on a few occasions by individual poets. It would seem, then, that the romantic anecdote repeated by a number of fiction writers and popular historians, according to which Richard fell in love with Berengaria at a tournament in Pamplona during which he composed passionate verses in her honour, has no basis in fact. Some contemporary sources do, however, suggest that he formed an attachment to her during his youth.

Whether or not Richard ever visited Pamplona or any other Navarrese city is not a matter of record. English pilgrims had been coming to Santiago de Compostela for some time, but there is no record of any member of Richard's immediate family making the pilgrimage. After the martyrdom of Thomas a Beckett, Canterbury became the principal destination for English pilgrims, and the closest relative of Richard recorded as having made the pilgrimage to Compostela was his nephew Otto of Brunswick. We cannot of course rule out the possibility that Richard visited Navarrese territory in some capacity or other before his marriage. It is in fact quite likely that he did so, since he would have had to negotiate with the Navarrese over the status of the territories which formed part of the region of Ultrapuertos and the related question of the safety of pilgrims.

The absence of attested troubadour activity at the court of Navarre[38] does not mean that artists and scholars from outside were never welcome. The cultural activity of medieval Navarre is not accessible to us in great detail, but all the evidence suggests that Berengaria's father found time, despite his continuing political difficulties, to encourage music, architecture and other cultural activities. During his reign and that of his son and successor, libraries and scriptoria flourished and many important codices were produced, including two famous illustrated Bibles. A school of polyphonic music was established which was to become famous throughout Europe. Among distinguished foreign scholars were the English Augustinian canon Robert of Ketton, archdeacon of Pamplona in 1143, who was commissioned by Peter the Venerable to translate the Qur'an, and an English architect-landscaper named Richard, who assisted in the planning of the famous abbey of Las Huelgas in Castile.[39]

The burgeoning bureaucracy saw an increase in official record-keeping, and the use of the Aragonese-Navarrese dialect as an official language gave it a status parallel to that of Latin, marginalising both the Basque of the countryside and the Occitan of the enclaves.

These few examples suffice to show that Navarre, though small, was no mere provincial backwater. Outside the country and especially in France, the reputation of the Navarrese and the Basques was not high. Their names were often coupled with the Brabacons as mercenaries, and their activities on the Pyrenean frontier were feared and hated. The author of the medieval *Guide des Pèlerins*, Aimeric Picaud,[40] was no doubt expressing the jaundiced view of those who had suffered at the hands of toll-keepers on the border, or bandits in the mountain passes, when he described the Navarrese and Basques as violent, avaricious, dishonest and uncivilised. There may have been some substance to his complaint because in 1177 Richard himself as count of Poitou had occasion to come down to the border to stop the plundering of pilgrims en route for Santiago. Not all pilgrims, no doubt, behaved themselves with appropriate decorum at all times, and blame might be difficult to apportion in the absence of detailed evidence.

An important area of French influence was the Church. The older, Mozarabic liturgical rites and other customs had been displaced by the Roman rites common to the churches of England,

France and Italy under the influence of French-born clerics like Pedro de Roda, bishop of Pamplona from 1083 to 1115. The great monastic movements which were to transform the architectural and spiritual landscape of the Christian West were thoroughly French in their inspiration. The earliest Christian kings of Pamplona, the descendants of Iñigo Arista, had been fiercely hostile to the Franks, even to the point of allying themselves with the 'renegade' Bani Qasi of the Ebro valley, the descendants of an old Visigothic aristocracy converted to Islam. But the dynasty which succeeded it, the Jiménez dynasty, was itself connected with France, and was quick to welcome French monks and prelates. The cult of San Fermín in Pamplona derives from a French tradition represented both in Toulouse in the south and Amiens in the north. The monks of Cluny had been established in Navarre for over a hundred years when Berengaria's father encouraged the Cistercians to settle in his kingdom.

The new radical Cistercian spirituality took root quickly in Spain and many monasteries accepted the Cistercian rule: Fitero in 1140, La Oliva in 1150 and Iranzu in 1176. Many women were attracted to the movement and were ultimately accepted into its cloisters; among these were Santa María de la Caridad at Tulebras, founded in 1157. The famous abbey of Las Huelgas, founded in 1186 by Alfonso VIII and ceded to the abbot of Cîteaux in 1199, was directly descended from these earlier beginnings. Its religious were women of noble rank and of considerable learning, and for a while its abbesses, such as the famous Dona María Sol, enjoyed great prestige and authority in the Church at large.

One of the most difficult areas to explore in a period as remote from our own as the mid- to late-twelfth century is that of family relationships. Despite the strong growth of family studies as a historical discipline over the past thirty-odd years, and the intense interest in the history of private life generated by the activities of the *Annales* school and writers like Le Goff and Duby in particular, some areas remain less accessible than others through lack of documentation or of appropriate methodologies. Medieval Spain is not as immediately encouraging a prospect for the study of family life as later medieval England or France.

Family dynamics can, of course, often be inferred from the course of external events. The unhappy relationship between Henry II of England and his sons in the years leading up to his death, and the manipulative behaviour of their mother Eleanor, demonstrate that this was a dysfunctional family by any criterion. The relationship between the women in the immediate family and between the sons and their sisters appears to have been closer, but this too has been questioned. Women's involvement in political matters was less obvious, and the rivalries which entangled their male siblings did not touch them so directly. Chroniclers also sometimes appear to be following a very old convention by attributing rivalries and even wars between men to the clandestine jealousies and intrigues of women – the Helen of Troy factor.

The lives of some of Berengaria's closest relatives seem to demonstrate certain common characteristics: tenacity, stoicism, loyalty and longevity. Her father is remembered chiefly for his political adroitness, his success in steering his relatively new country through prolonged periods of external threat, his protection of minorities and his concern for administrative order, seen in the issuing of a number of *fueros*. Economic standards rose during his reign and the arts flourished. In external matters he was a pragmatist, quick to realise where the political realities lay and resourceful enough to compromise, ready to negotiate with Christian and Muslim alike. As his recent biographer, Juan Elizari, notes, it was a fellow Navarrese, Rodrigo Jiménez de Rada, who summarised his merits concisely but effectively: '... *prudens, magnanimus et strenuus in agendis*' (wise, magnanimous and energetic). His daughter Berengaria seems to have inherited some of these qualities, but circumstances and above all, gender, meant that she could never match her father's achievements.

Such was the political face of Sancho's long reign, but what do we know of the private man? Apart from the public qualities demonstrated by the external events of his career, the answer is not a great deal. He does not seem to have attracted the same anecdotal interest as his son, Sancho El Fuerte, did later.[41] But there is one brief glimpse of his private feelings in a comment made by the annalist Moret, presumably on the basis of earlier sources, such as

Jiménez de Rada. On 5 August 1179 Queen Sancha (also known as Beata) died after twenty-five years of marriage. 'It appears,' comments the annalist, 'that it was his conjugal love for her which prompted the king to remain a widower for the rest of his life, even though his age – not much more than fifty years – would have been no obstacle to a new marriage.'

In 1181 Sancho confirmed a donation to Benedictine nuns of Marcilla in memory of his wife, also known as a lady of great piety and devotion. The word *widow* and its cognates mean bereft or separated, but its primary reference is always to women. Words for 'widower' in almost all Indo-European languages are derived by analogy, indicating that the condition itself is an accidental rather than a defining category in the case of males. So perhaps the implication here is that King Sancho was unusual in demonstrating a conjugal affection which endured beyond the grave. Not only was this a perfect embodiment of the ecclesiastical ideal of marriage[42] – and perhaps one which went even further, since the Church did not frown upon the remarriage of the bereaved – based on monogamy, consent and mutual affection, but it appears that the king was faithful in life to his spouse, since, unlike his son and his contemporaries, he does not appear to have had many, or perhaps any, illegitimate children. Other members of the family were famous for their conjugal devotion: Queen Sancha's brother, Sancho of Castile, had married Blanca of Navarre, the king's sister, who died in childbirth at the age of twenty-five. A few months later her husband died of grief, whereupon tradition conferred upon him the romantic title of 'El Deseado' – the Longing or Sorrowful One!

Some time later, both Berengaria and her sister Blanca were to spend over twenty years as widows without remarrying. In an age when young widows were encouraged to remarry and frequently disadvantaged when they did not, it may be that the memory of a father's devotion was a formative influence on his daughters. Of Queen Sancha herself, apart from her piety, we know nothing. It appears that she died soon after giving birth to her youngest child, Blanca. If the sources are to be believed, she must have possessed exceptional qualities to have inspired such strong devotion in her husband.[43]

Other women in the wider family were remarkable for their strength and independence and, when fate pushed them into the forefront of political events, they inevitably incurred the usual criticisms levelled at women who usurp the male prerogative of power. One such was Berengaria's paternal aunt, Margarita, who married William the 'Bad', Norman king of Sicily, in 1150. The Sicilian court, with its luxurious atmosphere and its exotic trappings – including, it was said, the king's own royal harem – earned this ruler great notoriety elsewhere in the Christian world.[44]

Margarita was strong-willed and was often accused of exercising undue influence over her husband, even though he is described as having lived more like a Muslim than a Christian ruler – a charge sometimes levelled at the Christians in places like Sicily or the Latin kingdoms of Palestine. She had three sons, the first of whom, Roger, died at age nine, according to one version by a misdirected arrow, according to another, more sinister account, from a kick aimed at him by his own bad-tempered father. The third son, Henry, died from injuries received in battle, but the second and remaining son, William 'the Good', lived to succeed his father in 1166 at age thirteen. Margarita then became regent for the next five or six years, difficult and troubled ones during which she tried to maintain a balance between her powerful male relatives who had arrived on the scene with ambitions of their own and the local population which consisted of Muslims and Greeks as well as Normans.

The locals resented French and Navarrese influence and blamed the foreign queen for it, accusing her of being both a virago and promiscuous. Recent studies of medieval queenship have shown how common such accusations were, especially when the queen was a foreigner. No doubt Margarita was pleased when her son attained his majority and acceded to the throne. This son, handsome, engaging and virtuous, by all accounts, married the young Joanna Plantagenet, Henry II's daughter and Richard's sister, who was herself to be widowed at twenty-four. History loses interest in the queen regent at this point and she is thought to have died before reaching the age of sixty.

A similar pattern appears in the life of Berengaria's younger sister Blanca, who also married into a powerful family far from home, was widowed young and spent a long and difficult period as regent during her son's infancy. Like her aunt, she too has been portrayed in a negative way, described as 'amazonian' and subjected to sexual innuendo: doubts were cast on the paternity of her son Thibaut, and the frequent references to her 'beauty' added spice to the allegations.

Blanca married Thibaut de Champagne, younger son of Marie de Champagne (and thus grandson of Eleanor of Aquitaine by her first marriage, to Louis VII of France) on 1 August 1199. Barely two years later, Thibaut died at twenty-one, leaving Blanca – or Blanche as she is better known – with an infant daughter and once more pregnant. Blanche's regency lasted twenty-two years and was marked by bitter conflict with the relatives of her dead husband's elder brother, mistrust of her ruthless and ambitious overlord Philip Augustus of France and constant niggling from churchmen. Blanca and Berengaria remained in contact with each other; they tried to support each other as best they could during the long years of widowhood and died within two years of each other.

The similarity in fortunes of these three Spanish princesses points very clearly to their role as pawns in the political struggles of the males who controlled their destinies.[45] None the less, each of them demonstrated courage and fortitude in the face of adversity. None of them, it would appear, succumbed to the easier strategies of 'pleasing' or even 'manipulating': on the contrary, they did not hesitate to sustain and perhaps even to initiate hostile relationships with powerful men in the defence of their own interests or those of their infant children.

The best known of Berengaria's siblings is her brother Sancho,[46] who succeeded his father in 1194, starred at the decisive battle of Las Navas de Tolosa in 1212, where a Christain coalition drove back the Muslims into the south, and died a virtual recluse in 1234. Even in the earliest sources it is hard to disentangle fact from fantasy where this prince is concerned. Like Richard, his brother-in-law and companion in arms, Sancho seemed to attract colourful legends both before and after his death. Both Jaume of Aragon[47] and Archbishop Jiménez de Rada left detailed accounts of the monarch whom they knew well. They describe him as huge, powerful and aggressive, loyal, energetic and brave but also avaricious, impulsive and naive. In the end, despairing and disillusioned, he shut himself up in the tower of Tudela and died alone after a long period of ill-health. Prince Jaume, who was a close associate,[48] describes his huge stature – just over two metres – and the increasing obesity which made him incapable of mounting a horse in later life. His family life, unlike that of his father, is something of a mystery: he married at least twice but the identity of these wives is not certain and he left only ex-nuptial children, several of whom went on to enjoy prominent ecclesiastical careers, the usual avenue of advancement for the illegitimate.

The thirteenth-century statue of Sancho VII in the collegiate chapel of Santa María at Roncesvalles is striking and powerful, with its heavy features, large, prominent eyes and the surprisingly realistic rendering of the deformed leg, which was probably caused by a varicose ulcer rather than the 'cancer' of the sources. Equally noticeable are the abnormally large, long-fingered hands. Arachnodactylism is a significant feature of the condition known as Marfan's Syndrome, from which Abraham Lincoln is thought to have suffered. Hyperactivity and cardio-vascular problems are often associated symptoms, as are 'staring' eyes and enlarged facial features. It seems possible that Sancho may have suffered from Marfan's Syndrome. This would partially explain the persistent aura of strangeness which surrounded him in the eyes of his contemporaries and encouraged the growth of folkloric or legendary accretions.

Family background and cultural milieu may enable us to focus more closely on the figures within a group, but individuals still have their own personality traits and sometimes break the mould. Education is often a catalyst. This was no doubt less true in the middle ages than in periods of greater social mobility, but, even in the case of women, education and training left their mark. Many of the comments made by the chroniclers at the time of Berengaria's marriage to Richard single out her moral and social qualities and refer to her 'education' in the broader sense. We shall return to these accounts later, but in the meantime, the question arises: what kind of formal education would she and her sisters have received in twelfth-century Navarre?

Medieval childrearing is a particularly difficult area, because most of the sources are prescriptive rather than descriptive and because many of the most interesting descriptions come from a later period than the twelfth century. Not so long ago the notion of childhood as a medieval concept was challenged by a number of scholars. Although the revisionist view was ultimately discarded, the depiction of childhood in medieval art, fiction and non-fiction varies considerably. The prescriptive literature, inevitably, tends to concentrate almost exclusively on the upbringing and education of boys.[49]

The education of aristocratic women in Europe during the high Middle Ages is not known to us in detail, but the general picture which emerges makes it clear that, as in so many other respects, in the area of education and training 'being born female is that first factor that defines women's experience [and] separates it from men's'.[50]

For women of noble birth, as much as for townswomen, marriage was the principal end to which their youthful training, whatever form it took, was directed. For aristocratic women there was also a social role for which they needed preparation, and this meant the acquisition of appropriate skills and accomplishments. Even where an heiress could and did inherit the all-important property, land, she was still – perhaps even more so – a marriageable commodity. In an age of faith, both boys and girls needed religious instruction. Some women destined for the cloister were permitted a more academic training, including literacy skills and, in the twelfth century at least, some Latin. Finally, the notion of correction, so strongly associated with both religious and customary morality, was particularly emphasised in the case of women, whose nature was seen as weaker, more prone to temptation and more dangerous as an instrument of temptation to others, that is, to men. Women could not escape the stigma of carnality and the age-old dual standard meant that they had a double responsibility: not to sin themselves and not to give offence to others or bring shame and disrepute to their families (menfolk).

A woman who accepted these constraints might, particularly in the courtly milieux of the later twelfth and early thirteenth centuries, lead a gracious and leisured existence and the various skills and arts which were practised – music, singing, weaving, embroidery, falconry, board games and elegant conversation – may have been a source of pride and pleasure to many. But to step outside the gilded cage was risky.

Courtly literature offers many glimpses of the ideal woman of male fantasy: noble, beautiful, accomplished and always available. As wife or fiancée she must be obedient, loyal and chaste. The only other alternative was to be cast in the role of seductress, distant, haughty and unattainable. Neither image reflects woman as she really was.

Some poets could, and did, expose, through satire and humour, the essential artificiality of these images. Chrétien de Troyes, particularly in his last and most mature work, *Perceval*,[51] uses comic effect to show how, when human feelings become overheated, the courtly veneer melts away and characters express themselves, by word or action, in ways which are brutal, spiteful and vulgar – in a word, human![52] The didactic writers did not appear to possess the same sense of humour. In the writings of Jacques de Vitry, Gilbert de Tournai, Vincent de Beauvais, Philip of Novara and the Chevalier de la Tour Landry, the same messages keep repeating themselves: 'Chastity, humility, modesty, sobriety, silence, work, charity, discipline – throughout the centuries, women heard these words repeated endlessly.'[53]

Some medieval families shared close and affectionate relationships. Both fiction and non-fiction depict parents and adults kissing and hugging children and taking pleasure in their company. Medieval illustrations show children playing with dolls, puppets, balls and so on. One of the best-known of medieval romances, Chrétien's *Perceval*, paints an engaging portrait of a typical adolescent boy, clumsy, unsubtle, exuberant and always hungry. Later in the same text, we meet an amusing little girl, equally spontaneous and uninhibited, turning the tables on her bossy elder sisters, to the quiet amusement of her indulgent father: this is the quaintly named 'Maiden with the Narrow Sleeves' who coaxes an unwilling but good-hearted Gawain, an aging former 'ladies' man', into fighting as her champion in a tournament.

Our sources of information concerning women's upbringing in medieval Spain are not abundant.[54] Heath Dillard's *Daughters of the Reconquest*[55] deals mainly with urban women in Castile but offers some insights into areas of difference between Spain in general and northern Europe. Survivals from Visigothic law appear to have favoured women in respect of their rights of property and inheritance. Hispanic canon law coincided with Visigothic practice in upholding the freedom of women to resist forced marriages. The *Fuero General de Navarra* allowed women the right to refuse two offers of marriage but obliged them to accept the third.[56] Luis del Campo[57] calls this the traditional Navarrese right of first refusal, and suggests that women could exert some limited bargaining power with their fathers and brothers. Dillard claims that Popes and churchmen were less prone to interfere in matters pertaining to lay marriage, which may suggest that the 'secular' model, which attracted such hostility from the churchmen because of its obvious abuses, may have been rendered less objectionable by practices and attitudes peculiar to Spain. Unfortunately the evidence is not sufficient to say whether this was so or not.

On the other hand, it is interesting to note that the penalties for molesting women appear to reverse the common medieval interpretation of the parable of the sower. Molestation of a married woman was more heavily penalised than that of a widow or a virgin and much more heavily than that of a woman of loose living ('*de mal vivir*'). This reflects the priority given to a husband's proprietorial rights and public 'face'. Although married women and especially mothers enjoyed a great deal of respect in Spanish lay society, adultery was a crime if committed by a woman, and the husband was seen as the injured and therefore compensable party. Similar conduct on the part of a man remained relatively unscathed. The position resembles in many ways the situation in Muslim societies today, where women face greater restriction outside the home but enjoy wide powers and great respect within its walls. Perhaps there were cross-cultural influences at work in this area of medieval Spanish society.

We can only speculate as to the type of education Berengaria may have received. F. Lopez Estrada points to evidence from the *Partidas* of Alfonso X of Aragon which suggests that aristocratic Spanish women were encouraged to learn to read if not to write.[58]

Medieval iconography, too, frequently depicts women reading or holding books, perhaps more frequently than men, and the Virgin herself is commonly portrayed with books in her vicinity. Berengaria and her sisters may have been educated by their mother or by women tutors specially appointed for the task, as was common in a wide variety of medieval cultures. Berengaria herself was asked to take on this role shortly after her marriage in Cyprus, when Richard entrusted the daughter of the defeated ruler of the island to his queen '*por enseignier e por doctrine*' (to be instructed and educated). When her mother died, Berengaria may have assisted with the education of her younger sister. She must have acquired some of the social graces and accomplishments appropriate to her status, if the comments made by some of the chroniclers at the time of her wedding are to be believed.

Almost nothing is known about Berengaria's early life. This is not unusual: medieval childhood is not well documented and girls in particular were raised in the privacy of their father's home, until such time as they were sent away to be married, or betrothed. We do know, however, that at the age of around fifteen or so, Berengaria assumed a public role, albeit a limited one. In 1185 King Sancho honoured his daughter with a '*tenencia*' or fief, commemorated in a document which describes her as '*habitante apud Monte Regale*' or Monreal (de Navarra), perhaps to be identified with the Monreal located a kilometre or so from Tudela.[59] Women members of royal or noble Spanish families if unmarried or widowed were sometimes given *tenencias*, but a male member of the nobility would generally administer the fief in their name.[60] There are a handful of women recorded as *tenentes* during the twelfth century, most of them honoured in this way during the reign of Berengaria's father Sancho El Sabio. Neither of her sisters appears in the list compiled by the Navarrese scholar A. Ubieto Arteta in his study of women *tenentes*. Berengaria would have been about fifteen at this time, and her nomination may have been in recognition of her coming of age, but it is not impossible that it was connected with betrothal negotiations, as we shall see later, and perhaps it was this occasion which gave rise to the notion of a prior attachment between Berengaria and Richard.

Two comments which occur in a much later letter to her sister Blanca, countess of Champagne, from Adam of Perseigne,[61] the influential Cistercian abbot prominent in the affairs of the Angevins at the end of the twelfth century, may reflect the shared background of the two sisters. Blanca (Blanche) had apparently written to the charismatic abbot whose reputation as a preacher and counsellor was widespread, requesting a copy of one of his sermons. Adam's reply was somewhat terse, in contrast to the warmth and eloquence which characterises much of his correspondence with both women and men, lay and religious. He gives a brief outline of basic Christian doctrine and a lot of advice about public matters. At one stage he tells the countess that she should have the letter translated, since she does not know Latin. Although Berengaria may have acquired some Latin at a later stage in her life, this would certainly imply that Latin was not part of the childhood curriculum of Sancho's daughters.

The other comment is rather surprising. Adam expresses disapproval both of the countess's involvement in politics and of the frivolous atmosphere of her court. It is all the more surprising, he comments, that she should need to be reminded of the right priorities, since he has heard that she had expressed an interest in entering the religious life in her youth. Nothing in the existing records confirms this suggestion and it is of course possible that Adam was misinformed. On the other hand, it was not uncommon for girls to be promised to the Church in infancy. At the very least, this suggests that one or more of the infantas of Navarre may have contemplated entering the religious life.

They may have intended to join the magnificent Cistercian convent at Las Huelgas, founded by their cousin Alfonso VIII and his English queen, Eleanor Plantagenet, Richard's sister, or one of the other convents of nuns, such as Marcilla or Tulebras. Some of the comments made by the chroniclers at the time of her marriage suggest that Berengaria was both serious and dutiful, and this, together with the life-long religious devotion praised by Archbishop Jiménez de Rada, lends some credibility to this idea. But whatever may have been the case, fate decreed that her life should take another more perilous course.

Eleanor of Aquitaine is reputed to have complained that in Louis VII of France, her first husband, she had married a monk rather than a man. It may be that a similar incompatibility contributed to the estrangement of her son Richard from his wife in the stressful first years of their marriage, giving rise to the bizarre suggestion, repeated by a handful of writers, that the marriage was never consummated. There is a profound mystery at the heart of this marriage, a clue to which must lie in the complexities of Richard's life both in private and in public.

Paradoxically, while much is known about Richard as king, his private life is the subject of considerable disagreement. Berengaria, on the other hand, is described as 'enigmatic' because so little detailed information of any kind has survived. The 'enigma' of the marriage lies in Richard's behaviour, rather than Berengaria's, which was essentially reactive. Women had limited choices in the twelfth century, even in Navarre.

Let us leave Berengaria then, in the year 1190, on the eve of her momentous journey across the Alps, through Italy to Sicily and Cyprus and ultimately to Palestine. A serious young woman, educated, devout, she had lost her mother at an early age and was as far as we know never to return to her native land. She might well have preferred to join the nuns at Marcilla, Tulebras or Las Huelgas, where she might have become a respected abbess, a scholar or even a mystic. But she was not free to choose. As so often happened, a political agenda stood in the way. She would certainly have heard of the powerful King Henry of England, whose arbitration her father and his rivals had sought on more than one occasion, of his famous Queen Eleanor, sovereign lady of Guyenne and Gascony, and perhaps of their son, the count of Poitou, merciless fighter, toast of the troubadours and already the subject of barrack-room gossip. He may even have been an occasional companion in arms of her brother Sancho as popular tradition suggests. Now she too would become embroiled in the turbulence which surrounded this ruthless dynasty and their Capetian rivals. And, like the turtle-dove, medieval emblem of life-long fidelity, whose likeness would be imprinted on her seal, she would be faithful till death.

CHAPTER THREE

Bride

Li gentils reis, li coers de lion ...

Richard Plantagenet, king of England, count of Poitou, duke of Aquitaine, count of Anjou and duke of Normandy, was, on the eve of his marriage to Berengaria in May 1191, the most powerful monarch in Christendom. He had inherited from his father, King Henry II, a realm which extended from Scotland to the Pyrenees. He had established, while still in his teens, the military reputation of a man twice his age. Already he was celebrated in the poetry of the troubadours as the epitome of youthful and insouciant vigour. In an age when a woman's status was derived from her standing as daughter, wife or mother, marriage to this man would have been an honour and a challenge.

It is unlikely, however, that Richard would have regarded his impending marriage as much more than a necessary formality and and perhaps an agreeable occasion for pageantry and display, even though one of the contemporary sources describes him as 'ardently longing' for the arrival of his bride to be. In spring 1191, not so long after acceding to the throne, he was after all on the threshold of a momentous venture: the third crusade.

It is above all as crusader king that Richard is remembered today, and the word crusade itself still retains a certain epic resonance. In modern usage, it also suggests impractical idealism, impetuosity and perhaps even irresponsibility, and these character- istics have also been imputed to Richard. Richard's modern biogra- phers have strenuously defended him against this particular charge, pointing to his many acts of statesmanship, but the older view is still held and was probably the dominant one in the late nineteenth and early twentieth centuries.[1] If we add to this an inevitably anglocentric perspective which expected English kings to occupy themselves appropriately with domestic matters, it is not difficult to see why Richard's reputation should have called for rehabilitation.

Although the crusades are regarded more negatively today – and even in the Middle Ages there were critical voices raised – for the medieval mind Jerusalem was literally the centre of the universe. The holy places were as important to twelfth-century Christians as those of the Arabian peninsula are to Muslims today. Richard had taken the Cross in November 1187 as count of Poitou, pledging his intention to go to the the Holy Land, and nothing would have deflected him from his purpose. He was not the only twelfth-century monarch to do so: it was a matter of national honour. In the many contemporary narratives which give a full and detailed account of this crusade, Richard is rarely absent from centre stage. The contrast between poor, 'shadowy' Berengaria and her flamboyant hero of a husband is inevitable.

What kind of a man was this hero, for whom posterity quickly adopted the title 'Lionheart'? His career was recorded in considerable detail by historians of his own time and by later writers. A composite picture emerges from a rich variety of sources, contemporary and more recent. There are a dozen or so major chroniclers belonging to what has been described as the 'golden age' of English historical writing. These chroniclers recorded the events of the reigns of King Henry and his son Richard in Latin prose (and occasionally verse), and there are also freer, more literary accounts in Anglo-Norman or Old French prose or verse, which cover the same ground. None of these writers are neutral observers, though some adopt a more cautious tone than others. Their writing is variously prudent, circumspect, tongue in cheek, snide, barbed, emotive, hortatory or grandiloquent.

Another, less reliable source of information follows quickly in their wake. As living memory recedes, so folklore and legend assume their own momentum. During the thirteenth and fourteenth centuries new traditions appear – the eating of Saracen flesh, the literal snatching of the lion's heart, the Blondel story – but all these themes, as B.B. Broughton correctly indicates, are derived from or suggested by episodes from the earlier biographical tradition, showing clearly how the two traditions have begun to intertwine.[2]

Many of these legendary elements – Richard the daredevil warrior, Richard the master of disguise, Richard the inspirer of undying loyalty – reappear in the fictional Richard. Modern scholarship has ensured the appearance of at least half a dozen recent biographies of Richard which draw together all the information contained in the earlier sources and further explicate and elaborate upon the context.

While a great many of the facts are indeed known, the truth is still in many ways as elusive as ever. The question of Richard's sexual preference is an obvious instance. The position can be summarised very quickly: there is no direct evidence to prove that Richard was exclusively homosexual, and some indirect evidence to suggest that he was not. Yet many, perhaps the majority of modern commentators believe that he was. There are puzzling aspects of Richard's conduct which are more easily understood if he was an active bi-sexual with a preference for male partners. His relationship with Berengaria is one of these aspects and, although these modern biographers have little to say about Berengaria, their judgement is inevitably shaped by their attitudes to Richard, his statesmanship, reputation and sexual orientation.[3]

In this crucial and sensitive area, the neutrality and objectivity of the texts cannot be taken for granted: it can be argued that, in some cases, care has been taken to set the record 'straight', while in the case of modern biographers, subjective bias and contemporary social attitudes towards sex and gender are inseparable from matters of historical judgement. As John Boswell has often pointed out, in a number of books and articles, it is dangerous to impose inflexible and simplistic typologies of sexual orientation on cultures remote from our own in time or place.

Richard was the third-born son of two distinctive personalities, whose marriage was contracted in haste for a mixture of political and personal reasons and ended, as far as we can judge, in a truce after years of bitter enmity. Henry II of England was of Norman parentage on his mother's side. The 'Empress' Matilda was the grand-daughter of William the Conqueror, and a woman of considerable learning, piety and political common sense. Henry's father, Geoffrey, count of Anjou, nicknamed Plantagenet because of the sprig of broom (*Plantagenista*) which adorned his headgear, was descended from a long line which included such notables as the violent and tyrannical Fulk Nerra, the Black Falcon of Anjou. Henry inherited his vast 'empire' through the alliance of his Norman and Angevin ancestors. He was an energetic monarch, always on the move, emotional, hot-tempered, intellectually curious and conventionally religious. From contemporary sources we learn of his restless energy, his enthusiasm for hunting and riding, his support for men of letters and his taste for political intrigue. He is also shown as violent, vengeful and adulterous. Giraldus Cambrensis (Gerald of Wales), one of the best-known contemporary chroniclers, was originally a protegé of the Angevins, but when the advancement for which he had manoeuvred and manipulated failed to materialise, he turned against the king and his sons and used his considerable eloquence to paint a picture of a family in which the sins of the father had brought about the corruption of the sons. It is to Giraldus that we owe the dramatic picture of the young eagles destroying the nest in which they were reared.[4]

In his last days Henry appears as a pathetic and disillusioned figure, his wife alienated by his numerous extra-marital affairs, and his restless young sons in constant revolt against his authority. Only the youngest, John, because he 'lacked land', i.e. had no safe base from which to attack his father, remained innocent in the old king's eyes, while, as Giraldus observes, with a certain satisfaction, the ex-nuptial son Geoffrey, later to be archbishop of York, proved to a be a better son to his father than any of the princes of the blood royal. Henry was intelligent, courageous and capable of great charm, but many of his personal relationships turned sour, as his fatal clash with Thomas a Beckett illustrates clearly. His marriage to Eleanor of Aquitaine must have appeared in the beginning to promise a renaissance of spectacular achievement. A young dynamic monarch and his beautiful, spirited consort would preside over the most powerful court in Europe, eclipsing by far the pathetic, feeble Louis

VII of France, for whom Eleanor had shown her contempt by remarrying almost immediately after her divorce. The outcome was quite different.

Eleanor of Aquitaine, Richard's mother, has inspired more biography, romance and general anecdotal comment than any other medieval woman, except perhaps Heloise. Simply by living to the age of eighty-two she stands out as unusual and all the more because she was both physically and mentally active and mobile until well into old age, as evidenced by the amount of travelling she did at the end of her life and the energetic role she played in the political affairs of her royal sons. It is unlikely however that she would have attracted such concentrated attention from both romance writers and literary critics alike if she had not also been renowned for her beauty and for her alleged sexual indiscretions, which may have little foundation in fact. In terms of the survival strategies available to women, Eleanor was for most of her life both a 'pleaser' and a 'manipulator' – a powerful combination.

Some of the mystique surrounding Eleanor is a reflection of her own immediate ancestry. Her grandfather, William IX of Aquitaine, was the first of the Occitan troubadours. An intriguing and colourful figure, he is credited with 'inventing' the troubadour tradition because his work is the earliest surviving example of the genre. He was violent and quarrelsome, a compulsive womaniser who was excommunicated three times, a warrior and sometime crusader and an accomplished poet. His surviving work comprises just eleven poems, which combine crude sexual humour with lyricism and apparently genuine religious piety. William's marital vicissitudes were not unusual for his time, but he was particularly aggressive in his relationships, driving two long-suffering wives to retreat by turn into a monastery and defiantly cohabiting with his long-term mistress, the aptly named Dangerosa, or 'la Maubergeonne', the wife of the count of Chatellerault. The abbey to which his first two wives retreated was the famous foundation of Fontevraud, which was to be so closely linked with the Angevin dynasty. William's response was, it appears, to proclaim the foundation of his own abbey, an 'abbey' of prostitution, at Niort, in mocking parody of the 'Madeleines' – fallen women – of Fontevraud.

Eleanor was the child and heir of William's son by his second wife Philippa of Toulouse, and her mother was Dangerosa's (legitimate) daughter. As her father's heir, Eleanor inherited the county of Poitou, the duchy of Aquitaine and the dependent territories of Gascony and Guyenne to the south. Her first marriage to Louis VII of France was not a success, despite the political advantages of such a union; she bore him two daughters, Alix and Marie, but no son; and matters took a turn for the worse when she accompanied Louis on the second crusade. Persistent rumours circulated concerning Eleanor's general lack of decorum and, more specifically, her conduct with her own uncle, Raymond of Poitiers. Historians have reacted in various ways to these traditions: some have dismissed them as mere gossip, while others have leapt passionately to her defence, blaming Louis for the failure of their marriage. Some of her recent biographers, influenced by their own anti-clericalism, have championed her cause because of the hostility she appears to have aroused in well-known churchmen such as Abbot Suger and St Bernard of Clairvaux – a tendency she shared with her grandfather, who was said to have publicly taunted a bishop about his baldness and roundly abused the various clerics who excommunicated him. Louis and Eleanor were divorced in 1152 and a few months later Eleanor had married the young count of Anjou, fifteen years her junior.[5]

Eight children followed in quick succession, five sons and three daughters. Eleanor was to outlive all but two of them. Richard, the third-born son, appears to have been her favourite. While his elder brother Henry the 'Young King' was destined to inherit the dukedom of Normandy and Geoffrey (the first-born, William died in infancy) that of Brittany, Richard was made count of Poitou and duke of Aquitaine, his mother's lands, and spent most of his childhood and adolescence in those territories. Occitan, his mother's language, was probably his own preferred idiom, though later, as king, in his dealings with his largely Norman and Anglo-Norman entourage, he would presumably have spoken the *langue d'oïl* of the north, with a north-western dialectal colouring. It is thus somewhat misleading to speak of him as 'French' except in a general and rather anachronistic sense.

He probably inherited his love of music and entertainment from his mother and may have been further encouraged in this by frequent contact with his half-sister, Marie countess of Champagne, herself a patroness of poets and men of letters. Richard's relationship with his father must have been coloured by the growing conflict between his parents. Eleanor's initial feelings for Henry seem to have worn off quickly: he feared her strong will and independence and she bitterly resented his public infidelities. The king's supporters claimed that Eleanor encouraged her sons in their frequent acts of rebellion, and perhaps this was the most effective way of protecting her own interests. Eleanor's devotion to Richard is clear on many occasions – in her reaction to his captivity in Austria in 1192 and the impassioned letter she wrote to the Pope imploring support for his release; in her constant presence at his side in her capacity as Queen Mother; and in the way in which Richard turned instinctively to her for counsel and support. But as some commentators have suggested, the relationship was perhaps a shade too possessive. Berengaria was unlucky to have had Eleanor as a mother-in-law and perhaps, unable to compete, she may have preferred to withdraw.

Events suggest that once Berengaria had outlived her usefulness by not providing Richard with a son and heir, Eleanor excluded her from participation in affairs of state and Berengaria responded by keeping out of the way. On the other hand, Constance of Brittany, wife of Eleanor's son Geoffrey, who did bear a son, the unlucky prince Arthur, fared no better in her mother-in-law's affections: many secondary sources have claimed that Eleanor disliked the ambitious Constance. But these claims may be due to the common habit of personalising the behaviour of women, attributing emotional or irrational motives to their actions, while men are more frequently described as acting 'rationally', that is, for political or economic reasons. Although claims have been made about the closeness of Eleanor's relationship with her daughter Marie de Champagne, at least one historian has claimed that Eleanor showed no particular affection for her own daughters, preferring to promote family interests by marrying them off strategically.[6] In the last resort, so much has been written about Eleanor that she has become a largely fictionalised construction.[7] Her energy, mobility and high political profile during a large part of her life are, however, a matter of historical record.

Richard was born in September 1157 at Oxford, in the 'King's house', sometimes called Beaumont Palace, at the bottom of Beaumont Street, opposite the present-day Worcester College.[8] Nothing remains of this wooden structure which was destroyed by fire, but some of the flagstones are said to have been preserved in a Carmelite monastery just outside the city. Richard divided his early years between England, Normandy and Anjou, in the company of his parents or of tutors and guardians, some of whom are known to us by name, as is his famous wet-nurse, Hodierna. A vivid account of the kind of activities he might have pursued in early childhood is provided by Anthony Bridge in the most colourful and discursive of the modern biographies. The education of boys is better documented than that of girls, and Bridge draws persuasively on this to show us the kind of tuition and guidance Richard would have received at the hands of these various preceptors.

Following normal practice, he was betrothed early in life, once to a daughter of the count of Barcelona, and then later to Aélis, Louis of France's daughter by his second wife, Constance of Castile. This betrothal was the subject of discord between England and France for many years to come. Aélis was brought to England to live at her prospective father-in-law's court, as was customary, but for some reason, which has never been satisfactorily explained, neither Richard nor his father seem to have been eager to proceed with the marriage. Perhaps Aélis was only useful as a bargaining chip. Richard's interests were in any case hardly those he could share with a fiancée. His youth, after his investiture as duke of Aquitaine and count of Poitou, in 1172, was spent almost entirely in these lands, engaging in active warfare with rebellious vassals or neighbours or intriguing with his brothers against his father or among themselves.[9] Unlike his older brother Henry, who loved tournaments and similar distractions, Richard preferred the real thing. As John Gillingham has shown, warfare and chivalry are two different things, and while many of the 'wars' of the time were more in the nature of tactical skirmishes, there were invariably serious strategic issues at stake. From the first, Richard was involved as a matter of necessity, as well as choice, in the defence of his own territories and the advancement of his family's cause.

Richard's life – and Berengaria's – might have taken a very different course if two of his brothers had not predeceased him. William died in infancy, and in 1183 Henry the 'Young King' (so-called because it was the custom, followed by both Angevin and Capetian monarchs, to nominate their own successor during their own lifetime) died as the result of sudden illness. Henry is now remembered as a paragon of chivalry, much addicted to fashion and jousting, less aggressive and hot-tempered than Richard, less devious and scheming than Geoffrey or John. These impressions are based not only on the comments of the chroniclers but also on the rather less reliable witness of the troubadours.

As H.J. Chaytor points out in an old, but useful book on the troubadours, the best-known of them all lived in lands under Angevin rule and they liked to give the impression that they were at the centre of events, dropping names and *senhals*, or pseudonyms, freely throughout their poems, particularly the less strictly lyrical *tensos* and *sirventes*. The Angevin princes appear frequently in these poems, under the labels Marinier (Henry), Rassa (Geoffrey) and Oc-e-No, Yes and No (Richard).[10]

However inflated may have been the troubadours' opinions of their own importance, the chroniclers never mention them or their writings. They were marginal *littérateurs* and their outlook was essentially artificial and narcissistic. None the less, the young Angevin princes were clearly people to be flattered and cultivated. They may have seemed like perfect models for the *jovens*, the young unmarried aristocratic males, to whom a certain licence was allowed to enjoy to the full that charmed interval before the inevitable assumption of adult responsibilities as head of a household and father of sons.[11] These bonded male groups appear in many medieval societies and despite their superficial differences, their one common characteristic is their essential transience. The condition is not necessarily predicated on chronological age but is bounded by puberty on the one hand and marriage on the other. Although he was married young, Henry did not evidently achieve the desired maturity but passes into legend as the golden-haired boy king, charming and frivolous, leaving a young widow and a people who hardly knew him.

Richard was harder and more practical, as active and mobile as his parents and with a violent temper, brutal on occasions but also capable of great magnanimity and tolerance. He was loyal to his mother and often considerate to his sisters, but his relationship with his father was shot through with rivalry and suspicion.[12] Gerald of Wales, the most hostile of the chroniclers, paints a dramatic picture of the old king on his death bed, abandoned and almost destitute, while Richard gazes down at the body in pitiless silence. Yet Richard was able to assure his father's most trusted retainer, William Marshal, that he valued his loyalty and service to the former king and would now expect the same loyalty to his own person. William was not the only one of his father's advisors and courtiers retained by his son, which suggests that Richard had a pragmatic streak and was capable of dispassionate judgements when it suited him.

No one knows exactly how and when the marriage between Richard and Berengaria was first mooted. Henry II had already set in place a network of alliances with the Christian kings of northern Spain, allowing his own southernmost territories to remain within the orbit of Aragon and Navarre, in part to keep in check the ambitions of the counts of Toulouse. When he gave his daughter Eleanor in marriage to Alfonso VIII of Castile in 1170, he nominated Gascony as her dowry, to be handed over on the death of Queen Eleanor. In theory, then, an alliance between his son Richard, who was duke of Aquitaine, would have been consistent with these policy objectives.[13] But the earliest mention of Berengaria in any of the chronicles is dated to spring 1191, when she and Eleanor are recorded as having crossed the Alps and commenced their journey down through Italy to meet Richard in Sicily or Calabria. Three brief references, one in a poem by the troubadour Bertran de Born,[14] the others in the rhymed Anglo-Norman *Estoire de la Guerre Sainte* and its Latin counterpart, the *Itinerarium Regis Ricardi,* have been the focus of considerable attention in this context. Bertran de Born was placed in Hell by Dante for sowing the seeds of discord, and of all the troubadours he shows the greatest interest in political matters. In this particular poem he speaks gloatingly of the shame brought to the king of France – Philip Augustus – by Richard's rejection of his sister in favour of the 'king of Navarre's daughter'. The poem cannot be dated very precisely. John Gillingham accepts Appel's older dating of 1188, but arguments for both an earlier and a later date have been advanced. The poem suggests familiarity with the king of Navarre and the many references to Spanish affairs in the poetry of the troubadours generally have lent credence to the belief that the marriage negotiations were not a secret.[15]

Ambroise, the author of the *Estoire*, was probably a Norman jongleur or professional minstrel who accompanied the crusading army. He was also a loyal supporter of the king. Both Ambroise and the author of the *Itinerarium* – the two texts are clearly related, though the nature of the relationship is not yet a matter of general agreement – state that Richard had fallen in love with Berengaria 'a long time previously, when he was count of Poitou'. On the basis of these brief references and other circumstantial evidence, historians have offered their own guesses as to when Richard and Berengaria first met or became attracted to each other: some suggest that it was as early as 1183.

Richard's father, Henry II, was enlisted as an arbitrator on more than one recorded occasion by the warring Christian monarchs of northern Spain. Roger of Howden mentions two incidents during which the kings of Castile, Aragon and Navarre visited King Henry and sought his counsel. Such consultations must have been based on more than a mere acquaintance. Moreover, as Susana Hereros has shown, the political activities of both Berengaria's father and later her brother demonstrate a long-standing preoccupation with trans-Pyrenean matters. It was thus extremely likely that the interests of Navarre and England should occasionally coincide. As count of Poitou, Richard was himself frequently involved in the affairs of Gascony and Guyenne and spent much time in the vicinity of his southern borders. Any of these contextual factors may have prompted a meeting between Richard and members of the Navarrese royal family.

The notion of a romantic attachment between Richard and his future fiancée has captured the imagination of novelists but is impossible to substantiate. It is not incompatible with Richard's reputation as a sexual adventurer during his youth. Unlike his father, his brother John and most of his royal peers, Richard fathered only one ex-nuptial child. We know nothing of the child's mother, who was unlikely to have been an aristocrat, but the episode is thought to have taken place during this precise period, i.e. when he was count of Poitou. Most 'bastards' acknowledged by kings and counts were born before marriage, rather than outside wedlock, and some languages, Spanish included, recognise the significant distinction between the two. The boy himself, significantly named Philip, was subsequently married to the heiress Amélie de Cognac but died without issue, fulfilling the grim prediction of Giraldus Cambrensis that the degenerate brood would reap its own harvest of sterility and self-destruction.

It is at this time, too, that Richard and his companions in arms acquired the reputation for the brutal mistreatment of the wives and daughters of the enemy. Later legends such as that of the nun of Fontevraud,[16] who was prepared to lose the beautiful eyes which had attracted Richard's lustful advances rather than submit to them, or the claim that he sent for prostitutes on his death bed, may have been inspired by these traditions. Needless to say, those modern scholars who reject the notion of a homosexual Richard rely heavily on this material, but as Duby, Flandrin,[17] Boswell and others have indicated, the amount of latitude allowed to young unmarried males in the twelfth century was considerable and included both homosexual and heterosexual experimentation. We hardly need to be reminded that active gay men can and do reproduce, and if, as seems likely, Richard's sexual preferences were not yet fixed, the odd pregnancy here and there is hardly a matter for surprise. Nor would this kind of brutal and unthinking promiscuity have precluded a more socially acceptable fleeting fancy for an inaccessible young woman, particularly a chaste and religious one. There have been very few societies in which men have not divided women into two classes, potential marriage partners and exploitable sexual commodities.

It is also possible that Richard may have formed a friendship with Berengaria's brother, Sancho, in the course of his activities on the Pyrenean border. The two men had much in common: both became the subject of legend and folklore and both were compared to lions for their outstanding martial virtues.

Perhaps the young Navarrese princes and princesses accompanied their father on visits to King Henry's courts on occasions similar to those recorded in 1172 and 1173. The younger Sancho may have been among the young guests invited by the count of Poitou to the feasts and hunting parties he held at his favourite spots, Talmont sur Jard in the Vendée and Chizé in Gascony. Sancho may even, like Kaherdin in the Tristan story, have spoken to his companion about his sisters. Perhaps Richard's predatory instincts were aroused by the thought of beautiful and virtuous young women who had decided to consecrate themselves to God. One of Richard's earlier biographers, Kate Norgate, believes that Richard formed an attachment to Berengaria around 1183, a year in which the twenty-six year-old Richard spent much time at Talmont, but only on the basis of one line in the *Estoire*. Gmelin dates the *sirventes* of Bertran de Born 'S'ieu fos aissi ...' to this period, which would suggest that firmer proposals may have been made.

J.M. Lacarra suggests 1185 as a more suitable period, because in that year, on 14 April, Richard met and established an alliance with King Alfonso II of Aragon at Najac in Gascony.[18] During this meeting, Richard's aid was sought in persuading the king of Navarre to return the castles of Trasmoz and Cajuelos captured in previous hostilities. Lacarra believes that '... the fact that Richard was chosen as intermediary argues that Richard was influential with Don Sancho ...' Why was this so? One plausible reason might well be that a marriage alliance had been proposed. It was not long afterwards, in the same year, as we have seen, that Berengaria was conferred with the honour of Monreal: an appropriate recognition of her status if she was to be the fiancée of the count of Poitou, whose political interests in the area were significant.[19]

If this was so, what Richard and his father planned to do about Aélis of France is not clear: perhaps Richard never took the matter of Berengaria very seriously or found it convenient to use it as a smokescreen to explain his reluctance to proceed with the French option. Norgate believes that the proposal was kept secret for several years, and there is some support for this suggestion in the

Anales of Moret, who, as we know, relied on Howden and presumably other lost sources of information for matters concerning the Angevin connection.

Richard's position in the family had, in the meantime, changed significantly with the death of his elder brother the young king in 1183. At twenty-six he was now the obvious successor to the throne. In 1186 his younger brother Geoffrey died, leaving Richard not only as heir but as chief rival to his father for the remainder of the Old King's life. Eleanor must have pinned all her hopes on her favourite son. At the same time, Richard was making new and more sinister friendships. Among these was the mercenary captain Mercadier who is recorded as having been present at Talmont in 1183 and who was to remain Richard's loyal lieutenant all his life.[20]

In the winter of 1186, however, Richard formed a new relationship, one which was to obsess him for the rest of his life: the consequences of this relationship were also to affect the future of Berengaria.

Louis VII of France, Eleanor's former husband, had subsequently remarried twice, once to Constance of Castile who died after giving birth to two daughters and then to Adela of Champagne. On 21 August 1165 the son he had so longed for was at last born. The new prince was named Philip and hailed as '*Dieu-Donné*', God-given. The chronicler Rigord was subsequently to confer on him the title Augustus. These auspicious names indicate the prominent place he has occupied in French historiography ever since, but his reputation has been consistently less glorious across the Channel. As he grew to manhood, Philip enjoyed none of Richard's physical advantages: although one modern French scholar, Robert Bautier, describes him as '*beau et bien bati*' (handsome and well-built), others have described him as red-faced, one-eyed, and prematurely bald. In addition he was greedy, intemperate and lecherous ('*luxuriae pronus*').[21]

He was also astute and calculating and, if only by outliving Richard, succeeded eventually in pegging back the English in Anjou, Normandy and Poitou, enlarging the boundaries of his small domain and extending French influence over a much wider area than ever before. Philip was crowned as his father's successor in 1179 and acceded to the throne on the death of Louis in September

1180. In doing so he became the titular overlord of the king of England in respect of the English possessions on the continent. The English king was his most powerful and dangerous vassal and rival. It was thus inevitable that he would lock horns with the aging King Henry and with his son and heir Richard.

In 1186-7 a truce of sorts was achieved and Richard and Philip struck up an immediate and intimate friendship. Philip was twenty-one and Richard nearly thirty. Although Richard undoubtedly used his friendship with Philip as part of his campaign against his father, there was an intensity about the friendship which caught the immediate attention of the chroniclers:

> After peace was made, Richard duke of Aquitaine, son of the king of England, went to stay with Philip king of France, whom he honoured so greatly for a long time, that each day they ate at the same table and drank from the same cup and at night they slept in one bed. And the king of France loved him as his own soul and their mutual affection was so strong that because of the vehemence of their mutual affection the Lord King of England was dumbfounded and wondered what this could be. And fearing for his own future he put off his desired intention to return to England until he could find out what such a sudden affection might mean. (Howden, *Gesta*, anno 1187)

John Boswell[22] sees in this the clearest indication that the relationship was homoerotic, a view strongly refuted by two of Richard's recent biographers, John Gillingham and Anthony Bridge, who both point out – quite correctly – that sharing a bed did not necessarily denote a sexual relationship in the medieval context. This is something of a red herring: the passage also goes on to stress the vehemence of the relationship which took all parties by surprise. The word *vehementer* is the same word used by Richard of Devizes to describe the state of Richard's feelings when awaiting the arrival of his bride to be some years later in Sicily. The adjectival form of the word is used by Peter the Chanter and other moralists to describe excessive manifestations of sexual love.[23] It hardly suggests mere mateship.

A more substantial objection has been raised by Stephen Jaeger[24] who points out that this kind of language is often used by and about kings, without any necessary homosexual implication. It has also been claimed that King Henry's dismayed reaction was essentially political rather than moral. These two arguments are not without merit, but in my view Boswell was correct in claiming that something more was involved.

No one has ever claimed that Philip Augustus was a confirmed homosexual – on the contrary, he was something of a libertine and had at least one long-lasting heterosexual relationship, with Agnes of Merania, with whom he contracted an irregular union not recognised by the Pope. At the time of his involvement with Richard, his Queen Elizabeth (or Isabelle) of Hainault was pregnant with his first son, the future Louis VIII. It is also true that many heterosexual men have at some time in their life indulged in non-coercive homosexual relationships.[25]

Whether or not the relationship was a physical one, its emotional intensity is suggested in the way in which intimacy turned later to bitter hatred, in the violently hostile language Philip uses when referring to Richard in official correspondence, and perhaps, too, in Richard's alleged deathbed revelation that he had not received the sacrament of holy communion for a number of years, because of the hatred he bore in his heart for the king of France. At least one commentator has suggested that this should be taken with a pinch of salt, though the source of the revelation can only have been one of Richard's familiars, if not one of his confessors. We know from other sources that Richard was not averse to prevaricating when challenged by churchmen about his behaviour, and he may, if the story is true, have used this as another excuse for infrequent communion. On the other hand, Roger of Howden tells us that in 1195, after a marital reconciliation, Richard also became a regular and devout mass-goer – though not necessarily a regular communicant. If this incident is not purely apocryphal, it would be in keeping with the special intensity of the hatred reserved for a former lover or intimate.

Richard saw Philip as his nemesis and bitter rival; Philip, for his part, was to speak of Richard as some kind of devil. Although these divisions had already begun to surface as they commenced their joint crusade, their fortunes continued to be linked; they shared the same disfiguring bouts of illness, the same disappointments and frustrations and were constantly caught up in a web of mutual mistrust, obsessed by each other's activities, reacting to each other's schemes, real or imagined, and seeking to undermine each other at every opportunity. The English view of Philip Augustus has always been a negative one:[26] he is seen as lacking Richard's redeeming qualities of bravery and magnanimity while possessing the very defects Richard lacked – deviousness, cunning and the discretion which is the better part of valour. Not for nothing did the Anglo-Norman public prefer Roland who was *'preux'* (brave) to Oliver, who was merely *'sage'* (wise)![27]

Philip was his father's only son and obvious successor, with no sibling rivalry to distract him and blessed with the apparent support of powerful neighbours such as Champagne and Flanders, linked to the French court not only by ties of vassalage but of marriage and kinship. Guarded and calculating where Richard was bold and impetuous, he had learned to gauge the measure of the ailing English king and his rebellious sons by the time he acceded to the throne in 1180. Having patched up their quarrels and backed away from open confrontation, the kings of France and England were shortly to be diverted by momentous news from the Middle East.

The disastrous rout of Christians by the Muslim conqueror Saladin at the Horns of Hattin was followed by the capture of Jerusalem. Pope Gregory VIII issued an appeal to the Christian kings in the bull *Audita Tremendi*. In Spain, where Muslims were not the frightening and unreal caricatures of French propaganda but neighbours, even if dangerous and hostile ones, the appeal had less obvious impact. In the North, however, the response was swift: Richard himself took the Cross in November 1187 and in January Richard and his father met Philip Augustus at the foot of the great oak of Gisors, in the Norman Vexin, and declared a solemn truce, in the course of which Philip and Henry also pledged to take up the cross.[28] By March the third great Christian monarch, the Holy Roman Emperor Friedrich Barbarossa, had followed suit, but he was ultimately unable to fulfil his pledge, as he died from drowning en route for the crusade a couple of years later.

In March Henry and Richard held council at Le Mans and drew up regulations for the conduct of the crusade, rules which clearly reflect the religious nature of the enterprise. Strict discipline was enjoined in a variety of respects, including the banning of all women but laundry assistants from the crusading ranks. Churchmen in both Europe and the Latin Middle East continued to fan the flames by their fiery sermons and emotional exhortations, but Richard and Henry appear to have been in no hurry to proceed. Richard's projected marriage was a minor but nagging issue in the background.

The agreement to marry Aélis had been ratified no less than five times since its inclusion in the Treaty of Mortain in 1169, and it must have looked to the outside world, in July 1189, two months before Richard's coronation, as if the wedding would finally take place and, with it, the final settlement of national differences on the status of the Norman Vexin, the crucial piece of land which had been allotted as the *maritagium*, or marriage portion, first of Marguerite, young Henry's wife, then of her sister Aélis. But with the death of King Henry, everything changed. Richard was now king and the need for an heir was more pressing.

The commonly held view is that Eleanor, alarmed at her son's reluctance to provide himself with an heir, and motivated by anti-French resentment, took the initiative and went herself to Spain to negotiate the terms of the marriage with Berengaria. If she knew of, or suspected her son's sexual ambivalence, the possibility of reviving memories of an adolescent passion might also have been an added incentive. This is the view taken by the fiction writers, who also suggest that Eleanor knew of Berengaria by reputation and judged her to be compliant and dutiful and thus unlikely to supplant her in her son's affections. The birth of an heir would certainly have been an important priority but, while the bride's consent was necessary – that much the Church had achieved – little thought was given to long-term compatibility. Companionate marriage was not unknown in the Middle Ages but it appears to have been accidental rather than habitual. Any young woman on whom the honour of a royal choice was conferred would have been expected to accept without question.

Courtly literature is not always a reliable witness but it does suggest that some notion of romantic love was current in the twelfth century. Literary fashions, however escapist, must in some way reflect or respond to current modes of thought. It may be that some aristocratic young women approached their arranged marriages with unreal aspirations. When the dream faded, a dignified stoicism was all that was left. For some, the reality was brutal and horrifying; for others it was a slower, sadder dwindling of expectations. Duby has described some of these cases in his study of the 'male' Middle Ages.

Eleanor herself would not have harboured any modern illusions about romantic love in marriage. Some literary historians have suggested that the popularity in the later twelfth century of adulterous love stories such as the Tristan and Lancelot themes was due to Eleanor's own disenchantment with marriage and possible extramarital affairs. Some of the popular biographies have greatly exaggerated this connection. But not all commentators accept that the initiative in Richard's matrimonial affairs was taken by Eleanor. John Gillingham has argued convincingly that it was Richard who initiated the proposal, pointing to a significant period of activity in Gascony and a particularly important meeting at La Réole which took place in February 1190, shortly before he left for the crusade, when marriage negotiations might have taken place. This is in no way inconsistent with the suggestion that the first moves were made five years previously. If the matter had been raised at Najac in 1185, the conference at La Réole may have been the appropriate occasion to ratify the earlier arrangement. This would certainly provide an answer to the rather puzzling question as to why King Sancho would have allowed his daughter to undertake such a long and dangerous journey apparently on the spur of the moment and without the appropriate undertakings.

Richard must have recognised the importance of ensuring the succession. Marriage to a pious and compliant spouse who would provide him with an heir might not have seemed incompatible with a growing inclination towards sex with men. From whichever quarter the initiative came, the king or his mother, King Sancho would have had little reason not to accept it. A stable situation in Ultrapuertos would allow more time and resources to be devoted to strengthening the borders with Aragon and Castile.

All this is, inevitably, speculative. The picture becomes clearer with the first mention of Richard's marriage in the eye-witness accounts of the third crusade, the *Itinerarium Regis Ricardi*[29] and the *Estoire de la Terre Sainte* of Ambroise,[30] and the *Gesta* and *Chronica* of Roger of Howden. Eleanor is recorded as having gone in September 1190 from Bordeaux to Navarre and thence, with Berengaria in tow, back across the Alps to Lombardy, Pisa, Rome and Naples, and finally to Sicily.

We have no direct account of this long and arduous journey, one of many that the apparently tireless Eleanor made in the course of her long life, with a political purpose in mind. We have to rely on parallel accounts of similar journeys and on the descriptive powers of historians like Margaret Wade Labarge and Norbert Ohler.[31]

The journey would have taken place in winter for the most part, when the beech and pine clad slopes of the lower Pyrenees become windswept and forbidding and the Alps a treacherous wilderness of ice and sleet. The women would have ridden in litters or carriages, over former Roman roads long fallen into disrepair, stopping perhaps at monasteries or castles, where they would have been received by local dignitaries. Travel was slow: a horseman might do 30-35 miles in a day, but travel through mountainous terrain might reduce the total considerably. We can only imagine what rigours the two women would have had to endure. Eleanor, advanced in age and rich in experience, was now for the first time for many years a free agent, a respected figure in her own right. She had outlived the two husbands who, in their different ways, had been such a source of disappointment. Now all her hopes were invested in this, her favourite son and the sons who would be born from his forthcoming marriage.

Berengaria, on the other hand, may never have left her native Spain before, and if she had, it was perhaps only to cross the mountains into Occitania with her parents or brother. The two women, one a queen already, the other a queen to be, were to spend long weeks in each other's company, as they pursued their journey through Spain, Occitania and Italy and rested at monasteries and castles along the way. In which language did they converse? Possibly in Occitan (sometimes referred to as 'provencal') since that language was widely spoken in the cities along the pilgrimage route – Pamplona, Estella and much of Sanguesa – and the Navarrese may have had some familiarity with it. It seems unlikely that Eleanor would have been familiar with any Hispano-Romance dialect, such as Aragonese-Navarrese. Latin was often used as an official *lingua franca*, as was French both in the Near East and Byzantium and, while Eleanor may have been conversant with these usages, we cannot be sure about Berengaria.

Did Eleanor consider it her duty to prepare Berengaria for what awaited her? Did Berengaria express the natural curiosity of a young woman on her way to be married to one of the most famous figures of the age? We cannot know, but we must surely be moved to wonder what might have passed between these two very different women. Berengaria had lost her own mother at the vulnerable age of nineteen or so: it seems very unlikely that Eleanor, by temperament or inclination, was prepared to fill the void.

At various points along the route, the two women were met by local dignitaries who accorded them the appropriate courtesies. We do not know who escorted them. José María Lacarra believes that Berengaria's brother Sancho was present for at least part of the journey but, as he is certainly recorded as active in Spain in July 1191, they must have parted company at some convenient point in Italy.

Richard, meanwhile, had arrived in Messina on 22 September, 1190, having left Vezelay for Lyons, in company with Philip Augustus and their two combined armies.[32] Richard's itinerary had taken him through Marseilles, Genoa, Rome, Naples and Salerno to Reggio di Calabria. His arrival in Sicily reads like the description of a stage set or a movie still: the chronicler tells how the local population gathered on the shore, and the sun glittered on the burnished sea as the great painted galleys swept into the bay. In the midst of the pennants and flags and banners, Richard stood erect on a specially raised platform, dressed to kill. (His various changes of wardrobe are recorded in some detail by the chroniclers, who say nothing at all about what his fiancée wore at any point in the narrative!)

Once garrisoned in the island, the English troops soon became embroiled in skirmishes with the local population as well as with the French troops already in the city of Messina itself. The chroniclers' accounts describe the behaviour of the troops: the French, we learn, were arrogant, and the English made a thorough nuisance of themselves.[33] Indeed, so unappreciative were the local Greeks, Franks and Muslims of the activities of the English that they referred to them as the 'long-tailed Englishmen' (*caudati*), though whether this referred to their devilish hooliganism or their physical endowments is not clear.

Once in Sicily Richard lost no time in rescuing his younger sister Joanna, widow of the Sicilian King William 'the Good', who had died in November 1189. Joanna had fallen prey to the ambition of an upstart relation of the royal family, Tancred of Lecce. Tancred had imprisoned the queen and seized her assets. Richard demanded and obtained the swift release of his sister and put Tancred on notice to deliver Joanna's dower entitlements as well as certain other valuables belonging to the late king and to his father-in-law, Henry II of England. Richard had other problems to settle: daily disputes between his men and local traders over food prices, profiteering and pilfering as well as the undercurrent of rivalry with the French which was always ready to break out into fisticuffs or worse. The French king, devious and scheming as ever, was quick to take advantage of the situation and encouraged Tancred in his refusal to settle with Richard.

By Christmas 1190 Richard had gained the upper hand and Philip was forced to agree upon strict regulations to control the conduct of the troops and the local merchants. It looked as if everyone could settle down to enjoy the seasonal festivities. But trouble was still brewing, because Richard would have been well aware of the imminent arrival of his mother and his fiancée and the fact that he was still officially betrothed to Aélis of France. He must have been working to a plan which necessitated very precise timing. Late in February he sent ships to Naples to meet Eleanor and Berengaria, but they chose to proceed by land, perhaps with Richard's approval, giving him more time to prepare the showdown with Philip. When the moment came, the French king was outmanoeuvred in a most dramatic way. Richard confronted him with a dramatic announcement: he could not possibly marry Aélis because his late father the king had seduced her while she was under his protection and made her pregnant. In case Philip was disinclined to believe this, Richard had witnesses to prove it. King Henry was dead and the princess herself several thousand miles away in the north, unable to confirm or deny the truth of the allegation.

It is impossible to know whether there was any truth in this accusation, and historians are divided on the matter, but whether the claim were true or not, to be spurned by Coeur de Lion must have reduced the market value of the princess considerably. It was not until August 1195 that Aélis's brother married her off to the count of Ponthieu. She was then aged thirty-three, and one can only hope that she found greater happiness in relative obscurity than in the frustrating years of her exile. Philip had no real choice but to submit to an agreement to release Richard from his engagement.

Tancred of Lecce had been bought off and Richard held the upper hand. The Treaty of Messina states that Philip 'concedes to the above mentioned king in all good faith that he may freely marry whomever he wishes, notwithstanding the former agreement made between us that he would take our sister Alice as wife'.[34] Philip also released Richard and any male heirs from dower obligations to Aélis, which in the event of Richard's dying childless should revert to France. Richard promised to return Aélis to her brother's tutelage on his return to his kingdom. The original text of the treaty is lost, but Delaborde's *Receuil* reproduces a copy. The French king swallowed his pride and left Sicily on 30 March, no doubt swearing to get even. Richard's mother and fiancée were only hours away and the way was clear for the wedding as soon as the penitential season of Lent was over.

Modern biographers have played down the significance of one incident which took place around Christmas of the previous year. It appears in the *Gesta* of Roger of Howden in these words:

> Meanwhile Richard King of England, moved by divine grace, recalled the foulness of his life: for the thorns of lust had departed from his head and it was not human hands

that uprooted them. But God alone who does not desire the death of a sinner but that he should turn from his ways and live, looked upon him with the eyes of his mercy and gave him a contrite heart so that he, gathering together all the archbishops and bishops who were present, prostrated himself naked at their feet, three penitential whips made of light rods in his hand and did not shrink from confessing to them all the foulness of his sins, with such humility and contrition of heart that none might doubt that this was the work of the One whose gaze makes the earth tremble. Then he abjured that sin and accepted the appropriate penance from these bishops and from that hour became a God-fearing man, doing good and backsliding no more into sin. O happy he who falls thus that he may rise the stronger! O happy the one who after penance does not relapse into sin![35]

The significance of this episode, which Howden recast in his *Chronica*,[36] with a few details added, seems to have been overlooked by many writers. Public penances were not unknown – the obvious parallel is Henry II's public expression of contrition for the murder of Thomas a Beckett. There is no doubt that for Richard the crusade was as much a religious as a military occasion. Confession and communion were appropriate preliminaries for those who in the medieval view were pilgrims as much as soldiers. We are not told if there were other public acts of penance prior to this, but Sicily was in a sense the final staging point (the subsequent visit to Cyprus seems to have been unplanned), the last farewell to what we would call Europe or (Western) Christendom, as the medieval world would have known it. It was customary to commence any journey with acts of piety and religious devotion and all the more so when the journey was itself in the nature of a pilgrimage.

But none of this really explains why Richard should undertake such a dramatic act of penance at this particular moment, nor indeed that Roger of Howden should record it with such emphasis (and write it up again in his later *Chronica*). It has been suggested that Richard was publicly confessing the same sins of which his own troops stood accused: plundering, fighting and generally terrorising the local citizenry. This appears unlikely. Whatever else he may have been, Richard does not seem to have been a hypocrite and even allowing for kingly licence, it would have been difficult for him to expect his troops to observe the strict disciplinary regulations already laid down twice while blithely indulging in such activities himself. It is true that these regulations applied mainly to drunkenness, brawling and gambling but, then as now, these disruptive activities often go hand in glove with sexual adventures.

We are entitled to ask whether Richard's motives were not more personal and complex and linked both to the troubling presence of Philip Augustus and the impending arrival of Berengaria. Roger of Howden was not only a trained public servant but also an apologist and an orthodox churchman who lost no opportunity to make a moralising comment. Happy indeed the man who turns away from sin ... but one cannot help wondering whether, knowing his king as he did, Roger may not have been expressing a pious hope rather than a confident prediction!

Richard must have been relieved to see the French king finally pack his bags and depart, no doubt wishing to avoid an embarrassing encounter with the two women who symbolised shame and loss of face for France, Eleanor who had treated his father with such contempt, and Berengaria the unknown Spanish princess for whom Richard had abandoned his sister.

As there are so few references by the chroniclers to Berengaria and her activities, it is a pity they have been so sparing in their treatment of those events in which she did play a more prominent role. Once again, we need to look at the way in which the texts have been structured so as to push the women characters effectively into the background.

Roger of Howden's authorial practice has been compared to the work of an efficient public servant. He carefully lists details of time and place, paying attention to the correct designation of the individuals involved: Queen Eleanor, mother of Richard, king of England ... Joanna, queen of Sicily and sister of the said king ... Berengaria, daughter of Sancho, king of Navarre and so on. He takes care to reproduce the correct order of events and adds background or explanatory details when appropriate.

Perhaps the arrival of Eleanor and Berengaria was kept a secret until the last minute. At any rate, the description of their arrival is much less colourful than that in which Howden describes the arrival of Richard's sister Joanna in Sicily shortly before her marriage to King William 'the Good' in 1176. This earlier passage, perhaps based on the report of an eye-witness, includes a couple of visual touches missing from the account of Berengaria's arrival: the lamps, we are told, were so bright that night that the whole city seemed on fire and the rays of the stars were eclipsed by this brilliance, while Joanna is described as regally attired and seated on a royal charger. Roger was clearly able to slip into discursive or descriptive mode when he felt so inclined – witness his curiosity concerning natural history and eschatology – but the arrival of Richard's bride-to-be is very much part of the official narrative and treated with the appropriate formality.

Fortunately perhaps, the other two eye-witness accounts, those of Ambroise[37] and the *Itinerarium* are more descriptive. This is Ambroise's account:

> For the news had been brought to him, that his mother had arrived there, bringing to the king his beloved. She was a wise maiden, noble, brave and fair, neither false nor disloyal. Her name was Berengaria, and her father, the king of Navarre, had handed her over to the mother of King Richard, who was longing for her to be brought to him. Then she was named as queen. For the king had loved her very much; ever since he was count of Poitiers, he had desired her.

It sounds very much as though this was something Richard had been keeping fairly quiet about. Ambroise certainly stresses the king's excitement at the arrival of his bride to be. He also praises Berengaria, using the vernacular vocabulary of courtly love. Berengaria is Richard's '*drue*' or beloved. She is also *sage, gentilz, preux* and *bele*, adjectives which I have translated as wise, noble, brave and fair. These terms are not gender-specific and their primary connotation is social. Medieval literature, reflecting the values of the class by and for whom it was produced, saw no distinction between inner and outer qualities: to be noble, in medieval romance or epic, was, with a few exceptions, also to be virtuous, brave and beautiful.

In the next line, the poet tells us what Berengaria was not – *fause* or *losiengiere*. *Fause* (false) once again often denotes low social status as do terms like *vil* (base) and *culvert* (cowardly) The lowly-born were rarely in the courtly texts credited with the higher virtues of loyalty, bravery and magnanimity. *Losengiere*, meaning treacherous or a slanderer, may just be a metrical 'filler' but it, too, reflects the same assumption that rank and virtue go hand in hand. So we see that although the text appears to focus more closely on an individual, the language is still to some extent conventional. What seems to me interesting is that, within the limited range of choices available, the poet has chosen to select qualities which are not stereotypically feminine. Berengaria is *sage*, which is echoed, in related Latin forms, in almost every contemporary or near-contemporary description of her, and she is *preux*, which is much more frequently used of males. We are, I think, entitled to see in this emphasis some distant reflection of her distinctive personal qualities.

Be that as it may, Ambroise's text concentrates on the joyful moment, as he speaks of the king's longing for the arrival of his beloved, adding that this love went back to the days of his youth. Whether this is mere barrack-room gossip or a romantic cliché from the jongleur's repertoire we cannot say. Other chroniclers, not themselves eye-witnesses though perhaps working from official accounts, comment in similar ways. William of Newburgh describes Berengaria as *'famosae pulchritudinis et prudentiae'* (of renowned beauty and wisdom),[38] Ranulph of Higden as *'virginem pulchram et disertam'* (a beautiful and learned maiden),[39] while the later vernacular chronicle of Pierre de Langtoft stresses her *'gentil lynage'* (noble lineage), her beauty and her *'parage'* – a vague term meaning something like turn-out, presentation, total appearance, an indicator in courtly texts of wealth or high status. A similar Anglo-Norman version, now lost, is supposed to have inspired the Middle English *Romance of Richard Coeur de Lion*:[40] The English poet speaks in similar vein:

His moder sent hym a faire present.
Elianore brought him Beringer,
The kynges doughter of Nauere[41]

One writer, Richard of Devizes, did not echo the general adulation.
In an often cited comment, he described Berengaria as *'prudentiore
quam pulchra'* (more wise/clever than beautiful).[42] Richard was not
an eye-witness: his most recent editor describes his work as an
'unimportant source of information' in respect of the third crusade.
If the Chronicle was written in 1193, before King Richard's ransom
and return, then it is unlikely that the author would have seen
Berengaria himself and he may have been relying on other people's
reports.[43] It is thought that his was a private diary compiled for a
close friend and this would explain the freedom with which he
expresses his views and, as his modern editor puts it, the 'strong
prejudices … which he airs at every opportunity'. One of these
clearly related to women.

Richard of Devizes' attitude to women is that of a malicious old
gossip-columnist. It is seen in the sexual tone of passing comments
on incidental characters such as Hadwisa, consort of William
Mandeville, and illustrated most clearly in his attitude to Eleanor,
whom he first attempts to flatter as an 'incomparable woman',
beautiful and virtuous, powerful and modest, humble and intelligent – qualities rarely found in women – and remarkably energetic
for her age. This rather fawning tribute is undermined by a titillat-
ing footnote containing a reference to Eleanor's alleged indiscretions
in Palestine during the second crusade: 'Many know what I wish
none of us did know. This same queen was in Jerusalem … Not
another word please! I know what I'm talking about. Hush!'

A later reference to Berengaria's leaving Sicily *'forte adhuc virgo'*
(perhaps still a virgin) is a further indication of this author's preoccupations. His sexist attitudes and in particular his dismissal of
Berengaria as an unattractive bluestocking have clearly struck a
responsive chord in some more recent commentators, as Anthony
Bridge's throw-away comment ('plain, dull and worthy') indicates.

Almost immediately after the arrival of Berengaria and Eleanor,
Richard handed his fiancée over to the care of his sister Joanna. The

two women, probably close in age, were to be travelling companions for the next couple of years. Pierre de Langtoft tells us, in a poignant little postscript, that they came together like 'birds in a cage'.[44] There is little indication that the close friendship continued after their return to France: the records point to occasions between 1193 and 1199 when Joanna, Richard and Berengaria may have been together, but Joanna died very shortly after her brother, in 1199, and circumstances had ensured that their paths diverge some years previously with the remarriage of Joanna to Raymond of Toulouse in 1196. Joanna's last testament is recorded in the archive of Fontevraud and there is no mention of Berengaria among the many beneficiaries, great and small. On the other hand, such testaments were usually formal documents and Joanna could not have foreseen Berengaria's later difficulties in obtaining her dower monies and subsequent need for assistance.

On the Wednesday of Holy Week, Richard's fleet set sail for Palestine. No doubt the intention was to marry Berengaria in the Holy Land, since the marriage could not have taken place in Lent and it would have been imprudent to delay the departure once the spring weather brought favourable winds to the Mediterranean. The women travelled separately in one of the larger ships, and the fleet, some two hundred strong, set out towards Crete and the eastern shores. On the Easter weekend, a violent storm erupted, scattering the fleet and throwing the king's ship off course. Medieval literature abounds in descriptions of storms at sea, and in the age of sail to be at the mercy of both wind and calm by turn was particularly hazardous. In addition, there were other dangers and inconveniences, including the diseases which resulted from vitamin deficiency and the presence of rats and contaminated bilge water. It was no wonder that medieval travellers, and especially sea-farers, felt the need to invoke special blessings and protection from the Virgin and saints like St Michael and St Nicholas.

Among the vessels unlucky enough to be blown far off course was the one carrying Joanna and Berengaria. When the storm abated, the royal fleet began to regroup and Richard sent galleys to look for the missing ship, which was eventually located just off the coast of Cyprus. The governor of this island, then part of the

Byzantine empire, was attempting to lure the royal women into port as potential hostages. They in turn had resisted this move, while politely requesting permission to take on water and provisions. The *Itinerarium*, Bk. 2, ch. 31 (pp. 187–8) gives a vivid picture of the two queens peering anxiously out across the storm-tossed sea, waiting to be rescued. Throughout this episode, Richard is shown as supremely confident and in charge, guiding his fleet by a lantern placed high in his ship.

Commentators past and present have warmed to the picture of Richard as knight-to-the-rescue, storming into the port of Limassol on 5 May, leading the charge up the beaches to demand the release of his men who had been taken prisoner, and triumphantly escorting his ladies to land. In fact it took barely a couple of days to subdue the island, chase off its governor, Isaac Comnenos, and establish control of the port city.[45]

English commentators have painted a black picture of this scion of an ancient royal dynasty, but the Byzantine chroniclers were equally negative in their comments. Isaac responded to Richard's challenge with deceitful obsequiousness. Richard appears to have decided to add Cyprus to the list of his conquests because he had already sent a message to the Latin authorities in Palestine, where the French army had already arrived, indicating a delay of some days. A delegation of nobles from the Holy Land landed two days after Richard's arrival in Cyprus, informing him of trouble in the Latin kingdom, instigated in part by the king of France. Richard invited the delegates to attend his wedding, which finally took place on 12 May in St George's chapel in the fort of Limassol.

May was traditionally a month of festivities linked to the rites of spring, with love-making and the temporary relaxation of social taboos. Popular Catholic tradition still celebrates it as Mary's month, devoted to the queen of the rosary. It would be difficult to imagine a more romantic setting for a royal wedding than a May day in Cyprus, where Aphrodite herself once rose from the flowering sea-foam. But unfortunately we have no detailed description of the occasion. Howden, as usual, gives details of time and place and lists the officiating clergy. Nicolas, the royal chaplain (later to become first dean, then bishop of Le Mans), celebrated the nuptial mass, while John, bishop of Evreux, assisted by the bishops of Apamea and Auxerre and the archbishop of Bayonne, crowned Berengaria queen of England. The king's clerk, Philip of Poitou, drew up a document setting out Berengaria's dower. Presumably Richard was wearing the outfit briefly described by the chroniclers: (*Itinerarium* 2, ch. 36, p. 197) a rose samite tunic with a scarlet cap, a gold embroidered cape and a silk sash and his scabbard was decorated with gold and silver. No one mentioned what the bride was wearing.

Once again, it is Ambroise who enlivens the account with a personal touch. Berengaria is described as beautiful and fair of form (*od la clere facon*) and her wisdom or intelligence is again stressed: she is the 'wisest lady you could find anywhere'. 'Look at the king!' the poet exclaims, 'How glorious he appears, overjoyed at his victory and because he has married the one to whom he had pledged himself!'[46] Is this the spontaneous reaction of an unlettered but devoted supporter or merely the uncritical language used by most royal commentators? On balance, one is inclined to give Ambroise the benefit of the doubt.

On that fateful day in May Berengaria assumed a dual role, that of wife and of queen consort. The first was one for which she would not have been unprepared, even if at some stage her preference had been for the religious life. Marriage was the norm for both sexes and it was the end to which the education of girls, such as it was, was primarily directed. It was the duty of a head of household to supervise the marriage of his children, thereby contracting new alliances, maintaining power balances, revitalising flagging fortunes or pre-empting potential hostilities. A wife's duty was to provide sons for the powerful group of males who controlled her destiny.

Despite the inbuilt tension between the secular and the ecclesiastical concepts of marriage, religious precept and secular politics often coincided. The Church's teaching, shaped by the writings of canonists and moral theologians, tended to stress the Pauline view of marriage as a concession to human weakness, and a remedy against concupiscence. It was also clearly in the Church's own interests to attempt to confine sexual activity within the sanctioned areas of conjugality and procreation. In promoting this agenda it also took up positions which threatened long-established practices such as the repudiation of wives and marriage with close relatives. It sought also to elevate marriage onto a more spiritual plane by stressing mutual consent and marital affection. Finally, a kind of equality was implicit in the notion of the conjugal debt, which enjoined each partner to agree to sexual relations at the request of the other.[47] In practice, however, not all churchmen were prepared to uphold this teaching, particularly in the case of kings and dukes and other powerful magnates. However clear-cut may have been the official teaching on the marital debt, widely held views about female inferiority must have ensured that, in practice, the needs and preferences of women were subordinate to those of their menfolk. In both the religious and the secular spheres the conduct constantly required of women was characterised by the same list of 'virtues': submission, humility, modesty. It is difficult to see how, without the explicit intervention of an impartial clerical spokesman, a twelfth-century wife could have demanded her conjugal rights from an unwilling spouse. Companionate marriage and mutual affection were certainly not unknown but the very clear separation of male and female spheres of activity in this period would have made this, too, more difficult to achieve. As for sexual compatibility, a major preoccupation of our own times, the medieval texts speak only of dysfunctional situations such as impotence, witchcraft or unnatural behaviour

Both Christopher Brooke[48] and Georges Duby have pieced together a detailed and intriguing picture of medieval marriage, citing many individual cases, real and fictional. Medieval art, too, is rich in images of courtship, betrothal and marriage. A feature of many of these paintings, carvings and tapestries is the growing importance of formality and ceremonial. Marriage in the late twelfth century had become a public event – '*al us del mustier, veant gent*' (at the Church door, before witnesses). Even in the bedroom there was little privacy in the modern sense: royal or aristocratic families were dependent on their servants to assist them in their rudimentary toilet routines, in rising and retiring for the night. There would have been few occasions on which a couple was left alone for any length of time.

Courtly literature sometimes provides a glimpse of such rare private moments. In the *Tristan* of Thomas, an Anglo-Norman romance of the late twelfth century often praised for its 'realism', Tristan, the reluctant bridegroom, is left alone with the wife he has married on the rebound, Isolt of Brittany. He spends a great deal of time analysing his own tortuous thought processes before deciding not to consummate the marriage, out of loyalty to his first love, Queen Isolt of Cornwall, his uncle's wife:

'The day is named, the hour is fixed, Tristan arrives with his friends. The duke is there with his followers and everything is made ready. He marries Isolt of the Whitehands, the chaplain says mass and all is done appropriately, according to the rites of the Holy Church. Then they go to eat a celebratory meal, and enjoy many sports of all kinds, as is customary and expected at such gatherings.

'The day dies away and with it the celebrations: the beds stand ready for the night. First they bring the maiden to bed then Tristan is helped to undress: as he takes off his tunic, which fits him closely and tightly at the wrists, they pull off by mistake the ring which Isolt had given him in the garden at their last meeting. Tristan gazes at the ring, and his thoughts carry him far away: greatly anguished, he does not know what to do ...'[49]

Some four hundred lines later he has managed to rationalise his double act of betrayal, but we are never given a parallel glimpse into the thoughts of the meekly acquiescent bride. She appears to have heard of the marriage debt, and indeed Tristan acknowledges that it is his duty to sleep with his wife, but he quickly abandons this thought out of loyalty to his former lover. This elevated notion of love as an autonomous moral code cannot disguise the fact that it is an adulterous relationship to which he is declaring his loyalty. The audiences who obviously enjoyed what Christopher Brooke has called a 'repellent tale brilliantly told' could take comfort from the inclusion in the tale of the love philtre – the '*viel unselig Trank*' ('the most unholy drink') as the German poet Eilhart called it – which served as an alibi, pre-empting the moral debate and reducing the culpability of the lovers. Thomas, who debates these issues continuously and obsessively throughout the poem, nevertheless tells us that this was not *fin'amors*[50] in the true sense because if it had been,

Tristan would not have married the unfortunate Breton princess in the first place. At least one twentieth-century novelist has, I believe, incorporated an element of this story in his depiction of the marriage of Richard and Berengaria.[51]

There are no grounds, however, for assuming as one or two recent commentators have done that the marriage of Richard and Berengaria was not consummated. Later accounts may give credence to the view that Richard and Berengaria became estranged in Palestine, but external events could hardly have been less conducive to the development of intimacy or companionship. More importantly, there is no evidence that Berengaria, unlike the bride of Tristan, was ever supplanted by another woman. If Richard's preference was for male partners, what has been interpreted as an estrangement may have been the inevitable beginning of a distance between the spouses.

Circumstances contrived to deprive Berengaria of the normal activities of a married noblewoman, such as the supervision of a household, the provision of hospitality and entertainment and the care and education of girls. Typical leisure activities would have included weaving, embroidery, music, singing, board games and perhaps horticulture and medicine. Even these activities require a stable environment. For the first few years of her marriage, Berengaria had no real home of her own. It was only much later, perhaps around 1195, that she and Richard purchased a property at Thorée near le Lude in western France, and there is no evidence that they ever lived there together.

Richard's arrangements for Berengaria's dower – the property guaranteed to a widow in the event of her husband's death – included 'all our possessions in Gascony and beyond the Garonne' during the lifetime of Eleanor, plus, in the event of Eleanor's death, certain properties in Normandy, including Falaise and Domfront and in Anjou.[52] As dowry – the properties pledged by the bride's father – the border castles of Rocabruna and St Jean Pied de Port were assigned by King Sancho. The exact location of Rocabruna has been a matter of some dispute, but Susana Hereros has recently suggested its location and suggested that the name which means 'brown rock' may be the romance equivalent of a local Basque name.[53]

Berengaria was also crowned as queen of a land that she was in all probability never to visit. The formal coronation of queens consort is of relatively recent origin and coincides with a significant shift towards lineage and pedigree. Before the eleventh century, it was still possible for a king to marry a slave girl or keep one or more concubines. David Herlihy, Lois Huneycutt and others have argued that the very same Church reforms which placed greater emphasis on monogamy and indissolubility resulted in losses as well as gains for women, as some of the earlier avenues of advancement were closed off.

With the growing institutionalisation of queenship came greater public responsibilities. Queens consort were expected to participate in affairs of state and were sometimes even consulted by popes and prelates on such matters. They were also supposed to fulfil the traditional role of protectress of the poor and needy and to intercede with the king on behalf of the disadvantaged. Here too, there was little scope for Berengaria to use her skills of prudence and judgement. Richard was driven by his own obsessive energy and sense of destiny: what counsels could his new bride have offered in a situation for which she was so ill-prepared and lacking in experience?

Excluded from her husband's counsels as well as from his military campaigns, Berengaria, with Joanna, was to be continuously moved from one crusader stronghold to another, under the watchful protection of officials like Bertram de Verdun, an experienced and trusted retainer from the days of King Henry II, and Robert of Turnham, who was to serve Richard and later John, in Anjou and Poitou. During their stay in Cyprus the two queens had also acquired a new travelling companion, the young daughter of the disgraced ruler of Cyprus.[54]

Ambroise tells how this 'young and appealing girl' had flung herself at the king's feet when the fortress of Kyrenia fell to the English attack. Richard took her into protective custody and handed her over to his queen. Some commentators must have hinted at a less than honourable intention on Richard's part, since other chroniclers are at pains to refute any suggestion of misconduct, but some recent French historians have repeated this rumour.

This has led, in turn, to the speculation that it was Richard's behaviour with the Cypriot captive which triggered the estrangement with his queen. Whether or not this was so, the subsequent history of this unnamed princess is a turbulent one: she accompanied the two queens back from Palestine to France, where she attracted the attention of the notorious Raymond VI of Toulouse, to whom she was briefly married after the death of Joanna in 1199. After Richard's death, her value as a hostage or pawn was nil and, with her father languishing in captivity, she seems to have been abandoned to fate. She may have succeeded in joining the fourth crusade in order to return to her homeland, in company with the French knight whom she subsequently married.

But this is merely an intriguing little postscript: the Cypriot princess is of no lasting interest to the English chroniclers. Beautiful and appealing though she may have been, history has not even recorded her name!

The story of these three women, two widowed queens and a princess in exile, now becomes a minor part of a much more substantial narrative, that of the third crusade. This narrative is dominated by the figure of Richard. Richard's temperament and interests inclined him towards action on such a grand scale. We do not know whether Berengaria shared these tastes, but the upbringing of medieval princesses would have made this unlikely. For an inexperienced young woman, a situation of this kind might well have created a sense of isolation and powerlessness, for which the sombre Christian teaching that life itself is but a pilgrimage, and humanity only a sojourner on earth, could only offer limited consolation.

Medieval people travelled for a variety of reasons, much as we do today, though recreational travel on a large scale was not common. Ambassadors were despatched from country to country, monarchs went on circuit in a visible display of sovereignty, and, in Rome, successive popes presided over a constant *va-et-vient* of nuncios, delegates and special envoys. Private individuals went on pilgrimage, or in search of fortune, while others were forced to leave their homes because of exile, banishment, famine, war and epidemics.

But religion provided a more conspicuous motivation for travel than it does today. For Christians and Muslims, pilgrimage was an essential part of the faith, while the Jews were very much an itinerant people for a variety of reasons, practical, professional or circumstantial.

The crusades were the most visible and dramatic expression of religiously motivated travel. We are inclined to think of a crusade first and foremost as a military expedition, but crusades were also pilgrimages, especially from the perspective of the individual participant. This duality of function is reflected in the part played by women on crusade.

Although there have been some societies, ancient and more recent, in which women have taken up arms, the warrior throughout history is quintessentially male and represented in religious, mythological and literary texts as a figure of unleashed virility. He is sometimes physically distinctive, set apart from the crowd or subject to the '*furor heroicus*' (warrior fury), as in the distortions of the Irish Cú Chulainn or the Norse berserker. His weapon, frequently phallic in its symbolism, is often depicted as an extension of his person. By contrast, women appear as his victims, the object of his conquest or the treacherous underminers of his virile force, like the biblical Delilah or the Greek Phaedra.

Warrior women were not unknown in the Middle Ages. The dominant image is of a young virginal woman – the Joan of Arc figure – with implicitly asexual associations. The virago or manly woman is an interesting and ambivalent figure in medieval culture. On the one hand, the term is frequently used pejoratively, as it is today; on the other hand, it could mean a woman who aspired to the virtues of a man, thereby transcending the limitations of the female condition. But most women who took up arms did so out of necessity, as widows or regents or in the absence of their husbands. Warrior consorts are not commonly represented in the literature of medieval Christian Europe, except in texts based on older, pre-Christian traditions, Celtic or Germanic, for instance. The Christian model of queenship is represented by such idealised figures as Queen Margaret of Scotland, St Elizabeth of Hungary rather than earlier queens like the legendary Meave of Ireland or Cartimandua and Boudicca of Britain, though Celtic mythology and semi-historical material have been appropriated to support exaggerated claims being made about early queens and women warriors.

Women of lower rank were less constrained by social etiquette and this reality is reflected in the documented activity of women during the crusades. In both literature and art we can find images of women crusaders fighting energetically alongside the men. Arab chroniclers also mention some of these cases. But such behaviour would have been unthinkable in a queen.

On the other hand, women had always been enthusiastic pilgrims. One of the earliest accounts of a pilgrimage to the Holy Land is that of a sixth-century Spanish nun named Aetheria (or Egeria). Women may have constituted as much as one third of the total annual number of pilgrims to Compostela. It was as pilgrims that crowned queens participated in the crusades of the twelfth and thirteenth centuries. One such queen was Eleanor of Aquitaine, who accompanied her first husband, Louis VII of France, to Palestine on the second crusade in 1147-9. Eleanor's independence and high profile provoked a certain amount of unfavourable gossip, as Richard of Devizes' snide little comment reminds us. The sexual innuendoes concerning her relations with her uncle Raymond of Poitiers may have no basis in fact but are typical of the reaction such behaviour provoked.

No hint of any such charge was ever levelled at Berengaria during the third crusade. Richard was unpredictable, prone to violence and, on occasions, inexplicably vindictive. His most widely publicised acts of magnanimity and compassion were directed towards males. Whatever his own shortcomings as a husband, he would not have tolerated the slight to his honour represented by any such suggestion of misbehaviour on the part of his bride or his sister. One inference which can be drawn from the silence of the chroniclers concerning Berengaria and Joanna is that they behaved with impeccable propriety.

They stayed in the background of events, constantly escorted and supervised and played no part in any of the decisions made. Richard, for his part, appears to have provided for their well-being with punctilious protectiveness.

Not surprisingly then, the main sources for the third crusade concentrate almost exclusively on the person of Richard and the progress of his army. Howden's semi-official record frequently summarises Richard's speeches and includes the text of some of his letters home. These latter, addressed to people like the abbot of Clairvaux, are very much official dispatches, reporting on progress of the campaign, on difficulties surmounted or anticipated, revealing a Richard preoccupied by military and strategic concerns, conscious of his image and not unmindful of English politics. They give no real hint of the personal, of Richard's frequent and severe bouts of sickness, for instance, the mysterious 'arnaldie', 'leonardie' or tertian fever, which may have been some kind of paludism, trench fever or malarial-style infection. Much less do they touch on domestic arrangements. What Berengaria, Joanna and their Cypriot companion did with their time is nowhere recorded.[55] Ambroise's account, and that of the *Itinerarium*, are more anecdotal and colourful than that of Howden but these too, concentrate firmly on the person of the king, his bravery and daring and the inspiration which he provided for his troops. This is a world in which women have no real place except as bystanders. Both the *Itinerarium* and Ambroise contain frequent references to the negative influence of women, mainly prostitutes, and link their presence with other distractions such as drinking and neglect of religious duties. Underpinning these culturally based motifs is an older and more persistent archetype, the notion that contact with women weakens and emasculates the warrior (the Delilah factor). This may be one of the reasons why it would not have seemed appropriate to the chroniclers to represent Richard spending time with his bride and her entourage.

The third crusade was launched by Pope Gregory after the fall of the strategically placed heights of Hattin in 1187 to the dynamic Muslim leader Saladin, whose head to head conflict with Richard has caught the imagination of history and folklore alike. The Latin kingdom of Jerusalem and its allied Christian principalities were now in desperate need of aid from fellow Christians in Europe, to whom their rulers were linked by ties of blood and lineage.

As Régine Pernoud has demonstrated,[56] the hundred-year-long history of these troubled states was for much of the time dominated by the fortunes and misfortunes of women, many of whom suffered vicissitudes worthy of a modern soap opera. Melisande, queen of Jerusalem from 1138, for instance, reigned jointly with her husband Fulk of Anjou for twelve years and then for a further nine on her own. Her two sons, Baudouin and Amaury, were to succeed her in turn. William of Tyre, major chronicler of the second crusade, described her as a wise and judicious ruler, while St Bernard of Clairvaux wrote to her in equally appreciative terms.

Another dramatic figure was Melisande's grand-daughter, the ill-fated Isabelle who outlived four successive husbands, including two claimants to the throne of Jerusalem, Conrad of Montferrat and Henry count of Champagne, grandson of Eleanor of Aquitaine by her first husband Louis VII of France. This latter connection was subsequently to prove extremely troublesome for Berengaria's sister Blanca, who married Henry's younger brother Thibaut in 1199. One of Henry's sons-in-law would launch a challenge to the position of Blanche (as she was subsequently known) and her infant son Thibaut and would prove extremely tenacious in the pursuit of his claims. This situation illustrates the problems besetting fiefs or principalities with no adult male heir, and it is precisely because of their situation as heiresses that the high-profile women of Christian Palestine have warranted such attention from the historians.

The societies in which these women lived were probably somewhat different from those in the lands of their ancestors. French and Anglo-Norman chroniclers often speak disapprovingly of what they saw as the lax and sybaritic lifestyles of the Christian courts in Outremer. Frequent bathing and homosexual activities were among the practices singled out for adverse comment. Be that as it may, in 1191 these communities were in total disarray, their very existence threatened by Saladin's successes to which their own internal political instability had undoubtedly contributed. Howden, Ambroise and other chroniclers emphasise the spoiling role played by the French king and some of his allies and their constant meddling in local affairs. French accounts reverse the roles. The Arabic sources, while themselves naturally somewhat partisan, enable us to assess the merits of the conflicting accounts.

The chronicles tell us little about social conditions in the settler realms. There are plentiful references to geographical and climatic conditions, to the heat, the lack of amenities and the terrible insects and vermin which plagued the crusader army, to the citrus and olive groves of the fertile coastal plain, to the prostitutes and camp followers who swarmed around the troops when they pitched camp at Acre and Jaffa. Ambroise, reflecting his own professional interests, sometimes speaks of singing and minstrels. But, for the most part, the chronicles devote their attention to the progress of Richard's army.[57]

Richard arrived in Palestine in June 1191 and left in early October 1192. He spent most of that time on the coastal plains, capturing in turn Acre, Arsuf, Jaffa and Ascalon. Although he came within sight of the Holy City, he was unable to take it and left Palestine vowing to return one day. We cannot know if he shared his disappointments with his wife. In any case, the women did not accompany the crusader army to all their locations. Berengaria and her new companions Joanna and the Cypriot princess spent their time at one or other of the newly consolidated strongholds. According to Howden, they arrived on the eve of Pentecost, 1 June 1191, with the major part of Richard's fleet. The king himself did not arrive until one week later, having engaged battle with a disguised enemy ship near the northern port of Tyre. Richard was already ill at the time, according to Ambroise, as he was on three further recorded occasions. None the less, he took an active part in the routing of the Saracen ship and was in high spirits when a fair wind finally allowed him to set sail for Acre. Ambroise again provides a vivid description of the port city – the hills and valleys covered with tents and pavilions both Christian and Muslim, the trumpeters blaring out a welcome to Richard, the Lionheart, the Conqueror of Cyprus. E.N. Stone's prose translation, despite its slightly artificial archaising style, captures the exhilaration of the original:[58]

> Forth came he to the land from out his galley. Then had ye heard the trumpets sound, honouring Richard, the knight without peer! All the people with one accord rejoiced at his coming; but the Turks that were within were filled with dread at his arriving, for well they wist that gone now was

their chance of sallying from the city and entering in again, whereby many of our people had been destroyed. The two kings accompanied each other, keeping ever side by side. Then did King Richard go to his own tents, meditating much and devising in his mind how Acre might be overcome and how it might most speedily be taken.

As the king sat in his tent, planning the assault on the fortress, wine flowed in the streets and from the ranks of the besiegers arose the strain of jubilant song. The defending 'Turks' rallied their forces and prepared to dig in. Shortly after his arrival Richard was again laid low by sickness and the chronicler tells us that Philip of France, who had arrived not long after Easter, was also suffering from the same disfiguring malady. Richard's illness was so severe that when the final assault began, on 6 July, he had to be carried on a litter to the front line to supervise events. In less than a week the beleaguered Muslims had surrendered and the two Christian kings entered the city in triumph.

On the 21st, Berengaria and Joanna, who had presumably been housed in tents well away from the fighting, were escorted into the castle to take up residence. During this time, according to Ambroise, Richard, despite his sickness, had thrown all his energy into the campaign and was furious with anyone who did not share his eagerness for action. Once victorious, he became embroiled in a petty skirmish with a fellow crusader, Leopold duke of Austria, who had the temerity to plant his banner on the ramparts of the newly captured city alongside those of England and France. When the English soldiers tore it down, the duke vowed revenge. Richard was to pay dearly for allowing or perhaps even encouraging his troops in this action. At the same time, Philip Augustus announced that he had had enough and was going home. He left on 8 August in an atmosphere of mutual recrimination. Ambroise, ever the sturdy patriot, remarks that his departure was accompanied more by curses than blessings!

Richard was now eager to press on and challenge the Muslims elsewhere. But the vanquished enemy had not yet fulfilled the conditions agreed upon at the surrender: to hand over the relic of the

True Cross, to release Christian prisoners and to pay an indemnity of 200,000 gold bezants. Tired of waiting and possibly giving credence to rumours that Saladin had already defaulted on the agreement, Richard now ordered the slaughter of all the Muslim prisoners, regardless of age or sex, with the exception of a few noble hostages. Appalling as this may seem to us, it was not an uncommon practice.

Anthony Bridge defends Richard against the charge of barbarism by pointing out that he had no choice: he could neither risk releasing the prisoners nor afford to feed and guard them indefinitely. He points out that Saladin had done the same thing after the defeat of Hattin and that such actions were not regarded as abhorrent by chroniclers on either side.[59]

Once the massacre was accomplished, Richard was free to move on. His men were less enthusiastic, because, as both Christian and Muslim commentators inform us, the newly liberated city was offering an interesting range of recreational activities – wine, women and much more. Richard was clearly unsympathetic. He was a man with a mission.

But what were Berengaria and Joanna doing at this time? Richard had brought them, with their Cypriot companion on 21st of July to the royal palace, where they were put under the guard of Bertrand de Verdun[60] and Stephen Longchamp. But Richard and Berengaria had spent very little time together since their wedding day, and this brief four-week period had seen Richard under considerable stress, seriously ill for part of the time, frustrated by his own weakness, embroiled in hostilities, dogged by the hateful presence of his nemesis, the king of France, and, finally, supervising a largescale massacre of prisoners, combatants and civilians alike. Berengaria and her companions could not have been unaware of the event and may indeed have witnessed it officially.

Women's cultures have not in general desensitised them to bloodshed or rewarded them for aggressive behaviour in the same way as they have done to men. To Berengaria, Richard was still a virtual stranger. He was no longer 'En Ricart', the young count, toast of the troubadours, as he was, perhaps, when they first met, but thirty-five years old, the most powerful monarch in Christendom and obsessed by one idea. Even if the royal women shared the fervour attributed to the crusaders by the chroniclers, and the general view that 'pagans are wrong and Christians are right', as the *Song of Roland* so memorably puts it, it is difficult to imagine that they were not affected by an event of this kind. Berengaria may not, like Pilate's wife, have attempted to stay her husband's bloody hand, but she cannot have been unaffected by the terrible choice he was obliged to make. At least one of the romantic novelists has suggested that Berengaria suffered a miscarriage in Palestine as a reaction to events and conditions during the crusade: the suggestion has of course no historical basis, but it adds another element to the conundrum.[61]

The impact of this mass slaughter, which took place before the city walls of Acre, is made worse by the fact that relations between Christians and Muslims in Palestine were not always characterised by implacable hostility. The Arab chroniclers reveal that there were significant differences between the 'Franj', as they called the crusaders from the north, and the local Melkite and other Eastern Rite Christians. The northerners, for their part, regarded the Eastern Rite Christians with suspicion and mistrust. After Saladin's capture of Jerusalem in October 1187, most of these latter signalled their intention to stay on in the city, reassured by Saladin's promise that Christian shrines would be protected.

Even between the Muslims and the 'Franj' there were occasional truces, during which Frankish and Muslim officers entertained each other with the appropriate civilities. Baha al-Din refers to several occasions on which Richard is alleged to have initiated contact with Saladin, both before and after the siege of Acre, even though neither side had any illusions about the purpose of such initiatives. The Muslim chroniclers praised Richard for his bravery and his leadership but also saw him as violent, rash and lacking in subtlety. Saladin himself was a more complex figure, resolute and courageous but also cautious and introspective. Popular tradition, with its tendency to personalise and polarise, has found the contrast between these two heroic figures irresistibly attractive.

The Arab chroniclers take pleasure in recounting individual acts of compassion on the part of Saladin, many of which involve women and children. Some of these stories may be apocryphal, or at least exemplary, in keeping with the finest tenets of a faith which regularly invokes the name of Allah the Compassionate, the Merciful. It is significant that no such anecdotes are told about Richard, who seems to have reserved his expressions of magnanimity for fellow knights, former adversaries or companions in arms, such as the unfortunate Guillaume des Barres, who incurred his wrath during a bout of horseplay in Sicily and was only forgiven some months later on account of his heroism in battle. Bridge, with all the zeal of a modern Ambroise, defends Richard against the charge that he was 'a brutal oaf, bloodthirsty and a bugger', but if the decision to massacre the prisoners was dictated by hard-headed military logic rather than momentary fury, the action is no less morally repugnant. Richard and Berengaria were now to remain apart for a few months while the Crusading army headed south for Jaffa. It was hardly a propitious moment for tender farewells. It was a poor start to an already precarious relationship.

On 22 August Richard led his army south, intent on the ultimate prize – Jerusalem, leaving Berengaria and Joanna behind in Acre. The 'way of the sea', as it is called in the Bible, was safer than the more direct inland route, where the rugged, hilly terrain afforded many opportunities for ambush. As many commentators have pointed out, the march which took nineteen days to complete, was taxing enough, given the normal weather conditions of Palestine in late August. All along the way, the Frankish armies were shadowed by their Muslim adversaries who sallied out from time to time to attack their flanks as part of a campaign of attrition. Gillingham sums up Richard's leadership as 'a classic demonstration of Frankish military tactics at their best'. Richard's own patience and coolheadedness and the loyalty and discipline of his troops attracted the praise of friend and foe alike. Ambroise and the *Itinerarium* also include the occasional glimpse of Richard the epic hero, darting out of the ranks to rescue his beleaguered rearguard, shrugging off the inconvenience of a flesh wound, riding up and down his lines, regrouping his men and constantly urging them on to victory. The enthusiasm of these writers is echoed in the moving tribute to Richard after his death by the troubadour Gaucelm

Faidit.[62] His admirers were not altogether blind to his faults, but believed that his merits outweighed his defects.

Of the two poems attributed to Richard himself, the one allegedly composed during his captivity in Austria speaks first and foremost of his men, his Gascons, Angevins, Normans and Englishmen and in these crusade accounts we find these same groups mentioned. Loyalty to Richard was the single factor which held them together and made them such a redoubtable force.

The next great victory for the crusaders was at Arsuf, a hot dry plain adjacent to a thickly wooded area where Richard had been expecting an ambush which did not eventuate. Most commentators agree that it was a sound tactical move on Saladin's part, to surprise the Franks as they emerged, relieved, into the open. This they did with great effect, swooping down from the surrounding hills in a volley of cavalry, archers, drums, discord and war-cries. Bridge's description is based on primary sources like Ambroise: 'Swarms of dark-skinned Arab pikemen and black-faced Nubian archers yelling and screaming and looking so like demons from hell ...' These frightening images are replicated in the Old French *chansons de geste* and represent the demonising of the enemy characteristic of military propaganda.

Richard's troops won a decisive if not final victory at Arsuf, despite heavy losses on both sides and he then proceeded to Jaffa, arriving on the 10th of September. He set up camp there in the citrus groves outside the town, which had been destroyed by the retreating enemy. Work began immediately on refortifying the town. A month later, Richard returned to Acre and brought Berengaria and Joanna with him to Jaffa. They stayed there as far as we know, for about six months. Once again their activities have not been recorded. The limited range of pursuits available to noble or royal women would very likely have been further restricted by the dangers of the location, as the anecdote concerning Richard's narrow escape while out hawking illustrates.

Richard and a few companions were out on a reconnaissance patrol and exercising their trained falcons at the same time. The king was almost captured in an ambush and was only saved by the quick wits of one of his knights who called out in Arabic that *he* was the king. If danger lurked so close to the camp it is highly unlikely that the royal women would have been allowed out of its limits for one moment.

What other activities might they have participated in? Ambroise in particular mentions minstrels and entertainment on several occasions. Some of these incidents are quite intriguing, including for instance, the occasion when rude and insulting songs were sung by rival factions about each other. It seems highly likely that at least one known troubadour, if not more, was present on the crusade.[63] From the frequent references to Alexander, Roland and other heroes, we can imagine the subject matter of the epics which would have been recited in some form to inspire the troops or to praise the king. Unfortunately there is no surviving text, apart from the crusade chronicles, of which we can confidently say that it was composed during the crusade. The troubadours were prone to name dropping but they also employed, for a variety of reasons, a number of pseudonyms or *senhals* which may conceal the identity of real people. Very few of these, and almost none of the female ones, have been decoded with confidence.

The novelist M. Hewlett, who had clearly read a great deal about the general cultural background, cleverly invented a *senhal* for Berengaria: he called her 'Frozen Heart', in keeping with the negative role he assigned to her in his historical romance. It is certainly possible that songs and poems were composed on the spot by the minstrels and entertainers in the king's retinue and that some of these would have included the usual courtly tributes to the two queens and other women in their entourage. Unfortunately however, no such material has survived and the only known reference to Berengaria in the poetry of the troubadours is the brief allusion to the 'king of Navarre's daughter' by Bertrand de Born mentioned earlier.

Richard's sister Joanna makes her appearance in the chronicles at this point as the subject of a bizarre deal proposed by Richard to Saladin and his brother 'al-Adil during their lengthy negotiations in the month of October 1191. Richard is said to have offered Joanna in marriage to 'al-Adil if Saladin would agree to hand over the control of Palestine to his brother as the prelude to a kind of joint rule.

Most modern commentators believe that this offer was never meant seriously. The Muslim chronicler Bohadin records Saladin's amused reaction to the suggestion. It may have been part of a sparring tactic, and the angry reaction attributed to Joanna by the chroniclers may have been very much what Richard expected.

Whether or not this was so, Richard resumed his campaign on 31 October, when he left Jaffa for Jerusalem. It was a long and arduous process, not assisted by the onset of winter and heavy rains. The reinforcements expected from home did not materialise. Saladin withdrew his army to Jerusalem, confident that climate and the terrain would make it impossible for the enemy to break through.

The Frankish forces finally came to a halt at Latrun near Beit Nuba, and once again the queens were brought to the camp to celebrate Christmas with the king's party. A select advance group then proceeded to Beit Nuba, some twenty kilometres from Jerusalem but went no further. For a variety of reasons, Richard ordered a retreat to the coastal town of Ascalon, where he was to remain until late May, adding to his list of victories the fortress of Darun to the south. In early June he decided to make another attempt on Jerusalem. He is said to have wept when he first saw the Holy City in the distance. All the while, the dissension in the ranks of the crusaders, the persistent intrigues of the local Christian kingdoms and defection among the French added to the daily problems.

Little headway was made, the obstacles seemed once again insurmountable and Richard once more signalled a retreat. It seems as if he had decided to turn the attack towards Egypt, Saladin's main source of supply. When Richard left Jaffa briefly for Acre again, the Muslims took the opportunity to attack Jaffa the very day after his departure. In desperation the defenders sent a message to the king, who promptly despatched the Templars and Hospitallers under the command of the count of Champagne to the rescue, while he himself returned by sea. Once more we see him playing a dashing role in the recapture of Jaffa, leaping out of his ship and charging up the beaches to take on the enemy. But this was to be the last battle.

Apparently neither Richard nor Saladin believed, in the last resort, that there was any point in further prolonging hostilities.

War and sickness had taken their toll of both men, and it did not take long to settle on a truce. By early September Richard had received an assurance that coastal cities would remain in Christian hands. But the greatest of all prizes, Jerusalem, the city over which the greatest king in Christendom had shed bitter tears, would be denied him. The promise of safe conduct to all Christian pilgrims, which was to be taken up by many, was one to which Richard could personally never accede. With a sad heart he prepared to return to his own country. He left for Acre and, after a brief period of convalescence, made ready to set sail. His intention was apparently to return one day, and this sense of unfinished business may have contributed to the restlessness which seems to characterise so much of his activity on his return from captivity.

We must assume that Joanna and Berengaria had been for some time at Jaffa, perhaps returning to Acre in advance of the king, since it was at Acre that he took his leave of them and from Acre that they themselves left on 29 September. Richard was to sail straight into another and totally unforeseen set of adventures involving shipwreck, disguise, capture and ransom. His wife and sister, still accompanied by the princess of Cyprus, were to find their way back to Angevin territory by a safer and more leisurely route, via Brindisi, Rome and Aquitaine.

Berengaria's absence from the principal accounts of the third crusade is frustrating and discouraging but by no means unexpected. In writings such as these and in the perspective which inspired them, there is, literally, no real space for women. Their presence could only be marginal and limited to the gendered roles of fiancées, brides, widows, heiresses, prostitutes and camp-followers. These roles reflect the polarised view characteristic of so much medieval writing. The absence of any sexual innuendo comparable to that which flavours references to Eleanor's participation in the second crusade may perhaps tell us something about Berengaria's character and conduct but it is far more likely to reflect the differing attitudes of the chroniclers towards the husbands of the two women: Richard was feared and respected by Howden, Ambroise and the author of the *Itinerarium*, while the pious, bookish Louis VII of France may have been regarded less deferentially.

Berengaria had been a wife and a queen for just over sixteen months in conditions which could not have been more taxing. Her experiences, and those of her female companions will never be known to us in the way that the thoughts, hopes and fears of women in more recent times caught up in war, calamity, class struggle and emancipation are available to us today. We may infer from this silence that she endured the vicissitudes that came her way without breaking the rules by which women's lives were circumscribed. But even in our own day, piety, patience and endurance do not make good copy, without the titillation of beauty or sexuality. Judgements such as 'plain, dull and worthy' are the ultimate male put-down. 'Beautiful, exciting and irresponsible' would obviously have been more acceptable, reinforcing the convenient image of women as decorative accessories or dangerous threats.

In the end we are left with speculation, which is both tantalising and frustrating. Eight hundred years later we might have found memoirs or extracts from a diary, or from letters, left behind either by the young queens themselves, or by women in their retinue, similar to the recorded experience of vicereines and other administrators' wives in imperial India or Malaya. But this type of writing belongs to a later age: even if the experiences of Berengaria and Joanna had been considered fit to be recorded, they could not have found a place in the kind of chronicle written by Howden, Devizes and the others. Nothing illustrates better the divide between private and public spheres than these documents. As recent studies of medieval queenship have effectively demonstrated, queens consort, by the nature of their office, could and did move freely between public and private worlds, but the events of the third crusade and the dominant role played in the affairs of England by the widowed queen mother ensured that Berengaria remained very much on the margin of public affairs at this time. She could not know what fate awaited her husband nor indeed that they would be apart again for many long months.

CHAPTER FOUR

Queen

The years between 1192, the departure from the Holy Land, and 1199, the year of Richard's death, remain the most obscure and ill-documented period in Berengaria's life. Although there were some duties expected of a queen consort, many of which belonged to the private sphere, there were also less defined, liminal or interstitial areas in which she might make her own special contribution. But so much depended on the relationship between the queen and her husband and his family. Even a strong personality like Eleanor found her activities severely curtailed during the period of her virtual house arrest by Henry.

First and foremost among the duties of a queen was to provide an heir and in a society where ecclesiastical sanction restricted the frequency of sexual relations, where reproductive physiology was imperfectly understood and male infertility virtually unrecognised, a queen who failed to provide a male heir was at considerable risk.[1] However pious or dutiful she may have been, however genuine the ties of personal affection which bound her to her new family, she had still to prove her worth or face an uncertain future, which might include repudiation or even accusations of adultery or witchcraft. Failure to produce an heir was regarded as a disaster which evoked the old notion of sacral kingship, where the fertility of the ruler guaranteed that of the land.

Richard's captivity meant a further obstacle to the success of the marriage in this and other respects. He left Palestine for Marseilles on 9 October 1192 but his ship became separated from the rest of the fleet and he was forced to change vessels. Straying from his chosen course, he changed his route in order to avoid unfriendly territory. He landed first in Corfu, then turned north-west to Ragusa, from whence he headed towards Venice. From there he travelled through Austria with a few companions, disguised variously as a merchant, a pilgrim and, as tradition has it, a cook. Various legends arose from the events of this period, most of which have Richard revealing his true identity either by some impetuous gesture or by allowing one of his followers to use some item which revealed their master's identity. In late December he was captured by a new and dangerous adversary, Leopold duke of Austria, whom he had insulted in Palestine by ordering his banner to be torn down from the walls of Acre. Leopold handed him over to the German Emperor Henry, Richard's bitterest rival. Many of the legends later associated with Richard owe their origin to events from this period: Richard as a master of disguise, the betrayal of his identity by a ring or a jewel, or, most enduring of all, the romantic fiction of the young minstrel Blondel singing beneath his master's window.[2]

During his imprisonment, first in the castle of Dürnstein on the Danube, later in various castles in Germany, Richard issued a stream of messages, while his mother Eleanor railed against prelates and princes and even the Pope himself, demanding her son's release. Her impassioned letter to Pope Celestine, accusing him in effect of standing by while the enemies of Christendom held in ignominious captivity its noblest and bravest champion, resonates with righteous indignation and maternal despair.[3]

But others were working against Richard and endeavouring to persuade the emperor not to release him. Chief among these were Philip of France and Richard's younger brother John, both of whom promised the emperor large sums of money to keep the Lionheart in confinement. Relations between Philip and Richard had soured to such a degree that Philip, in a letter of 1193, could speak of the man with whom he had once shared a cup and a bed as '... the most impious king of the English' who had behaved 'perversely against both God and man ...' He tried repeatedly to bribe John into an alliance, offering to make him king of England and duke of Normandy and even suggesting that he should marry Aélis, Richard's cast-off fiancée. John, who was a lot bolder when Richard was not around, was desperate to see his brother's confinement extended so that he could build up a power base in England and Normandy.

Whether or not Richard anticipated such machinations, in addition to his official communications, he expressed his frustration in a more personal way in a poem, allegedly penned during his captivity. This poem contains much that is interesting but it is cited here because of a single line in one variant reading. The poem survives in two versions, differing slightly in content.[4] One is in standard medieval French, with a slight southern colouring, the other is in Occitan, the *lingua franca* of the lands south of the Loire. Experts differ as to whether Richard wrote both versions or whether one is a translation, and if so, which is the original version. Among the most reputable of these experts, two well-known scholars, Martin de Riquer and Reto Bezzola, believe that Richard wrote both versions. The Occitan has an extra verse. It concludes with an envoi, or coda, in which the troubadour regularly asks a confidant or friend to take his message to a third party, usually the real or imaginary object of his love. According to one reading, Richard's verses conclude like this:

> Sister, Countess, your sovereign worth
> may God preserve, and guard the fair one
> whom I love so much, and on whose account
> I am a prisoner here.

The countess addressed here is generally assumed to be Marie, countess of Champagne, Richard's half-sister, with whom he was on familiar terms, and who may, through the French connection (she was also a half-sister of Philip on her father's side) have been in a position to exercise influence on his behalf. Who then is the 'fair one' for whom the royal captive languishes?

This last line may represent an echo of that preciosity characteristic of the troubadour poetry where the 'captive' is in thrall to love itself or to love for a particular lady. No doubt Richard, who as count of Poitou was well-known to the troubadours and their particular milieu, was as able to play these literary games as any of his peers, but if this is merely a bit of literary scribbling, it seems out of place in a poem which is generally sombre in tone. Could this possibly be a reference to Berengaria? If so, it would be the only recorded expression of marital affection on Richard's part.

This view would be more persuasive if the countess addressed could be identified with Joanna. But Joanna would not become countess of Toulouse until 1196, and at this particular moment she was still the widowed queen of Sicily: Richard would have addressed her as 'Dame, Reine ...' (Lady Queen) or something similar. Neither of Richard's other two full sisters was styled countess – Matilda was the duchess of Saxony and Eleanor the queen of Castile. The other half-sister Alix of Blois seems an unlikely candidate. Exaggerated claims have been made about the closeness between Eleanor of Aquitaine and her daughter Marie of Champagne, but Marie may have occasionally visited her mother in Poitou or Anjou and Richard might possibly have assumed that his wife and sister had already reached the safety of Angevin territory. The reading containing this reference is only a variant and may not be genuine. No other candidate has been suggested, however, and the allusion remains tantalising. If Richard himself did not write these lines, who added them and to whom was he referring? Brief affairs like the one which produced Philip of Cognac did not usually inspire courtly verse, and the legend of the king of Almayn's daughter, with whom Richard is supposed to have fallen in love, is a much later creation.

Berengaria and Joanna had left Palestine on 29 September 1992 and sailed without incident via Cyprus to Brindisi, which they reached in November, before heading for Naples and Rome. Their stay of six months in Rome is attested by a charter granting security for a loan dated 9 April '... in the first year after our return from Syria' and signed by 'Berengaria Queen of the English, Duchess of the Normans and Aquitanians, countess of the Angevins and Joanna, former queen and Lady (*Domina*) of Sicily.'⁵ When news of Richard's captivity reached Rome, the two queens added their voices to the chorus of pleas for papal action. Berengaria is almost totally absent from the body of legends associated with Richard, but there is one little anecdote which subsequently gained popularity. One day the queens were walking in the market place in Rome and Berengaria spotted a jewelled belt for sale, which she recognised instantly as belonging to her husband. She knew at once that something was amiss and raised the alarm. Perhaps this story is just a doublet of an anecdote in Roger of Howden's chronicle in which, in Palestine in September 1191, William of Tornebu, one of the crusaders, found and returned to the king a gold and jewelled belt which Richard had lost in a scuffle.[6]

In June, the two queens left Rome, escorted by Cardinal Melior and the loyal Stephen of Turnham, and made for Marseilles via Pisa and Genoa. From thence King Alfonso of Aragon and Raymond, count of Toulouse, escorted them with all due proprieties through their respective territories to Poitou.[7]

The record is disappointingly scrappy for this period, during which Berengaria was a queen in waiting and a bride without her groom. New to her duties both as queen and wife, she was overshadowed in both roles by the dominant figure of Eleanor, now virtually governing alone in her son's absence. She was also on her way to take up residence in a new country, different in significant respects from her own. Unlike many other medieval princesses, she had not been sent at an early age to live with her prospective husband's family. Although the outcome in such cases was not always happy – witness the fate of the tragic Aélis of France – it is thought that the custom grew up precisely to assist foreign brides to adjust to their new context, to learn the language and become familiar with different customs.

Berengaria was given no such chance. She had to forget her mother tongue and learn to speak the Poitevin or Angevin dialects, the first a form of Occitan, with which she may have been already familiar, the latter a variation of the *langue d'oïl*[8] of northern France and England. Anjou, the homeland of Richard's grandfather, was a land with a turbulent history of robber barons and unorthodox religious cults, into which Henry II had introduced strong government for a brief period. It would soon revert to disorder.

Meanwhile, the Navarrese stood loyally by their new alliance. In 1192 Berengaria's brother Sancho came to the assistance of the ailing seneschal of Gascony, under attack from supporters of the

French and at the same time strengthened his own hold on the territories north of the Pyrenees called Ultrapuertos. The French king continued his intrigues: the ill-fated Danish marriage, which took place in August 1193, was designed to isolate further the English king, and, when Philip learned at last that the 'devil' was loose, he began to prepare for war.[9]

Richard's release was finally obtained early in 1194 with the promised payment of a large ransom and the handing over of hostages, among whom was Berengaria's brother, the Infante Fernando. Some years later, the pipe rolls note that sums of one hundred marks and one hundred pounds were incurred in his release. Once again, the Navarrese showed their loyalty. The Cypriot princess too became part of the bargaining process. Richard and his mother, who had gone to Germany to assist in the negotiations in person, came back to England in March, and Richard quickly resumed the reins of government, which had been entrusted to a few of his most reliable 'familiares', the small circle of Norman bishops and laymen such as the doughty William Marshal. Not all was plain sailing, however: the chroniclers frequently describe him as angered by what had happened in his absence. It is this period which inspired the development of the Robin Hood legend, although Robin, if he ever existed, probably belongs to a later context and a different reign.

As if in recognition of his triumphant return, Richard was crowned again at Winchester on 17 April 1194. This second coronation, which is described in some detail by Roger of Howden,[10] was perhaps above all to demonstrate that the status quo had been restored and, as one scholar has put it, to 'purge the shame of his captivity'. It was not unusual for medieval kings to renew their coronation rites, perhaps to demonstrate that they were still in control. John was a notable example of this: he is recorded as having put on his crown on at least three or four occasions. At this, Richard's second coronation, Eleanor was present with her ladies but not Berengaria, and this omission has been seen as further evidence of a marital estrangement.

A simpler explanation may be that there was insufficient time for the younger queen to make the journey from Anjou to England.

Richard returned to Normandy a bare two months after his first landing at Sandwich and only three and a half weeks after his coronation, which he had himself arranged at two weeks' notice. Berengaria had already been crowned and anointed queen of England, at the time of her wedding in Cyprus. Advisors may have deemed it impractical or even unnecessary for her to make the long journey, and Eleanor would probably have been receptive to any such suggestions.

Upon his arrival in Normandy, the records suggest that Richard spent what were to be the remaining five years of his life in ongoing military campaigning. The chronicles and administrative documents which furnish a step by step account of his movements have virtually nothing to say about his domestic arrangements at this time. With one significant exception, Berengaria is almost entirely absent from these records, but that particular exception, to which we shall return, suggests a possible explanation for the silence.

It is, however, not the only explanation. Recent studies of medieval queenship by scholars like Parsons and Huneycutt suggest that a significant change in the position of queens may have taken place around the middle of the twelfth century, perhaps in association with the growing reliance of kings upon an inner circle of *familiares* and palatinates.[11] Evidence from Capetian France is particularly significant: from the reign of Louis VII onwards, queens appear as witnesses to charters and other royal documents much less frequently than in the preceding century. Even Eleanor of Aquitaine, who has been cast in the role of a dominant woman from the days of her first marriage, was not a high profile queen of France on the evidence of the written record. Her presence in the royal curia is not noticeable. Neither of Philip Augustus's first two queens appears as witnessing or even 'assenting' to royal acts. Moreover, it is from this late twelfth-century period that queens begin to have their own separate quarters, tables and households. While kings continue to be peripatetic, queens tend to stay put. Courtly romances by writers like Wace and Chrétien de Troyes frequently describe situations of this nature.[12]

If the fictional image of the bold, capricious Eleanor has coloured historians' views of her earlier years, perhaps the nineteenth-century view of Berengaria as the '*mal mariée*' or neglected wife has prompted a similar reading of these early years of the marriage. If some of these older scholars saw her as a pitiful victim, abandoned by the husband who had once courted her so ardently, the motif of the '*mal mariée*' fits better with another young princess from the periphery of Christendom who in 1193 had undertaken a disastrous dynastic marriage to a man who would treat her with unparalleled callousness for twenty years, for reasons which are still not clear today. Her story is of one of the saddest in the history of medieval queenship.[13]

The eighteen-year-old Ingeborg of Denmark was the sister of the Danish King Knut VI. She was selected for political reasons to be the bride of Richard's old rival and one-time intimate, Philip Augustus of France, six years after the death in childbirth of his first wife, Isabella of Hainault. The wedding took place at Amiens on 14 August 1193, and what followed quickly became a matter of some notoriety and one which attracted the attention of most of the major chroniclers of the day.

On the morning after the ceremony, and shortly after the queen had been crowned, Philip publicly and violently repudiated his bride. He was subsequently to claim that the marriage had not been consummated, due to sorcery, although when the compliant French bishops eventually pronounced the marriage dissolved three months later at the assembly of Compiegne, it was on the more convenient, if factitious grounds of consanguinity. On that occasion, Ingeborg, according to the official record noted by Pope Innocent III, unable to speak French and weeping copiously, none the less had the presence of mind to appeal to Rome. '*Mala Francia!*' she is alleged to have said, '*Mala Francia* (Evil France), *Roma! Roma!*'

Pope Celestine responded quickly and upheld her appeal. Then began a long struggle between France and the papacy which only ended when Innocent III, Celestine's successor, finally prevailed upon Philip to restore his queen to her rightful place, which he did in 1213.

Whatever the reason for Philip's conduct, he was not averse to another attempt at 'marriage', this time to Agnes of Merania, with whom he contracted a marriage on 1 June 1196 and who bore him several children. Perhaps, like other princes in more recent times, he thought that his rejected bride would accept the situation and go quietly. When she refused to accept the sentence of dismissal, he treated her with great cruelty. She was banished from the royal domain and imprisoned in one castle after another, in oppressive conditions, with the smallest possible retinue, in the hope that affliction and duress would break her spirit. Régine Pernoud's sympathetic study of the 'captive queen' reproduces the text of her heartfelt appeal to the Pope and the pleas of support issued on her behalf by sympathetic churchmen.

Despite protracted appeals from the Pope, ranging from paternal admonitions to the imposition of an interdict on the realm, Philip refused to give up Agnes and restore Ingeborg as queen. Because they had sided with the king rather than the Pope, many French churchmen saw their prospects of advancement temporarily curtailed. Only after the death of Agnes did negotiations even begin to take place. But bow though he ultimately did to papal pressure, Philip continued to treat his estranged wife with implacable hostility, exacerbated probably by a guilty conscience, and it is most unlikely that they ever resumed full conjugal relations as directed. Certainly no children were ever born to Philip and Ingeborg.

The events of the wedding night remain a mystery. Philip's official apologists repeat the king's claim that he was unable to consummate the marriage because of sorcery or witchcraft. This has given rise to strange speculations, some of which are not free from misogynistic prejudice. Although some contemporary commentators described her as beautiful, Ingeborg 'must have' suffered from some horrendous deformity. Halitosis was one contemporary suggestion, though that would hardly have been uncommon in that day and age, and there are even prurient hints at deviant sexual behaviour. Unless the whole thing was stage-managed to get rid of an innocent victim, it seems more likely that Philip became temporarily impotent and sought to blame the bride for the loss of face such a crisis would entail. Régine Pernoud[14] suggested that he may have suffered a psychosomatic crisis when he saw, in his new bride with her pale Nordic beauty, the image of his first wife Isabella lifeless on her bier. Ingeborg's insistence that the marriage had been consummated was due, according to this view, to her lack of sexual experience.

Ingeborg's psalter, annotated in her hand, survives as a testament to her stoicism, while the memorial masses she later instituted for her faithless husband are a further indication of the piety for which she became famous. Her plight reminds us forcibly of the unenviable position of the foreign bride totally dependent on the goodwill of her husband, readily abandoned by her own kinsfolk when politics were at stake, a potential object of suspicion and a ready-made scapegoat.

There is no evidence that Berengaria and Ingeborg ever met. Though there are some similarities in their respective situations, there are also differences. In Richard's case there is no known mistress. Berengaria's rivals are at least as likely to have been male as female, but the names of these two young brides are often coupled as victims of male mistreatment in the so-called age of chivalry. A far cry indeed, as Georges Duby has often observed, from the literary fiction of the haughty and capricious lady worshipped from afar by the love-struck suitor! Or perhaps an example of the truth so cynically expressed in the *Romance of the Rose* that 'if you abandon yourself so much that you give them (i.e., women) too much power, you will repent later, when you feel their malice.'[15]

Much of the period succeeding Richard's release from captivity was taken up with fighting against the French. Hostilities recommenced almost immediately after his return to France from England, shortly after his second coronation. The intermittent hostilities in which kings like Richard and Philip were so often engaged should not be compared to full-scale war in the modern sense. Although they were frequently quite bloody, they were mainly limited in scope and objectives, confined to fairly small areas and quickly concluded with truces, exchanges of territory or occasionally stand-offs. Theoretically, warfare between Christian princes had been outlawed by the Church and, as the type of stoushes described in the entertaining 'biography' of William Marshal demonstrate, these localised encounters were often the way to achieve promotion and acquire portable gear such as horses and weaponry.

None the less, if modern English writers like John Gillingham and J.C. Holt are correct in attempting to show that Richard was not just a '*rex bellicosus*' (bellicose king) but also a statesman who led from the top, it is still true that by inclination as well as necessity, he was the quintessential man of action, most of it physical. Even the mysterious bouts of illness to which he was often subject seem to have made him more determined to prove himself. He clearly enjoyed a certain amount of risk-taking, and his favourite leisure pursuits were the traditional male ones of hunting, falconry and sword-play. Although he founded abbeys and made the appropriate charitable donations, the general verdict is that he was not particularly pious: he had wandering thoughts during mass and if he did not indulge in clergy-baiting to quite the same degree as his redoubtable ancestor William IX of Aquitaine, who taunted a bishop about his baldness and threatened to found an abbey of whores, he certainly handed it out robustly from time to time. The verse biography of William Marshal records a dressing down Richard gave to the papal envoy, Peter of Capua, when the latter came to ask for the release of the bishop of Beauvais:

> Have you been bribed? You, Sir, are a lackey and an idiot! If you were not an ambassador, Rome itself couldn't stop me giving you a beating to remember me by – and to take back and show the Pope ... Get out of here, you wretch, traitor, liar, deceiver, simoniac, and make sure I never see your face again!

The narrator goes on to say, with obvious enjoyment, that the legate couldn't get out quickly enough, scared out of his wits, and fearing he might even be emasculated ...[16]

Most of the things Richard enjoyed doing, and excelled in, were activities in which a woman, particularly a medieval woman, would have found it impossible to participate. Even Eleanor, on her son's release, did not accompany him on the campaign trail, but sought semi-retirement at Fontevraud. It seems likely that Berengaria's company, whether a pleasant but fading memory, or an irksome reminder of his marital duty, was not a high priority. And Berengaria, too, who, as her later life suggests, was capable of enduring a difficult situation with dignity and stoicism, had to make a virtue of necessity.

Be that as it may, in May and June of 1194, Richard was much on the move, passing rapidly through his Norman strongholds – Barfleur, Caen, Lisieux, Verneuil – and then further south to settle scores with two of his rebellious Poitevin vassals, Geoffrey of Rancon and Ademar of Angoulême, who had renounced their allegiance and taken sides with France. The Infante Sancho once more came to the aid of his brother-in-law, in the attack on the stronghold of Loches, which was ultimately successful. Richard's arrival, in mid-June, while the Navarrese maintained the siege, sealed the fate of the defenders. The *Chronicle of St Aubin* states that Richard took only a few hours to take the fortress despite the fact that it was 'both by nature and artifice heavily fortified.'[17]

Some scholars think that it was here for the first time that Berengaria was reunited with both her brother and her husband. There is no record of this but it is not unlikely. The meeting would have been all the more poignant because not long after this, in early July, came the news that the king, Sancho El Sabio, had died some ten days previously, either in Pamplona or Tudela.[18] His death brought to an end a long life of faith and endeavour. The younger Sancho now left the battlefield to be '*alzado*' – raised on the shield – as king in his turn, and a truce was quickly concluded. Richard returned to Normandy where he celebrated Christmas at Rouen. Neither his wife nor his mother were with him. Berengaria remained in Anjou, mourning her father, perhaps at Chinon, Saumur or Beaufort en Vallée, a secluded spot in thick woodland, close to the '*grand chemin mansays*' which linked Angers and Le Mans. This seems to have been the place in which she chose to stay for most of the remainder of her short married life.

The ruins of Beaufort castle today, atop its mound close to the centre of the small market town, are not those of the original castle in which Berengaria lived, but are part of the edifice which replaced it a hundred years or so later.

Berengaria seems to have established a small household of her own there, for it is there that we find her at the time of Richard's death. She does not appear to have spent much time at Fontevraud, where Eleanor made her final home and where many of the dynasty were buried.[19] There was no place for her in this sanctum and perhaps she was always seen as an outsider. When her name is mentioned in charters issued by Eleanor from Fontevraud after the death of Richard, it is always simply as *'regina Berengaria'* and never *'carissima'* or *'dilectissima'* (dearest) as the queen mother styled her own daughters. Although these documents are written in a formal and somewhat impersonal style, details such as these afford valuable insights into personal relationships. Some tenuous connection between Berengaria and Fontevraud must have continued after the death of Eleanor, however, for among the foundation documents of the abbey founded in 1230 is recorded the purchase of land in Maine belonging to the abbess of Fontevraud.

Richard's return to Normandy signalled a temporary lull in hostilities, during which, as John Gillingham has put it, 'peace talks were resumed on and off', and the chroniclers show Richard devoting time to more statesmanlike pursuits.

Roger of Howden mentions, for instance, the legislation entitled *Capitula Judaeorum*, which penalised the murder of Jews and probably as a consequence encouraged the migration of many Jews from French territory into that controlled by the Angevins. He then goes on to recount with some relish the grisly fate which overtook Leopold of Austria. Because of his misdeeds, his land eventually became blighted and he himself broke his leg in an accident. This led to his death. The episode is told as a vindication of divine justice: 'The heart of Leopold, duke of Austria, was hardened and because the aforementioned evils which God had allowed to befall his land were unable to affect him, God chastised his person in this way.' The passage introduces one of Howden's familiar themes, the need for rulers to be subject to the law of God. As we shall see, this leads into a discussion of good and bad kingship.

The year 1195 begins, in Howden's *Chronicle*, with another episode narrated in homiletic mode. Richard, the magnanimous ruler, pardoned his illegitimate half-brother Geoffrey, archbishop of York, who had been disloyal to him during his absence and had been fomenting discord. The archbishop became boastful and over-confident as a result, and Richard's response was swift and summary: he deprived him of his offices. Howden then introduces a lengthy denunciation of the tongue, that 'small member' which can destroy the whole body, just as a great ship can be turned around in its course by a small instrument at its helm.

The next passage is linked to the preceding by a somewhat imprecise phrase: 'in that same year'. Thematically it is linked by the image of the small and insignificant member, which can be an instrument for good or for ill, by the power of the word and by the larger theme of righteous and unrighteous rulers.

The passage reads as follows:

> ... in the same year a certain hermit came to king Richard and, preaching the words of eternal salvation, said: 'Be mindful of the destruction of Sodom and abstain from unlawful things; or else God's just retribution will overtake you.' But the king, intent on earthly things rather than the things of God, was not able to turn his mind so quickly from unlawful conduct, without seeing some sign from above. He scorned the messenger, not understanding why and when the Lord reveals to the lowly what is hidden from the wise. It was to the leper that he announced the salvation of Samaria and it was Balaam's humble servant who recalled his master from his evil conduct.
>
> The hermit left and removed himself from the king's presence. In the fullness of time, perhaps, the king might have set aside the hermit's warning, but, prompted by divine grace, he retained some part of it, having faith that God, who recalled to repentance the publican and the Canaanite woman, would, in his great mercy, grant him too a contrite heart. Whence it came about that, on the Tuesday of Holy Week, God chastised him with an iron rod, not to confound him, but so that he should recognise this chastisement as coming from above, the Lord brought great sickness upon him that day, with the result that, summoning to his side holy men, the king did not flinch from confessing the foulness of his life, and, having accepted penance, *received his wife, whom he had not known for a long time, and, renouncing unlawful intercourse, was united with his wife and the two became one flesh; then God gave him health of*

both body and soul. Oh happy the child whom the heavenly father chastises in this life, for amendment not for death. For the Father corrects his son sometimes gently, sometimes severely, and in this way or that brings him back to good practice. For thus God tries his gold in the furnace of his justice, thus He tests His saint through adversity and brings him to his crown. Truly great and wonderful are the works of God and His mercy is the greatest of His works. For this king, whose head had been crowned with so many iniquities, was adopted as a son of Christ and, turning from his depravity to the Lord, was received as a son ...[20] (italics mine)

Other good works followed: the king rose early and went to mass (and stayed till the end!). He ordered the poor to be fed both in his castles and in his cities and he ordered chalices to be made to replace the ones taken from churches to raise his ransom.

This episode is found only in Howden, though several other writers refer in more general terms to the king's bad habits and new resolutions.[21] There is another, closer, parallel in Adam of Eynsham's life of St Hugh of Lincoln, the *Magna Vita Sancti Hugonis*.[22] Both are variants on the theme of 'king and holy man', in which a royal sinner is rebuked by a fearless cleric and shamed into amending his ways.

Popular for obvious reasons with clerical writers, from Gildas onwards, this motif was probably inspired by the biblical story of King David and the prophet Nathan, where the fearless man of God rebuked the powerful king for his sins. Adam's version, which is corroborated in less detail by the other early biography of Bishop Hugh, by Gerald of Wales, is set in the year 1198, when the charismatic and well-loved bishop was in Normandy to remonstrate with Richard – not for the first time – over his irregular dealings with the Church. On this occasion he also charged his 'parishioner' (Richard was born in Oxford) with marital infidelity as well as the sale of offices. In Adam's vivid and simple narrative, Richard admitted some of the charges and denied others! But, unlike the incident in Howden, this episode is narrated succinctly and in a very specific context. Despite the hagiographical emphasis, it has a ring of authenticity about it and the portrayal of Richard as mercurial, quick to anger and with a somewhat undisciplined conscience corresponds to what we learn about him from other sources. His magnanimity, a traditional virtue of kings, makes him respond with generosity to the moral authority of one who was not only an outstanding spiritual leader but a fellow aristocrat. Common to both Adam and Roger's accounts is the specifically sexual nature of the sins with which the king was charged.

In Howden's text, the unknown hermit, unlike the revered bishop, is not a person who commands instant respect. He could even be fictitious, though hermits, sylvans and other recluses were numerous in Maine and Anjou and were often quite influential because they stood between the ordinary people and their overlords: the *Tristan* of Beroul,[23] composed somewhere in the 1190s and written in a western, perhaps Norman, dialect, features a hermit who acts as a go-between in this way, helping the fugitive lovers to recognise their sin and offering to facilitate their return to court.[24] Richard, blinded by love of this world, fails to hear in the words of the humble hermit, the voice of God Himself: the hermit, unlike the bishop, does not attempt to remonstrate further, but quietly leaves the royal presence. But his words had not fallen on entirely deaf ears, Howden assures us, and almost without recognising it, the king himself had not lost all hope of repentance. A sudden bout of illness – unspecified, but perhaps a recurrence of one of those acute infections which frequently laid him low during the crusade – hastened the process. Richard's repentance was a public one, probably in the presence of his regular confessors and Howden is quick to demonstrate that the fruits of his contrition were immediately seen in the amendment of his life, both in the private and the public sphere.

Although Adam's text refers to simony as well as marital infidelity, Howden's reference is only to sexual sins: the king was told to abstain from illicit things, later clarified as unlawful intercourse (*concubitus illicitus*). This unlawful intercourse, which had caused him to neglect his marital obligations, is not described in detail, but the reference to the destruction of Sodom has been seen, correctly in my view, as referring primarily to homosexual practices. This is rejected by those historians – almost exclusively English – who deny that Richard was homosexual or bi-sexual. John Gillingham argues that references to the destruction of the biblical city of Sodom were commonly applied to any kind of sinful activity. No doubt there is some truth in this view: it is, however, equally noteworthy that in a very large number of homiletic texts and commentaries the terms sodomy and the 'sin of Sodom' refer unambiguously and consistently to male homosexual intercourse.[25] The term *concubitus illicitus* is, admittedly, more general and could refer to heterosexual adultery as well as homosexual acts.

The bout of illness with which Richard is conveniently and dramatically visited is a central motif in this episode, unlike the incident in the *Magna Vita Sancti Hugonis*, where the person of the messenger himself adds to the credibility of his message.[26] Was this a recurrence of the same illness which plagued Richard in Palestine and from which, significantly perhaps, the king of France also appeared to suffer on occasion? The exact nature of the illness is not important: the significance of the theme of disease here has more to do with the longstanding association of disease with sexuality.

The reconciliation with Berengaria is placed at the heart of this episode and is followed by the assertion that God granted the king healing of both body and soul. The other good works are the classic effects of the firm purpose of amendment necessary for absolution. There is a distinctly homiletic tone to this whole section.

The language in which the marital 'reconciliation' is described is very precise; it is both biblical and sacramental: the verb *cognoscere*, to 'know' is used in the biblical sense; *adhaesit*, imperfectly rendered 'remained faithful to' in Riley's translation, is better conveyed by the older 'cleave to' of the King James Bible and the phrase *facti sunt duo in carne una*, perfectly expresses the biblical teaching on marriage.[27] Implicit in this passage is the notion of the reciprocal marital debt, a principle from which Church teaching never departed but which has, in practice, frequently conflicted with older and more deeply rooted notions of female subservience. Although the passage does not spell this out, the clear implication is that Richard's sins included withholding 'for a long time' from his wife the conjugal rights to which she, as much as he, was entitled.

It appears as if the chronicler wished to emphasise the theme of a new beginning, in keeping with the spirit of Richard's second coronation. Just as the ceremony in Winchester purged away the shame of captivity and reasserted the king's dignity, so this solemn reconciliation with Berengaria signals a new start to the marriage and ushers in an era of peace and prosperity.

Roger was both a churchman and a loyal public servant. Although he is thought to have been present for at least part of the third crusade, this final part of the chronicle, which recounts events in France after Richard's return, is unlikely to have been based on his own eyewitness observations. As John Gillingham has shown,[28] the chronicle represents a writing up of detailed notes made during the crusade, which in their original form appear in the *Gesta Regis Ricardi*, formerly attributed to 'Benedict of Peterborough'. The differences between the two texts, in the sections which cover the same ground, are often instructive. Details of time and place are often added to flesh out the briefer record of the *Gesta*. Sometimes events are rearranged and the authorial comments are expanded.

These events which took place after Richard's return from captivity are more loosely coordinated and structured in a more reflective way. The brief lull after the truce of Tillières would have been an appropriate time to place the king's reunion with his wife, for whom he had had little time during the first hectic months of his return from captivity. Easter, the most important festival in the Church's year, when Catholics are under an obligation to seek the sacrament of penance (reconciliation), may have seemed the right moment for this long overdue rendering of the marital debt.

A vigorous editorial peroration in sermonic mode makes clear the central message: no sinner, however egregious, is beyond the reach of divine mercy, if the pilot light of conscience still flickers. That sinners backslide is inevitable, but Christ himself decreed that forgiveness should be seventy times seven, that is, unlimited. The eloquent lament, or *planh*, composed by the Occitan troubadour Gaucelm Faidit, echoes this sentiment. In the final verse, the troubadour alludes to Richard's sins and asks God to forgive him: 'Ah,

Lord God, you who are truly forgiving, true God, true Man, true Life, have mercy! Forgive him, for he needs your mercy, and overlook his fault, but remember how he strove to serve you.'[29]

There is an obvious similarity between Howden's text and an earlier passage, found in the *Gesta* and repeated, with minor alterations in the *Chronicle*. This passage, to which attention was drawn previously, describes the public penance undertaken by Richard in Messina in December 1190, shortly before the arrival of Eleanor and Berengaria. In that episode, there is no holy man present to issue a warning to the king. Richard himself, prompted by his own conscience, called together leading churchmen in his retinue and abased himself before them, confessing the 'foulness' of his sins and accepting penance. After this he returned to the paths of virtue. The language is very similar in the two passages and once again the sexual nature of the sins is made clear. The first public act of penance takes place just before a major Christian festival and, significantly, it is followed by the arrival of Berengaria. There is an obvious symmetry between these two events and it is difficult to believe that the author did not intend to highlight this.

Howden's writing is didactic but it is also partisan. In this section of his chronicle, written when he was at the end of a long career, he was further from the day to day workings of the court and more interested in church matters in England, especially in his own province of York. His narrative is sketchier and he pads it out with more correspondence. His treatment of Richard's final years is more of a reflection on the theme of kingship and the verdict of Providence on rulers, good and bad.[30] Richard's public act of penance follows other examples of that magnanimity which is characteristic of true kingship: he pardons his rebellious and disloyal brothers and prelates for their 'anger and malice', he gives laws to his subjects, and does not neglect the well-being of the Church. But unlike Geoffrey, the bastard son who became proud and insolent when fortune favoured him, or John the younger, weaker brother who broke faith when Richard's back was turned, or Leopold the petty tyrant who failed to heed divine warnings, Richard was ready to humble himself before God's representative and acknowledge himself a sinner in need of absolution. Like the precious gold which is refined in the fiercest furnace, the true nobility of a king's nature will shine afresh. Not only does this episode exemplify the Gospel teaching that those who would be forgiven must also forgive, it sets up an exemplary icon of Christian kingship.[31]

How accurate a picture of the king's behaviour this was is, of course, something which we cannot determine. It is certainly possible that Roger himself, loyal though he was, may have been troubled by certain aspects of his king's behaviour or reputation and felt the need to engage in a vigorous defence. However idealised this picture may be, it does appear to represent a period of relative stability before hostilities with France once more broke out. Lionel Landon believes that it was at this time that Richard and Berengaria bought the property at Thorée, which Berengaria made over to the Hospitallers in 1216. It would be pleasing to think that this period was a happier one for Berengaria, whose life had so often been, in the words of Agnes Strickland, 'replete with hope deferred'.

We hear little more about Berengaria after this, but it is possible that she was present with Richard at Christmas in Poitiers, and later in the following year she would certainly have been present at the wedding of Joanna to the count of Toulouse, which took place in Rouen in October 1196. This was a political marriage arranged by Richard to neutralise the count of Toulouse, and it brought Joanna no joy. A son was born the following year but before the child was much more than two years old she would be fleeing for her life, with another child on the way. Richard, meanwhile, had other preoccupations in Normandy: he was building the great castle named Chateau Gaillard at Les Andelys which was to be his headquarters during the renewed campaign against the French. Its ruins still command a sweeping view of the river valley below. There is no record of Berengaria's presence there, if indeed she ever visited it. Richard seems to have spent a great deal of time there and was particularly attached to the place, for strategic and personal reasons, according to the chroniclers. He even called it, significantly, his 'child'. In March 1204, just short of five years after Richard's death, it was to fall to Philip Augustus.

Some historians have seen this activity in Normandy, together with the neutralisation of the count of Toulouse through the marriage to Joanna, a major shift in importance, away from the south towards the north of the so-called Angevin 'empire' and a corresponding decline in the importance of the alliance with Navarre. The Navarrese historian L.X. Fortun Pérez claims, without specific evidence in support, that Richard conferred the government of Gascony on his wife during the period 1196-9 in order to strengthen his position in the south. At the same time, Fernando and the other hostages were released from captivity in Germany. Those who suggest that the Navarrese alliance was under strain have even speculated that Richard may have been considering repudiating Berengaria.

This period in the history of Navarre is a complex one and not easy to summarise quickly. A bizarre story, repeated by Roger of Howden and attributed by some to this period, tells of Sancho El Fuerte's visit to Africa, where the daughter of the 'king of Morocco' had fallen in love with him from afar and insisted that he marry her. Moret suggests that Howden heard this story from Berengaria but the whole episode savours of folklore, in keeping with other traditions concerning Sancho. What is beyond doubt is that during this period the Navarrese monarch was actively negotiating new alliances, including some with the Muslim rulers in Andalucia.

J.M. Lacarra, in his invaluable multi-volume survey of the political history of Navarre, and in other more detailed studies of the period, has provided a useful summary of these decades when the independence of Navarre was again under threat from neighbours great and small. From an anglocentric point of view, the alliance with England may seem to have been the most important of the Navarrese engagements with the outside world, but, viewed from a Spanish perspective, the situation is and no doubt was different. For Sancho as for his father before him, two dominant and interlinked problems threatened the stability of his kingdom. One was the rivalry with Castile and, intermittently, with the other Christian kings, of Aragon and Leon: ever since the time of Sancho's ancestor Garcia Ramirez, one or other of these two neighbours had aggressively questioned its legitimacy and claimed areas of its territory. The other was the importance of access to the sea.

The Pyrenees form a natural barrier, but Pamplona controlled one of the most important land passages or 'ports', and a combination of the Basque provinces of Alava and Guipúzcoa, giving access to the sea at Fuenterrabia and the coastal road to Bayonne, with an increased stake in the region known as 'Ultrapuertos' – the land on the far side of the mountains – was clearly the best guarantee of a secure northern border. This in turn allowed more resources to be devoted to defending the disputed territories in the Ebro valley to the south and the frontier with Aragon.

Susana Hereros has demonstrated the importance of the territories of Ultrapuertos to successive rulers of Navarre. Tension between the 'Navarrese' and Richard in his capacity as count of Poitou and duke of Aquitaine was evident in the year 1177 when he suppressed revolts in Dax and Bigorre and enforced the submission of people described as 'Basques and Navarrese.' Again, in the following year, 'Basques, Navarrese and Brabacons' sacked Gascony as far as Bordeaux and Taillebourg. These troops appear to have been mercenaries, working for the highest bidder, rather than regular troops owing allegiance to the ruler of Navarre. However, in 1189, Martín Chipia was designated '*tenente*' of the regions of Cisa by curial degree and this may represent a first move by the king of Navarre to extend his protection over territories left in a vacuum after Richard's reprisals against the count of Labourd, Arnaldo Beltran.

John Gillingham drew attention to the possible agenda for Richard's visit to Gascony shortly before leaving for the crusade in 1190, suggesting that the marriage to Berengaria may have been part of a deal to ensure that the Navarrese would keep an eye on this notorious trouble spot, and Susana Hereros has argued that the *quid pro quo* would have been a tacit acceptance of the extension of Navarrese power in Ultrapuertos. Sancho's successful military actions in 1192 and 1194 further strengthened that power and influence, to the extent that the count of Toulouse, whose interests in the area were obvious, offered his daughter in marriage to Sancho as part of a pact.[32]

By 1194 the castles of Rocabruna[33] and St Jean Pied de Port, assigned by Sancho El Sabio as Berengaria's dowry or *arras*, were held by *tenentes* of the king of Navarre, Martín Chipia and Fortún Rodrigo de Bazton respectively. In 1196 Arnaldo Ramón de Tartás, viscount of Dax, swore allegiance to Sancho, and he was followed in 1203 by Bibiano de Agramont; and the following year the burghers of Bordeaux did the same.[34] Sancho remained a loyal ally of King John and, even after his death, a much later record attests the continuation of Navarrese support for his son and successor Henry III.[35] Whatever political events lie behind these declarations of support and allegiance, it seems clear that as long as the English retained control of substantial parts of south-west France, the Christian kings of northern Spain needed to retain good relations with them. None of this precludes the occasional ripple of disagreement.

In 1196 after the death of King Alfonso of Aragon, his young son, Pedro II, influenced by his mother Sancha, allied himself closely, albeit as a weak junior partner, with the 'Emperor' of Castile. This appears to have altered the balance of power within the recently established alliance between the three Spanish kings and the king of Portugal against the aggressive Almohad Muslims in the south. Lacarra saw the agreement with the viscount of Tartás and Bearne as part of this general Christian alliance and its subsequent collapse into a succession of shifting coalitions and counter-coalitions as part of the ongoing struggle to ensure access across the Pyrenees either by land or by sea. To this context belongs Sancho's attempt to marry one of his sisters – probably Costanza – to the young King Pedro of Aragon, a marriage vetoed by Pope Innocent on the ground of consanguinity.[36]

John Gillingham drew attention in 1981 to a reference in the text of the 1196 agreement with the viscount of Tartás to the king of England. This reference, he suggested, implied that the Navarrese alliance was under strain, and it may have been this cooling of relations which prompted Richard's request to the Pope in 1198 to press Sancho to hand over the dowry castles. The terms of his request are no longer extant, but the Pope's response was one of formal support for the English king.[37] The papal directive does not appear to have been complied with, and Sancho's relations with John after Richard's death make it clear that it was with John's support that Sancho concluded the alliance with the city of Bordeaux and that a sizeable colony of Bordelais then established itself in St Jean Pied de Port. Since the Castilians were poised to seize the two Basque provinces of Alava and Guipúzcoa, which they did in 1199-

1200, the Navarrese depended on this link with Bordeaux for access to the sea.

It appears then that the differences over the dowry castles represent a minor hiccup rather than a serious rift: Sancho continued to enjoy papal favour despite his apparent non-compliance with the request to hand over the two castles, and whatever grievances the king of England may have had against the viscount of Tartás, their consequences must have been limited and quickly contained.[38] There is certainly no evidence, even circumstantial, that Richard was planning to repudiate Berengaria in 1196-8, and indeed had he contemplated doing so it would have made matters considerably worse.

Had he repudiated his wife, he would no doubt have been expected to marry again, if only to provide an heir. There is not the slightest indication that Richard considered remarriage, and the language of some of his edicts at the time suggests that he had already designated John as his heir in the event of no children of his own. If he had been in any doubt as to his capacity to father a child – and the assumption that the lack of an heir was the 'fault' of Berengaria is based on little more than sexism – it would have been unwise to make this obvious by contracting any new union, with the risk that this too might prove infertile. We shall never know exactly how Berengaria 'felt' about her marriage, but the fact that she received the unfailing support of so many prominent and discerning churchmen who were also close to her husband suggests that they at least neither blamed her for the lack of an heir nor encouraged her exclusion from the royal circle.

By 1198 Roger of Howden's chronicle is drawing to its close. Reading, as we do inevitably, with the benefit of hindsight, we sense that the Angevin 'empire' itself is in its dying throes. The signs are there: its old warriors like William Marshal are growing weary; Eleanor, its fading icon, is resting at Fontevraud, gathering her forces for one last desperate rally; John, the youngest, is waiting in the wings. But this is no David, no fresh-faced innocent from the fields. John is a wayward and weak-willed schemer who in the space of a few brief years will see his birthright reduced to a small kingdom in north western Europe. And what of Richard?

Hindsight too is responsible for some of the lush language used by otherwise sober historians: he is seen as a wounded Titan,[39] a hero without a quest,[40] or perhaps just another old soldier dusting off his medals. As far as the documentary record shows, the last three years of his life seem to have been something of a plateau, a period of low-level hostilities with France, skirmishes, false starts, transient truces, prodding from the German emperor, churchmen and other envoys scurrying around taking soundings and the occasional papal pronouncement.

We see Richard spending more and more time in Normandy, where his beloved Chateau Gaillard is at last complete. The last few Christmases were spent at one or other of the capitals or fortresses – Poitiers in 1195, Bur-le-Roi in 1196, Rouen in 1197 and perhaps again in 1198. Prompted by the remonstrations of a holy man, he may have brought his queen to be with him on one or two of these occasions, and there are some indications that she was beginning to assume a more public role. In mid-1199, according to Giraldus Cambrensis, all the parties to a dispute concerning the succession to the see of St David's, in which Gerald himself had a particular interest, appeared at Chinon before the new king, John, 'Queen Eleanor his mother and Queen Berengaria, his sister-in-law' in accordance with instructions issued previously by Richard.[41] Perhaps, in more settled times, Berengaria might have been granted an opportunity to assume a more public role.

But we shall never know. Her status changed irrevocably on 6 April 1199, the Tuesday of Holy Week, when Richard died from septicaemia or gangrene just over a week after being wounded by a crossbow shot during the course of the siege of the castle of Chalus-Chabrol in the Limousin. It has been seen as a pointless and unnecessary accident, brought on by the king's own well-known habit of risk-taking. But John Gillingham has shown quite clearly that the buried treasure which was supposed to have attracted the predatory monarch's attention is probably apocryphal and that the siege was a calculated response to French provocation in the border zone.[42] This gives point to the secrecy which surrounded Richard's sick-bed and the directions he gave to his inner circle:

All his companions were sent away from the entrance to the cubicle in which he was lying, with the exception of four of his nobles who were freely admitted to see him, lest the news of his sickness should become public. (Ralph of Coggeshall)[43]

The news could not, of course, be concealed for ever, but if a hiatus could be avoided, especially while there was still hope of recovery, the French would have had less opportunity to take advantage. This may also explain why Berengaria was not, apparently, summoned to her husband's death bed, or perhaps even told of his condition. The few messages which were sent out, to Queen Eleanor and William Marshal in Normandy, were sent in secrecy, but even if news of these messages had leaked out, the full truth would not necessarily have been immediately revealed. A summons to his wife, however, who did not normally accompany him on campaign and who had no direct political involvement, would certainly have revealed the situation.[44]

As usual, legendary elements begin to cluster, like iron filings on a magnet, around the episode of Richard's death. There is, for instance, doubt concerning the identity of the avenger who allegedly defied the dying king's final act of magnanimity and ordered the death of his assassin: according to one version it was Mercadier, the mercenary captain; in another version it was Philip of Cognac, the king's illegitimate son. Other traditions detail the events of his final hours: one chronicler claims, presumably from hearsay, that the king had not received the sacrament of Holy Communion for a long time because of the hatred he harboured for the king of France. Another late source, the fourteenth-century chronicle of Walter of Guiseborough, tells of Richard's insatiable lust, which drove him to repeated debaucheries even on his death bed, in defiance of his doctors' wishes:

The wound in his shoulder was deep and dangerous and because of that his doctors forbade him to embrace, or even see and touch his wife (*interdixerunt ei omnem uxoris amplexum, visum etiam et tactum*). But because he was very lustful and inflamed with the love of women (*mulierum*) he would not restrain his pleasures but ignored this sound advice and took no heed of his wound.[45]

This story may be an embellishment of earlier accounts such as that of the Cistercian Ralph of Coggeshall, thought to be based on the testimony of one of Richard's Cistercian confessors. According to Coggeshall, the king showed remarkable fortitude when wounded; he did not react when shot and 'carried on regardless, without heeding medical advice' (*incontinenter se habetur et praecepta medicorum non curante*).

The passage in Guiseborough is frequently quoted as evidence that Richard was not homosexual, and, curiously, is given almost literal credence by scholars who, in other contexts, counsel frequently against taking 'anecdotal' material in chronicles too literally. As 'evidence' in a debate which rests more on perceptions than 'facts' this passage in a relatively late source is of little value.

Even if this source is judged to be a reliable one, it has not been interpreted correctly. It is instructive to look at the use of the word 'wife' (*uxor*) in this text. If the Latin text is taken literally, the doctors appear to be warning the king, not against death-bed orgies but against any normal marital intimacies. One might argue from this that Berengaria was present, which seems unlikely, or that her presence was anticipated by the doctors or, at the very least, that the latter had no reason to doubt that the relationship between the spouses was a normal one. Perhaps we have overlooked the obvious here and the absence of Berengaria at the king's death bed was the logical consequence of these warnings, as the prima facie meaning of the text seems to suggest.

For whatever reason, Berengaria was not, in all probability, present and the king did indeed 'carry on regardless' – an opinion which Guiseborough, writing well over a hundred years later, interpreted in a particular way, in keeping with other late traditions. There may be a traditional element here too; a common element in the universal folklore of kingship, much of which is derived from an archaic belief in the sacrality of the monarch, is a set of customs and practices relating to the fertility of the monarch. Originally linked to the fertility of the land, the king's powers of procreation were sacralised and surrounded with rituals of various kinds. In early Irish tradition, so often closest of all the European mythologies to the common Indo-European base, a dying king or a warrior figure with kingship potential, is challenged by females, human or supernatural, in a sexually charged way. As in the old story of Samson and Delilah, female sexuality is seen as undermining or destructive of male vigour. The wounded King Conchobar of Ulster is warned, in an old Irish story which meshes new Christian values with archaic pagan ones, to abstain from anger, sex and physical exertion.[46] It may be that this anecdote reflects some of these ancient traditions which persisted in folklore long after they were displaced in 'high' culture.

Although we have no way of knowing, then, whether the dying king in his last moments remembered his absent bride, we do have a brief but touching picture of the young widow's grief, in the writings of Adam of Eynsham, friend and biographer of Bishop Hugh of Lincoln. The bishop had returned to Normandy in 1199, a year after warning Richard to amend his conduct. This time another touchy subject was on the agenda: the king had been attempting to seize the assets of clerics in Hugh's diocese.

Hugh was on his way to see the king when he learned of Richard's death. He decided immediately to go to Fontevraud to assist at the funeral but, despite the dangers of the location, first he would go to Beaufort en Vallée to comfort the queen. Taking only a few junior attendants he 'left the highroad and journeyed through a wild forest region to that town, in order to comfort her for the death of her husband. His words went straight to the soul of the sorrowing and almost heart-broken widow, and calmed her grief in a wonderful way.' Among the counsels he offered her, according to Adam, were the need for fortitude in misfortune and prudence in happier times. He celebrated mass for Berengaria and her retinue before passing on to Saumur.

It is clear from the text that Berengaria had her own retinue at Beaufort. The details are not recorded – a variant version specifies that they were women – but clearly they were of sufficient standing to earn an official blessing from Hugh. Adam on several occasions speaks of Hugh's respect for women, an attitude not always con-spicuous among his clerical contemporaries.

It appears that Berengaria did not immediately follow Hugh to Fontevraud, where the cortege was already entering the Church, though some later writers have assumed that she was present. After the solemn obsequies were completed, Hugh did not stay but returned with the new king, John, to Beaufort to celebrate Easter there. As the Benedictine scholar Dom Piolin observed, it can only have been the widowed queen's presence there which brought him back to Beaufort to celebrate the most important feast in the Church's calendar, when the message of the angel to Mary Magdalen, that 'He is risen, He is not here', is a reminder to all believers that just as Christ rose from the dead, the faithful departed too shall one day rise to glory. For the grieving queen, these words would have had a special significance.

Three days later Berengaria herself was in Fontevraud, where her name is listed as witness to a charter issued by Eleanor.[47] It was at that time too that the two queens, together with the papal envoy, Cardinal Pietro di Capua, and others, discussed the proposed mar-riage of Berengaria's sister Blanca to the young Thibaut of Champagne, who had succeeded to his brother's title in 1197 when his brother fell out of a window at Acre and died of his injuries. This marriage was solemnised on 1 July 1199 at Chartres and Berengaria took a leading role in the ceremony, escorting her sister, perhaps from Poitiers, and acting as a witness to the ceremony.[48]

This marriage was not only a shrewd political move, but it turned out to be providential for Berengaria herself. It was at her sister's new court that she took refuge in 1200, abandoned both by John and Eleanor, to whom she was plainly of no further use. Pope Innocent III, her true and tireless champion, described her plight there, reduced to the status of a beggar, as destitute and abject.

It is difficult to find, in the history of medieval marriage, such a poignant contrast between a beginning and an end, or such a dra-matic illustration of the effect of Fortune's Wheel. In the chorus of voices, from the troubadours of the early thirteenth century to the British imperialist historians of the nineteenth, bewailing the death of a hero and the loss of an empire, few have bothered to spare a thought for the young widow, now alone and facing an unknown future. But Berengaria was tougher than the passive image constructed by posterity. Having mourned her husband she entered a new phase of her life, in which, mindful no doubt of St Hugh's admonitions, she had to take control of her own future. Faced with opposition from powerful interests and with few supporters of her own, she fought for her rights and won. That it took her thirty years to do so is a measure of the difficulties and obstacles which lay in her path. But it is during those thirty years of widowhood that Berengaria emerges from the shadows to show us a small glimpse of the real person.

CHAPTER FIVE

Widow

Although it is as Richard's queen that Berengaria is best known in England, her marriage to Richard lasted only eight years, during which circumstances and perhaps inclination or mutual agreement kept them apart for significant periods. Yet it is on this basis that she has been consigned so dismissively to the footnotes of English history and saddled so unhesitatingly with the blame for Richard's lack of a successor. To the traditional English dynastic historian her life before and after Richard has been of scant interest.

The longest single period of her life was in fact spent as a widow, a member of a particularly disadvantaged group according to medieval canon law and, because of the political circumstances at the time, her individual position was unenviably precarious. The resilience and tenacity with which she confronted these difficulties were crucial to her survival.

Until recently medieval widows as a group have not attracted a great deal of scholarly interest. Both in official records and in medieval narrative fiction the same prejudices and stereotypes which shape the portrayal of women at other stages in their lives are alive and well in the depiction of widows, either as staid, pious seniors or as lewd, worldly-wise busybodies. The young widow posed, in reality, a particular problem for the dominant males in her family. An heiress or a dowager might present an opportunity for a strategic remarriage or she might be used as a potential bait. The speedy remarriage of widows and consequent reassignment of property was a regular preoccupation of kings and overlords, including Richard himself. A young widow with an infant son might be called upon to act as regent, as Berengaria's sister Blanca (Blanche) did in the county of Champagne: this inevitable propulsion into the public domain brought about new tensions and opportunities. Blanche's relationship with her new overlord, Philip of France, who quickly took her infant daughter into his protective custody, illustrates this clearly. Records show that she kept him supplied with presents, such as Brie cheeses, as well as offering the necessary expressions of loyalty and support.

For many reasons, a young widow of royal or noble standing was under considerable pressure to remarry. As feminist historians have pointed out, the need to control was a dominant aspect of the medieval male attitude to women. It manifests itself across the full spectrum of medieval texts, and its origins go back beyond Christianity to the ancient world. The power to give birth, 'inscribed' on the female body, has represented a force which, even when imperfectly understood, needed to be appropriated, controlled, socialised and codified. Religious sanctions could easily be invoked in order to ensure legitimacy in the agnatic line and the age-old dual standard fits easily with the apparent privileging of the 'feminine'. The commodification of 'femininity', as Howard Bloch and others have shown, underlies the essential misogyny of much 'courtly' culture.

As we have seen, religious literature often takes a different attitude towards male and female chastity: male saints, like some secular heroes are depicted as valiantly resisting the overtures of seductive women but their victories are moral ones, acts of will or judgment. They represent, literally, the victory of (male) mind over (female) matter. Women, then as now, were apparently seen as bodies before all else.

Church teachings were an important element in the medieval view of widowhood. These too reflect a certain ambivalence. The parable of the Sower in Matthew 13:8 was consistently reapplied to the three states of virginity, marriage and widowhood, but almost exclusively in connection with women rather than men. Virginity was regarded as the highest index of sanctity, and marriage came a poor third, with widowhood representing the middle term. It was almost as if, by ceasing to be sexually active, a widow regained in part her original integrity. This is represented in many different ways: in the later conventions of heraldry, a lady, whilst unmarried, bears arms on a lozenge, and, upon becoming a widow, bears again upon a lozenge the arms of her husband impaled with the arms borne by her father.

But a widow was also to some extent a loose cannon: her very experience of the world represented a potential threat. If she did not remarry, then consecration to the 'heavenly bridegroom' was the appropriate alternative, even if she did not formally enter religion, as many did.

A more positive, scripturally based image of widowhood was that of the pious widow devoted to good works. In the case of a childless widow, a sublimated spiritual maternity might be recognised in such activities as the endowment of monasteries, mass offerings and other charitable works. The seventh-century *Sacramentum Gelasianum* included a rite for the consecration of a widow, and in common usage a widow might be designated as an *ancilla Dei*, handmaid of God, just as a consecrated virgin was a *sponsa Christi*, bride of Christ.[1] The references to Berengaria in some of the Spanish chronicles, and particularly that in *De Rebus Hispaniae*, fit this pattern. At the same time, a widow's life-long devotion to her husband's memory was regarded with approval, as the medieval image of the turtle-dove, believed to be a bird which mated only once and for life, demonstrates.

One medieval writer, Guibert de Nogent, writes of his mother's experiences as a young widow.[2] He tells us that she was determined not to remarry, despite pressure from some of her own relatives, and finally, a few years before her death, she took the veil, against her son's objections. Peter of Blois, influential Anglo-Norman churchman and royal advisor, wrote that 'Scripture holds that conjugal fruitfulness is good but the chastity of a widow is better ... best is intact virginity but best of all is virginal fruitfulness.' He goes on to explain that nuptial fruitfulness populates the earth but virginal fruitfulness populates Heaven.[3]

Guibert paints a realistic picture of the young widow assailed by predatory relatives who even took her to court demanding that she hand over her late husband's property. But the pious widow put her trust in Christ alone and, by a combination of unswerving faith and verbal sophistry appropriate to the writer's homiletic mode, shamed her would-be persecutors into silence. Constantly devoting herself to self-denial and the regular practice of charity, she was a tireless attender at the offices, and her loyalty to her husband's memory was manifested in her regular offering of masses for his soul. The pious widow is promoted as both asexual and generally self-denying and keeps faith with her marriage vows.

This picture would probably not fit in with modern ideas of widowhood. Less controversial is the discussion of widows in the *Book of the Three Virtues* by the currently fashionable later medieval writer Christine de Pisan.[4] Christine, herself widowed young, writes in a practical way about the widow's duties, first and foremost to remember her husband's soul, but also, after the official mourning is past, to fulfil her responsibilities to the community. In the case of a royal or aristocratic widow, this involved instruction by both word and example. Once again, we see similar ideas in Jiménez de Rada's description of Berengaria's sanctity and good works as an example to other women.

Guibert's picture of his mother fending off both the attacks of greedy kinsmen and the unwelcome overtures of earthly suitors may appear somewhat idealised. None the less it testifies to the importance of widows in canon law, as members of a class of disadvantaged persons, or *miserabiles personae*.[5] To these, the Church through its ministers owed a special duty of care and protection.

Since this principle underlies much of the next part of Berengaria's story, it is important to understand that this was an important part of the medieval legal system, which formed the basis of a number of recorded judgments, including one involving Berengaria.

James Brundage has published a number of important studies of medieval canon law and has long sustained an interest in its application to marriage, sexual relations and poverty. He has shown how the teachings of medieval jurists were based on a body of authoritative teaching stretching back beyond the important fifth-century council of Chalcedon to Jesus' own teachings on poverty and riches and the Jewish tradition in which those teachings were grounded. Responsibility for implementing these laws rested squarely with the hierarchy, in the first instance the bishops, and consequently, all clerics under their jurisdiction. A complex body of case law evolved in time out of the implementation of these general principles.

As the examples given by Christine de Pisan illustrate, widows, like married women – and particularly queens consort – moved frequently between private and public space. Women who assumed too high a profile were often subject to criticism, even when the role was forced on them by circumstance rather than choice. These criticisms, from the pen of nineteenth-century historians, as much as from their own contemporaries, stemmed from a belief that such actions detracted from their femininity or tarnished their reputation. In other circumstances, a woman who 'rose above' the fallen condition bequeathed to her by the sins of Eve could be admired and praised. But this usually meant renouncing sexual activity and conforming in a sense to an androgynous model, something much easier to achieve in a religious context than a secular or political one, though both Joan of Arc and the later Queen Elizabeth I of England managed to combine these requirements. In most cases it was overtly political activity on the part of medieval women which was most strongly resented because it directly challenged a non-negotiable male prerogative.

In Berengaria's case, the political crisis brought about by her husband's death ensured further disadvantages. She was not only a poor, childless widow but a potential dependant on her brother in law John, the new king of England.

Ever since his return from captivity, Richard, by general acknowledgement Christendom's most powerful warrior-king, had kept the upper hand in his rivalry with the French. But on his death, his successor, John Lackland, was unable to hold back the French advance, and over the course of the next decade or so English possessions in north western France fell one by one like the proverbial dominoes. While some officials, both clerics and laymen, remained loyal to England, others, like the powerful seneschal of Anjou, Guillaume des Roches, sometimes described as a thirteenth-century 'vicar of Bray', were ready to switch sides when it suited them.

French inroads into Angevin territory were substantial at the time. Berengaria was a widow bereft of any power base; as a dependant, she was a financial liability in the eyes of her hard-hearted brother-in-law and, to her husband's enemies, an irritating reminder of past hostilities. Although her brother Sancho remained a loyal ally to Richard's successors, we have no record of his expressed concern for his sister's welfare. He may reasonably have assumed that her new family would honour their obligations. But Eleanor was now as strenuous in her devotion to John's interests as she had been to those of his brother Richard. Berengaria had failed in her duty to provide a son for her favourite and was of no further consequence. Whatever may have been the personal feeling between the two women, the relationship itself must inevitably have been to some extent adversarial. It would be difficult to imagine a more unenviable position than that in which the young widow now found herself.

In 1204 she came to live permanently in Le Mans. She was to spend the next twenty-six years of her life there. The circumstances in which she became the 'dame' or lady of Le Mans are somewhat complicated.

During the last years of Richard's life Berengaria appears to have spent most of her time in one or other of his Angevin castles. The anglocentric perspective of some nineteenth- and twentieth-century commentators have seen in this evidence of a voluntary or enforced withdrawal from her role as spouse and queen. But where else would have been appropriate? Not England, certainly, for Richard himself showed little inclination to spend time there, and the records show him as frequently impatient at the delays which kept him from crossing the Channel during the brief period spent in the island after his release. Like his father, he was a peripatetic monarch and few kings threw themselves so wholeheartedly into military operations. There was no obligation for a queen to follow her husband onto the battlefield and a number of obvious reasons why most would have preferred not to do so. In Palestine, in trying circumstances, Richard had provided care and protection for the royal women, but their presence must have been at times an added burden. As the episode in Cyprus shows, they provided an obvious bait for would-be ransom seekers.

So the young queen had lived mainly in the Angevin heartland – Chinon, Saumur, Beaufort, Angers. On Richard's death, however, these territories were in the hands of his successor, whose hold on them was already under challenge from France. Although a number of properties in Normandy and England and the south-west had been assigned to Berengaria as her dower lands, once again, it was not until after the death of Eleanor that these territories would pass to the younger queen. Eleanor lived on until 1204 when she was past eighty but by then the Angevin Empire was itself crumbling fast. Berengaria was thus effectively denied access to those territories, nearer to her homeland, which might have provided a more secure refuge.

John was a monarch whose reign was beset with problems, financial and administrative, from its inception. Berengaria was not the only loose end from the past. His late brother Geoffrey of Brittany had left a young son, with the significant name of Arthur, whose claims were being championed by some influential functionaries, including for a while Guillaume des Roches.

Some historians have suggested that antipathy between Queen Eleanor and Constance, Geoffrey's widow, fuelled the flames of enmity between John and his young nephew. Popular tradition has often portrayed Eleanor as hostile towards other women, including, notoriously, her husband's mistress, Rosamund Clifford, the 'Fair Rosamund' of legend, whom Eleanor is alleged to have murdered in various gruesome ways. For whatever reason – perhaps in deference to her dead son's wishes – Eleanor now sided vigorously with her surviving son against her own grandson and his mother.

Guillaume des Roches was Arthur's choice as seneschal of Anjou, Maine and Touraine, replacing the tried and true Stephen of Turnham. With French support, Arthur quickly installed himself in Le Mans and was immediately pursued by John. In his account of the three-cornered contest between John, Philip of France and the seneschal, Henri Chardon, Berengaria's nineteenth-century biographer, uses the florid language of his day. He sees Philip as Pontius Pilate, Guillaume des Roches as Judas Iscariot and the boy Arthur as a sacrificial victim. His most thunderous denunciations he reserves for John – 'a coward, base and vile, a barbarous, perfidious tyrant, whose life was one of crime after crime and continuous debauchery in a world where courage could still redeem a good many vices'.[6] To this paragon of evil he assigned the ignoble role of the executioner. The attempts of revisionist historians to provide a more balanced view of a traditional villain have not been able to absolve John of all responsibility for the death of the young prince in 1203. Whether, as tradition has it, he himself blinded and strangled the boy, before throwing his body into a moat, or whether he merely left the job to others, the effect was the same.

Le Mans, which the French king had cynically assigned to Arthur as the weaker of the two Plantagenet rivals, was left in the hands of Guillaume des Roches. The dangerous situation which prevailed in Anjou and Maine at the time is described in the *Chronicle of St Aubin*: 'The wretched state of affairs in Maine, Poitou, Anjou and Brittany grew worse daily, so that towns, castles and fortresses were plundered and neither age nor condition could save those within them.'[7]

Between Richard's death and her own arrival in Le Mans, Berengaria had lived at Beaufort, Chinon, and occasionally Fontevraud. For a brief interlude she had sought refuge with her sister in Champagne. She may have been present at another even more unexpected funeral in 1199, that of her sister-in-law and former close companion, Joanna, who died not long after her brother's dismembered remains had been dispatched to the capitals of his former empire, in keeping with Angevin practice.

Joanna's life was briefer and perhaps more tragic than that of Berengaria. Married in splendour at the age of eleven to William 'the Good' of Sicily, widowed twelve years later without a living child, she did not find peace or happiness with her second husband, Raymond VI of Toulouse. After the marriage in 1196 Raymond was involved in almost uninterrupted hostilities with rebellious barons and quarrelsome neighbours, hostilities in which Joanna herself became caught up. Early in 1199, already pregnant with her second child, she left him and was on her way to seek her brother's protection when she learned from her mother at Niort of his death. In desperation she sought to take the veil at Fontevraud, but her wish was not granted until after her own death, at Rouen, in childbirth. She was finally buried '*inter velatas*' (among the veiled ones) while her baby lived only long enough to receive the sacrament of baptism.

Her obsequies are not recorded in detail. If Berengaria was present she must have reflected on the fate of one with whom she had been as close as 'birds in a cage' and perhaps seen for herself the disadvantages of that 'beauty' which made her sister in law a sexual bait and political pawn – one which, for all his professed affection Richard himself had not hesitated to use on more than one occasion.

The Cypriot princess who had shared their travels is of little interest to the chroniclers, but she must have been in the vicinity too for Raymond VI lost little time in taking her as his third wife. For Berengaria the few remaining links with the past, immediate or more distant, were being broken one by one, with little to replace them.

Only Blanca her sister, whose marriage she had helped to arrange, remained to offer her support. But Blanca's marriage to the young Thibaut was shortlived, for her bridegroom died in May 1201 at the age of twenty-two, leaving her with a young daughter and another child on the way. Blanche, as she must now be called, was obliged to turn to her overlord the king of France for her protection during the long years of her regency.

The two young widows would continue to support each other loyally through the difficult years which followed. Each had to fight for her rights against powerful and often unscrupulous men, both laymen and clerics, and their tenacity and stubborn resolve did not always endear them to their contemporaries.

Similar qualities of endurance and tenacity, as well as a measure of self-interest, were demonstrated by the promptness with which King Sancho transferred to John the support he had pledged to Richard. In 1201 and again in 1202 he signed treaties of support with John for the protection of Gascony and the south. Berengaria may have elicited her brother's support in the first of many vain attempts to ensure payment of her dower monies by John which began as early as 1201 at a meeting with the new king at Chinon. Other negotiations with Navarre are hinted at in the issuing by John on 18 February 1202 of a safe-conduct to an envoy of Costanza, the remaining sister, whose projected marriage to Peter of Aragon had been vetoed in 1198. The document gives no indication of the purpose of the mission and the date of Costanza's death is nowhere recorded. One source states that she died at Daroca, another at Pradillas, possibly Pradilla, a district (*termino*) of Tudela or, alternatively, Pradillas del Ebro near Tauste. If the latter, then perhaps her presence in these areas was connected with other unsuccessful marriage negotiations.

With the death of Fernando in 1212, Sancho, though considerably older than his siblings, was ultimately to outlive them all. From the epic figure of the founding father, Garcia Ramirez, El Restaurador, to the doomed and brooding giant shut up in his tower of Tudela, the Jiménez dynasty of independent Navarre lasted a mere hundred years – a graphic illustration of the fate which befalls small nations with powerful neighbours.

As one by one the Angevin possessions fell to the French, Rouen in 1204, Chinon in 1205, Berengaria's safety became increasingly at risk. In August and September of 1204 a settlement was reached with Philip Augustus: in a treaty of that date she agreed to hand over her dower properties in Normandy – Falaise, Domfront and Bonneville-sur-Touque[8] – in return for the city of Le Mans and one thousand marks sterling. Her authority would extend only over the city itself and its '*quinte*' or suburbs, which consisted of about thirty-seven parishes, from which she would be entitled to exact the appropriate tithes and other duties. In return, she formally acknowledged Philip as her overlord. Guillaume des Roches was named as seneschal of Maine, Anjou and Touraine, but she was allowed to nominate her own appointee, Herbert de Tucé, as seneschal of Le Mans. Herbert came from a prominent local family, and, like many of Berengaria's officials, was to render her long and loyal service throughout the period of her incumbency as dame or lady of Le Mans.

Some French historians have seen in this settlement a gesture of generosity and magnanimity on the part of the French king to the destitute widow of a former enemy, and one appropriate to a monarch designated by his people as 'Augustus'. From a less partisan perspective it can be seen as a shrewd act of political expediency, designed in part to weaken further the English position and in part to ensure a balance between the ambitious magnates of the region by the old strategy of divide and rule. One cannot help wondering too, whether Philip, whose intimate friendship with Richard had turned in time to a stubborn rivalry fuelled by an obsessive mutual animosity, may not have felt some sympathy for the widowed queen and seen in her a fellow victim of Richard's mercurial affections. From what we know of Philip's disposition, however, he does not seem to have been a naturally compassionate man: his treatment of both his legitimate wives was harsh and, in as much as it is possible to judge such matters, his religious disposition was purely formal.

Berengaria never again designated herself as duchess of Normandy or countess of Anjou, titles which had belonged to her as Richard's queen, and although posterity has bestowed on her the title of lady or dame of Le Mans, it was always as '*humilissima regina quondam Anglorum*' (most humble former queen of the English) that she styled herself in charters and letters and it is this title which appears on the later (1602) inscription on her tomb.

The extent of her new domain was probably quite restricted. It would certainly have been an area smaller than the modern municipality of Le Mans. The old city – '*le vieux Mans*' – is today a well-preserved tourist precinct adjacent to the grand cathedral, bordered in part by the river Sarthe and the remains of the old Gallo-Roman wall. Its picturesque cobbled streets and half timbered houses are of more recent vintage than the time of Berengaria, but many of these constructions rest on earlier foundations and the lay-out of the city in the thirteenth century would have been very similar to what survives today.

Contemporary documents speak of the 'Queen's chamber' overlooking the rue Héraud and this refers in all probability to the still standing palace of the counts of Maine, and the collegial church of St Pierre de la Cour, rather than the so-called '*maison de la Reine Bérengère*', a fifteenth-century edifice in a picturesque alley adjacent to the cathedral, now used as a tourist museum. The palace is part of the outer perimeter wall of the old city, its fortress-like aspect softened for the visitor by the neat lawns and flower-beds added by heritage-conscious city fathers. It is not difficult to picture the widowed queen sitting alone at some 'casement high and triple arched' looking out over an undulating panorama of copses and meadows, where the modern city now stands, to an empty horizon, as she had done so many times before in her semi-reclusion.

Berengaria was still a young woman – little older than Eleanor had been at the time of her second marriage – and her prospects of remarriage would have been reasonable. But neither of the two men under whose tutelage she now fell, her brother-in-law John and her overlord Philip, would have been eager to arrange a marriage with potential political consequences. It is likely too that Berengaria herself was not attracted by the prospect. Luis del Campo, the Navarrese amateur historian and forensic medical expert, who, in a brief but interesting comparison of the 'Four Navarrese Infantas' attempted a psycho-historical analysis of the marriage of Berengaria and Richard, believed that Berengaria was 'profoundly disappointed' by her experience of marriage to a man whose sexual ambivalence led him to outbursts of violence and excess. Be that as it may, there might have been other valid reasons for preferring not to marry, or making a virtue of necessity. Later events reveal a strong streak of independence in the widowed queen's character and perhaps, too, the example of her widowed father's lifelong devotion to his dead queen's memory helped to strengthen her resolve.

Not much detailed information is available about Berengaria's household during this period. We know from other sources how many and what type of officials, lay, clerical and domestic, would have constituted such a household. As kings and other nobles were frequently on the move, they were invariably accompanied by large retinues whose expenses were recorded, often in detail. Literary sources, too, delight in describing the processions which accompanied noble lords and ladies, right down to the cooks, scullions, grooms and minstrels. Berengaria's household would of necessity have been fairly modest but, even so, a number of officials – bailiffs, *prévots* (a kind of magistrate), sergeants, *voyers* (highway officers) and toll-collectors would have been needed to oversee the collection of dues of one kind and another on which the maintenance of the estate depended. The activities of some of these officials have been documented, and a list of the most prominent names can be drawn up from the records covering a period of over twenty years, during which Berengaria was involved in litigation and disputes of one kind and another.

In addition to Herbert Tucé her steward,[9] there are Paulin Boutier, one of her most loyal knights, Pierre Prévôt her cantor, Simon and Garsia her clerks, Martin and Pierre her sergeants, Walter of Perseigne her chaplain and a number of others. Although at least one of these, 'Garsia', was a Spaniard who served at St Quiriace in Provins (Champagne) and another may have been 'English' (i.e., Norman), many of them were local men, perhaps people who had already served under the Angevin kings in one capacity or another. Some may have belonged to the queen's household in Beaufort en Vallée and followed her to Le Mans.

Of the women who attended her and, perhaps, provided her with some form of closer companionship, the records say nothing. There must have been such women, like the two maids Beatrice and Alix mentioned in the last testament of Joanna,[10] whose loyalty was again rewarded by King John in 1200 by a donation of fifteen and ten Angevin pounds respectively, for the lifetime, after which it would return to the royal exchequer, except for a donation of 100 sous to Fontevraud where they had taken the veil.[11] Once again, literary texts help to bring life to such bare data.

The 'demoiselle', confidante or lady's maid is an important figure in courtly romance. Loyal, resourceful and courteous like Lunete in Chrétien's Yvain or clever, manipulative and bold like Brangain in the Tristan story, she is never far from her lady's side, counselling, covering up, acting as a go-between or decoy. A grimmer and perhaps more realistic picture is painted in texts further removed from the courtly tradition: maids are scolded, whipped or sexually exploited by ladies and their knights. Visual representations too always show noble ladies attended by female retainers, some in nuns' habits, others in lay dress. In a society where the sexes were to some degree segregated, close friendships must have developed, even across social boundaries. But, with the exception of a certain Julianeta Brodaresse mentioned in a document from Champagne, the names of these women, Spanish or Angevin, religious or lay, with whom the widowed queen shared her private moments have passed into silence.

Berengaria's life in Le Mans might well be forgotten today in English histories had not her financial problems left their imprint on the public record. A considerable part of this documentation concerns the protracted campaign, waged over a period of more than twenty years, to obtain the dower monies promised by John in lieu of the properties assigned to his wife by Richard. Once again, the particular political circumstances in which the protagonists found themselves further complicated an already difficult situation.

This long struggle for justice, with its many attendant frustrations and few small triumphs, has been misunderstood by ill-informed writers. One such, contrasting Berengaria unfavourably with the romanticised figure of Eleanor, described her as a passive creature constantly whining about her dowry, and even the sympathetic Henri Chardon was led to remark that Berengaria's story seems at times to be little more than the history of her dowry problems.

The truth is that Berengaria was fighting for her survival. Unless a woman was an heiress in her own right, she was totally dependent on her husband and his family, and the dowry system was a vital part of the protection extended to a widow on her husband's death. The medieval practice, which varied from place to place, was not a tidy and neatly codified system, but one which, like many medieval institutions and practices, had evolved from a mixture of Roman law and Germanic custom.

Strictly speaking the words dower and dowry (and their French equivalents, *dot* and *douaire*) should be distinguished, though they tend to be used interchangeably. Dowry or *maritagium*, known in Spain as *arras*, was the gift bestowed on the newly married couple (effectively the husband) by the bride's father. The origin of this form of dowry, which is widespread, is remote and may represent a survival of the old Germanic *Morgengabe* (morning gift). In Berengaria's case, her father King Sancho had given as dowry the two castles in the Pyrenees, St Jean Pied de Port and Rocabruna, over which Richard and the younger Sancho had apparently quarrelled in 1198. The original record, unfortunately, no longer survives. Dower, on the other hand, was the property assigned by a husband to his bride, to the usufruct of which she would be entitled after his death, for the remainder of her own life. The principle was simple enough but the practice, inevitably, gave rise to legal disputes, partial attempts at regulation and problems for widows where the dower was claimed by someone else.

By the time Richard and Berengaria were married it was both customary and sanctioned by Church law to assign the dower rights at the time of the wedding. In Cyprus in 1191, Richard had dowered his bride with his territories in Gascony, and, after the death of his mother Eleanor, all the lands which his father had assigned to her, the so-called 'douaire des reines' or queens' dower. These included lands and castles in England, Normandy, Touraine and Maine. It was a generous settlement and no one could have foreseen the tragic circumstances which would reduce it to mere promises, dependent on the word of a monarch who was desperate, unprincipled and avaricious.

The details of the transactions which began in 1200 when Berengaria first raised the matter with the new king, are complicated and somewhat tedious. John, in a charter (now lost) whose contents are summarised in a letter from the king to his bankers,[12] agreed to pay Berengaria one thousand marks per annum in respect of her dower properties and a portion of the revenue from the castle of Segré, not included in the original dower but granted by John in recompense for other territories already lost to the French. Papal approval of these arrangements was communicated to the queen in a letter of Pope Innocent, dispatched in 1201. In 1204, Innocent instructed John, abbot of Casamuri, who had acted as the papal agent in the case of Queen Ingeborg of France, to press for the restitution of Berengaria's rights. For many long years, however, despite a steady stream of papal admonitions, instructions to churchmen entrusted with monitoring the agreements and hypocritical prevarications from John, no money changed hands.

On the death of Eleanor in March 1204, Berengaria should have received the traditional queens' dower rights in Normandy and elsewhere but these were already largely in French hands and it was in exchange for the remaining territories of Domfront and Falaise that she was given Le Mans by Philip. But the revenues which resulted from this exchange would not have been sufficient to maintain a household let alone the charitable donations dear to the heart of the widowed queen. Nor, it seems, did Berengaria ever receive the so-called 'queen's gold' which had been paid to Eleanor.[13] As Pope Innocent's letter so movingly records, Berengaria had been left virtually penniless at the time of her husband's death. She had no choice but to fight.

John was already in deep trouble with Rome over a number of contentious issues, including the matter of Archbishop Stephen Langton, which had resulted in a papal interdict. In 1213 he appears to have succumbed to papal pressure, and arrangements were made for Berengaria's envoys, Garcia ('Garsia') and William, to go to England to begin the transfer of funds. An enigmatic letter from John to Berengaria, dated spring 1215, advises that negotiations were still in progress and urges her to keep the matter confidential. These details may have prefigured the agreement dated 25 September 1215 whereby John promised to pay Berengaria two thousand marks including arrears and a further one thousand pounds stirling in two instalments. She was also free to pursue her entitlements outside England without interference – a rather hollow promise – and the king granted her a permanent safe-conduct into his territories. There is no suggestion that she ever contemplated a voyage to England in person, but she may have considered passing through those territories in the south still nominally held by England, perhaps on the way to Spain.

Despite this agreement, ratified by Pope Innocent in several communications with his bishops and with the queen herself, John did not live to keep his promise, if such was ever his intention. In 1216 he sent a letter to his 'dearest sister' regretting his inability to honour the agreement. The war with the French had absorbed all his money ... he knew she would understand![14]

The lengths to which Berengaria was forced to go can be inferred from the surviving documents, which reveal how closely enmeshed were political, pastoral and private issues. The letters also bring to life the interaction between three strong personalities: Pope Innocent himself, one of the greatest of medieval churchmen, who raised in the queen's defence a voice as eloquent and magisterial as that of any Hebrew prophet thundering from Zion in denunciation of unrighteousness; John; two-faced and venal;[15] and the widowed queen, polite but persistent.

Not every letter survives. Most of the papal letters do and many of those written by John.[16] Two of Berengaria's letters, in the impersonal style of a chancery official, are preserved in the Public Records Office in London and reproduced in two collections, *Letters of Queens and other Royal Ladies*, the nineteenth-century work by Mary Anne Everett Wood,[17] and a recent one by Anne Crawford.[18] Much can be gathered from the papal letters about the queen herself and about John, the backsliding monarch. Both the letters and Treasury records list the envoys used by Berengaria in her dealings with the English.

The hollow nature of John's promises, in particular, is obvious in his final letter, a masterpiece of prevarication. Those revisionist historians who have attempted to correct the traditional image of 'bad' King John point to more important aspects of his political career, against which these petty injustices may well seem trivial. It is certainly true that for much of his reign he was plagued by serious financial difficulties which he was never able to surmount. But obviously, then as now, for those who hold the purse strings, justice for the orphan and the widow was less important than balancing the budget.

John's death put an end to the worst of these prevarications, and his son and successor, Henry III, proved more amenable to papal pressure. Innocent's successor, Honorius III, was no less prompt in his response to Berengaria's appeals as his letter of December 1216 to the archbishop of Tours shows: in this letter he reminds the prelate of his sacred duty to defend widows and describes the plight of 'our dearest daughter in Christ, the former queen of the English (who) has had to endure frequent acts of injury and theft both by clerics and laymen ...'[19] On 9 April 1218, and again on the 28th of that month, he assured the queen of his special protection, in recognition of her unswerving devotion to the Holy See.[20] After a lapse of four years, Henry finally settled the outstanding debt which had risen to four thousand five hundred pounds sterling. The records show that this sum was paid progressively over a five-year period, with Gautier de Perseigne, Berengaria's chaplain, Simon and Garsia her clerks acting as emissaries and go-betweens.[21]

Gautier was the chosen successor of the former abbot of Perseigne, Adam, whose links with the Angevin monarchs were substantial and well-attested. Adam had been the trusted emissary of both King Richard and of Pope Innocent; he was also an eloquent writer, whose preaching was renowned and whose letters are full of interest for the historian as well as for the theologian.

These letters reveal a man of outstanding intellect and a warm, sometimes impulsive, deeply compassionate personality. Unlike the brilliant but self-centred Abelard, Adam seems to have sustained friendships with women, both lay and religious, without any hint of sexual exploitation. Although he was often austere and severe in his judgements, his piety was firmly grounded in the Incarnation and his Marian theology is sublimely poetic in its expression. By the standards of his day he was enlightened and open-minded, expressing doubts about the value of crusading and distaste for the persecution of the Jews. He was also disciplined at least twice for breaking the fasting rules in Lent by offering prohibited foods to guests!

His background is an intriguing one: he left the Benedictine order for the more austere Cistercian rule, but his origins were, by his own admission, humble and 'rustic'. His original home was in Champagne, where he may have dabbled in courtly literature and the poetic arts, which he subsequently renounced. His denunciations of the trappings of courtly society, especially women's fashions, with the long dragging trains which made them look like 'little foxes' and stirred up unbearable clouds of dust in their wake, are conventional enough, but they seem in places querulous enough to be based on first hand experience. Perhaps the dust irritated his sinuses! In some of his letters to laywomen, on the other hand, he slips effortlessly into a style reminiscent of the courtly romance. Some have argued that Adam was once a court poet, who turned his back on worldly frivolities.

We have no letters of Adam to Berengaria, although one of his letters, cited earlier, was addressed to her sister Blanche. However, his name and that of Berengaria appear together in a number of documents and he also witnessed a number of transactions between her and the king of France. These indications suggest that he enjoyed her trust as a friend and advisor. Berengaria was fortunate at least in this respect, that she enjoyed the protection and support of some of the most distinguished churchmen of her day. Adam was instrumental in assisting her with the plans which were taking shape for the foundation of the Cistercian abbey which was to be her lasting legacy and gift to the order which had meant so much both to her father's family in Spain as well as to her late husband.

The other outstanding voice raised on her behalf had been that of Pope Innocent, who had championed the cause of other women such as the French queen Ingeborg, when she was so shabbily treated by her husband Philip.[22] Innocent's marriage 'policy' was highly interventionist and did not always involve saving marriages: some proposed unions such as that of Pedro II of Aragon and the infanta of Navarre, as we have seen, were vetoed on the grounds of consanguinity. The case of Ingeborg, however, shows that the pontiff was also capable of recognising attempts by monarchs and others to manipulate the degrees of consanguinity to their own ends.

Innocent acted vigorously in defence of Church law, and in pursuit of a number of what we would today call social justice goals. This fact and a degree of latent anti-papist folk memory on the part of some anglocentric historians past and present has given rise to the view that his actions were merely 'political'. While he was certainly a skilled statesman and did not hesitate to wield each of the 'two swords', this view fails to acknowledge the centrality of the concept of *miserabiles personae* in canon law. It was certainly upon this fundamentally scriptural concept that papal defence of widows like Berengaria was based.

The doctrine, however, was not applied blindly and in the subsequent corpus of judgments and commentaries on canon law, we see that cases were often considered on their merits, that is on the facts themselves. One such case involving Berengaria as plaintiff did make it to the law books and provides a neat illustration of the conflict between general precepts and the ingenuity of lawyers.[23]

Unlike the castle of Loches,[24] which was part of the original dower but was appropriated by a powerful local lord and former crusader, Dreu de Mello, the castle of Segré was not part of that settlement.[25] In Chinon in 1204 John had assigned part of its revenues to Berengaria in lieu of other properties lost to the French and accorded her full access to the castle. It was subsequently seized by another robber baron, Guillaume de la Guierche, who swore allegiance to the king of France in 1214. John, desperate to shore up any alliances he could among the unreliable Angevin barons, recognised Guillaume's tenure in June 1215. His promises to Berengaria were, once again, conveniently overlooked. Berengaria appealed to Rome.

Pope Innocent set up a tribunal to hear the case, but died himself the following year. His successor, Honorius delivered the final judgment in December 1217[26] after a series of challenges by the defendant's lawyers. Some of these are listed in the text which is reproduced in Book 5 of the *Decretals of Gregory IX* in the *Corpus Iuris Canonici*. These objections range from technical quibbles about the spelling of certain words to claims of judicial bias. The basis for judgment in favour of the plaintiff, Berengaria, was that the interests of a disadvantaged person, even if a person of high status, whose property had been seized by force, should prevail in a possessory action.

Later commentaries on the case, including the important commentary of Pope Innocent IV,[27] were to refine and qualify the definition of *miserabiles personae* and the circumstances in which a person might bypass the secular authorities and go straight to Rome, but the case remains a landmark one. Unfortunately, as often happens, the moral and legal victory had little practical effect, and Berengaria does not appear to have benefited from the decision in her favour. Her recourse to the legal resources available at the time indicates none the less a willingness to stand up for her own interests in the face of powerful adversaries.

The anxiety generated by all these lengthy and stressful negotiations was made worse by the long time it took for messages and judgments to be delivered. The fastest messengers from Rome to northern France or England would have taken the best part of a month. Such time lapses frequently added complications. Politics intervened too, as when, during the course of the interdict placed on England from 1208 to 1213, John repeatedly obstructed traffic to the continent and the French did likewise with English messengers passing through their territories or lands under their influence.

The last recorded transaction with the king of England over the matter of the long delayed dower payments, in 1225-6, signals the closing of the final chapter in Berengaria's relationship with England, her adopted country. For the past thirty years and more, during which she bore the name of queen, the association had brought much pain and some little gain, as it would for many other foreign born princesses. The price of exogamy, with all its political, genetic and economic advantages, has usually been paid by women.

Yet it is as queen that Berengaria chose to be remembered. In keeping with the practice of the day, she continued to ensure that masses were offered for the repose of her husband's soul and the perpetuation of his memory. Whether her own memories were sad or happy or whether the image of her all-conquering bridegroom became in the end a blurred and distant one, we can only speculate, since she left no word of praise or of reproach. Only one man, if his biographer is correct, witnessed her inconsolable grief that day in April 1199 and there is no reason to suppose that all those memorial masses – and countless unrecorded mass intentions – were not also the genuine expression of a deeply felt loss.

The story of Berengaria's widowhood is not just the story of her struggles to regain the monies due to her as former queen of England. Popular French tradition, always equivocal about Coeur de Lion, remembers his widow more positively than the professional historians do. As dame or lady of Le Mans, her name is commemorated in a variety of colourful, if anachronistic tourist attractions. More importantly, she leaves in her wake, as Henri Chardon put it, a 'lingering perfume of charity' ('*un long parfum de bonté* …'). She has always been remembered by the Manceaux as a generous benefactor of the many churches and convents for which the city was and still is famous.

There is still some doubt as to the extent of the territory controlled by Berengaria, either directly or through the collegial church of St Pierre, of which she was patron and protectress. The 'collégiale', as it is known today, was originally the chapel of the counts of Maine. It was founded at the end of the tenth century and endowed by several of the early Anglo-Norman kings including William the Conqueror and Henry II.[28] Although the settlement of 1204 conferred on her the city and its '*quinte*' or suburbs, it is possible that outside these limits, there were other properties which owed her allegiance. Some earlier historians designated her, incorrectly, as countess of Maine, but this title is nowhere found, in an unambiguous form, in the early documentation, while at various times during her incumbency individuals referred to as 'counts' of Maine appear in the records. Even within the city there were certain parishes outside her control.

The cathedral chapter of St Julien exercised direct control over the *'lieue'*, or outer periphery as well as forty parishes (153 households) within the city, and it also exercised judicial rights over the barony of Courgenard and the castle of Assé le Bérenger. It was, in addition, responsible for the *prévoté royale* – the right to administer justice at first instance on behalf of the king – in respect of 270 dwellings within the city and twenty outlying parishes.

This separation of powers was not atypical of the times but was undoubtedly made less easy to accommodate by the power vacuum which had followed the death of Richard. It was unfortunate for Berengaria that this powerful body, the cathedral chapter, over which even the diocesan bishop exercised only limited influence, began to consolidate its power just at the time of her arrival in Le Mans. During the reign of Richard and his father Henry, Le Mans, and to a lesser extent the county generally, had remained loyal to the English kings. Important officials like Stephen of Turnham, former seneschal of the three provinces, and the bishops Guillaume Passavant and Hamelin were strong supporters of the dynasty. Nicolas, the former dean, who married the royal couple in Cyprus, was the last bishop of Le Mans with any connection to its former Angevin rulers, but his episcopate was a very brief one, from 1214 to 1216 and his successor was bound by no such ties of loyalty to the past.[29]

During the turbulence of 1200-2 the county became a battlefield, with French and English troops constantly trampling across its towns and manors, burning, razing and looting. Local barons, traditionally unruly, secular clergy and even the religious orders had all been caught up in this unrest. Although composed in a different part of France, the late *chanson de geste Raoul de Cambrai*, which belongs to the third great epic cycle, the cycle of the '*barons révoltés*' ('barons in revolt', rather than the Pythonesque alternative) probably reflects what was happening in Maine and Anjou as well as further to the north. In this extract, the poet paints a vivid picture of a convent set alight in the course of a local skirmish:

> Origny was a great and spacious town, greatly loved by the sons of Herbert, who had established there Marsent, the mother of Bernier, with a hundred nuns to pray to God. The fierce hearted count, Raoul, set the streets on fire. Burning were the dwellings, their floors caved in, while the wine was spilling everywhere, flooding the cellars and the bacon flitches were aflame as the larders collapsed. The burning fat made the flames leap higher, reaching the towers and the highest steeple until the rooftops gave way and crashed to the ground. Between the two walls the fire blazed so fiercely that the nuns were burned in the conflagration, all hundred of them in one calamitous stroke. There burns Marsent, Bernier's mother and Clamados, the daughter of Duke Renier – the smell is everywhere and the bravest knights weep with pity.[30]

After the settlement of 1204, relative peace returned to the region. The diocese already included a large number of Cistercian foundations and within a short time, all the major religious orders, including the new preaching orders, the Dominicans and the Franciscans, came to be represented in the diocese of Maine and the city of Le Mans. Several of these churches and convents are still standing and in use today and most of these had been closely associated with the Angevin kings of England.

Now in use as a parish church, the hospital of Coeffort was originally staffed by the brothers of Our Lady of Coëffort (Cauda Fortis). It looked after the sick and was also responsible for one of over a hundred leprosaria in Le Mans. It is supposed to have been founded by Henry II in 1180 in expiation for the murder of Thomas a Beckett, though its existence is attested in 1165. Young prince Arthur, during his brief incumbency, further endowed it and gave it a parcel of land, known as the 'terre de l'Epau', which Berengaria would subsequently buy back to build her abbey.

The abbey of La Couture (Cultura) was founded around the same time and also received royal patronage. There were numerous other foundations including the abbey of St Vincent, in which Richard had taken a special interest, granting it a charter in 1190 along with a number of other important abbeys, such as Bonport in Normandy and Lieu-Dieu near his favourite hunting grounds at Talmont-sur-Jard. As Dom Piolin points out, there is no evidence that Berengaria ever acted as a benefactor of any of the foundations associated with her husband.

The Cistercian order flourished in Maine and enjoyed the protection of powerful local lords like Juhel de Maine, a former crusader and loyal supporter of the French, who extended his special protection to the abbey of Notre Dame de la Fontaine-Daniel and encouraged the monks to develop a large agricultural area. The province of Maine was to become a fertile ground for Cistercian activities.

The area south of Le Mans to Saumur and the Loire is also, even today, largely rural. It does not attract large numbers of tourists, but the quiet charm of places like Pontvallain and Vieil Baugé, with their curious twisted church spires and manor houses set in thick woods, suggests that the physical landscape has changed little since the Middle Ages, an impression partly confirmed by seventeenth- and eighteenth-century accounts of populations, occupations and land use in these areas. There were numerous expressions of popular religion in these rural areas during the twelfth and thirteenth centuries, such as the pilgrimages to Our Lady of La Faigne, whose statue was associated with several 'miracles' and there were also an unusually large number of popular heretical movements, usually of short duration.

This was the situation into which Berengaria now came, with little experience of governing alone and with a gridlock of conflicting interests already in place around her. She had her small circle of trusted administrators, some of whose names have been mentioned previously, clerics, laymen and members of old local families, most of whom stayed faithful to her through many tribulations, men like her knight Paulin Boutier, whose support landed him in trouble on more than one occasion, and whose son, after his death, gave a substantial amount of land to Berengaria's new monastery in memory of his father.

It is unfortunate that the documentary record of Berengaria's administration is rather sparse and it is not possible to put together a very clear or detailed picture of the day to day workings of her court, as others have done for the better documented areas such as Champagne. English record-keeping was much more advanced than that of its neighbours, but once these continental possessions were lost by the English crown, the information dries up quickly. To make matters worse, much was destroyed during the wars which later ravaged north-western France on and off for over a hundred years, and material which escaped these ravages perished during the wars of religion or at the time of the Revolution, when many monastic archives were destroyed.

None the less, the existing record makes it clear that Berengaria enjoyed a special status in Le Mans: her authority was regularly acknowledged by the French king in his official dealings with the city, in developments such as the extension of the city boundaries or changes such as the enlargement of the cathedral precincts.[31] When presiding over a duel in 1216[32] between the champions of a brother and his sister respectively in a dispute over property rights, she is described as 'the noble Queen Berengaria formerly wife of King Richard and from that time lady of Le Mans in exchange for her dower'. Three years later she authorises the appointment of another of her supporters, Pierre Prévost, as cantor to the chapter of her chapel of St Pierre, and dispenses him from the usual residence requirements;[33] again, in 1226, she is named as the official arbiter between the chapter and a knight named Gervaise de Cogners.[34]

The dispute was quickly settled with a suspended fine of sixty pounds, but the report indicates some of the complexities of the local jurisdiction: Gervaise and his heirs are bound not to put themselves in a state of hostility against the chapter, its vassals or its possessions. Were these territories directly answerable to Berengaria as patroness and protectress of the chapter or only indirectly by delegation? What is clear is that, in both these capacities, she became increasingly committed to defending its interests and sometimes acting pre-emptively in promoting them.

Far more tendentious and uncertain in outcome were her attempts to levy the taxes and other revenues she believed to be her legal due and to pursue and even imprison defaulters. These activities brought her into immediate and inevitable conflict with the cathedral chapter of St Julien, which constantly challenged her jurisdiction, protected her defaulters and retaliated with excessive use of the power to interdict, which meant effectively the cessation of all church services including the burial of the dead, as well as with the frequent excommunication of individuals and their families. The main focus of these reprisals was the rival chapter, that of St Pierre de la Cour, and Berengaria as its patroness, and again and again she rose to its defence with vigorous appeals to the Pope and acts of defiance against the excessive use of these sanctions by the cathedral chapter.

Almost nothing remains today of the original holdings of the chapter of St Pierre. Its *Cartulaire*, apart from a few pages, exists only in a much later manuscript copy. It records a number of donations including gifts of land and money from Berengaria and traces in part the cause and effect of the various interdicts placed on it by the cathedral chapter. It also demonstrates the strenuous resistance of the queen to what she saw as attacks on her prerogatives, and the papal backing which she continued to enjoy on several occasions.

It was Berengaria's response to these difficulties which caused some later commentators to describe her as avaricious and obstinate – charges which have also been levelled at her brother Sancho, the 'banker of kings' who, despite all the problems which confronted him during his reign, is said to have amassed a considerable fortune in part from his transactions with the Muslims of Andalucia and Morocco. As far as Berengaria is concerned, careful study of the records and examination of the the grounds listed by Pope Honorius in his frequent personal interventions do not support a charge of avarice. Berengaria was forced by necessity to fight for her rights but this entailed a degree of political initiative which was sometimes seen as inappropriate behaviour on the part of a woman.

Such criticisms also ignore the harsher realities of medieval life. Side by side with the exquisite scenes of chivalry and dalliance depicted in medieval art and literature, which have captured the popular imagination, there exists a more sombre testimony which speaks of fires, plagues, epidemics, the violent destruction of towns and villages, the ruthless exploitation of the weak and powerless, the brutal exclusion of lepers and outlaws and the malevolent harassment of minorities such as the Jews. This view of the 'dark' Middle Ages has become more popular in recent times, with the success of films like *The Name of the Rose*.

In any case, Berengaria can scarcely be blamed for the ongoing hostilities between the two chapters, that of the cathedral and that of St Pierre. These hostilities were of long standing, and the first of the interdicts launched by the cathedral against its rival occurred in 1199, well before the widowed queen arrived in the city.[35] It arose over fairly trivial differences but the interdict lasted at least a year until a compromise was finally obtained, and not without papal intervention. It was as a result of this compromise, ironically, that the powers of the cathedral chapter were greatly increased. These now included the right to summon anyone, lay or cleric, even including royal delegates and office-holders, whom it deemed guilty of an offence against the dean and chapter. Refusal to appear or to make reparation would result in the immediate excommunication of individuals and the placing of the interdict on churches. Local landowners protested to their overlord, the king of France, who, already in enough trouble with the papacy over his marriage problems, evidently decided this was a trivial matter and declined to get involved. The chapter clearly saw this as tacit support for its position.

It was not long, inevitably, before Berengaria clashed with the cathedral chapter herself. The first occasion occurred somewhere between 1204 and 1206 when two of her officials, Martin and Luke, attempted to enforce payment of a tax on a certain André, who claimed in his defence allegiance to the cathedral chapter. The chapter moved promptly to excommunicate at least one of the queen's men. André, meanwhile, moved out of the city to avoid the queen's jurisdiction. The following year, when the same tax was again due, Berengaria ordered the seizure of his goods and later imprisoned him, together with another defaulter in the tower of Le Mans.

In retaliation for this action, an interdict was placed by the chapter on all the churches in the city. Its effect was immediate: the bells fell silent and the offices ceased. But the chapter of St Pierre, with the queen's support, defied the interdict and continued to ring their bells, only submitting after pressure from the papal legate.

In 1216, the last of the bishops loyal to the old Angevin rulers, Nicolas, was succeeded by a new and very different prelate with no previous English connections. Bishop Maurice was a native of Champagne, and Dom Piolin's old but invaluable *History of the Church in Le Mans* describes him as austere, devout, abstemious and a zealous defender of the rights of the Church, which in this instance seems to have included the cathedral chapter. Although they were to collaborate on other matters during Maurice's long incumbency, including support for the religious orders and conversion of the Jews, Berengaria clashed with him during the first five years of his tenure over several issues.

One of these was the ruse adopted by laicised former clerics who, in order to avoid paying dues owed to the queen as their overlord, claimed benefit of clergy, despite their married state and substantial involvement in commercial matters.[36] An additional source of friction was the attempt by Maurice to claim revenues from some of the city parishes around the periphery of the cathedral, a move opposed with equal vigour by the queen. Maurice appealed to Philip Augustus, and a boundary commission was set up under the supervision of Guillaume des Roches, Robert count of Alençon and the abbot of La Couture. A jury of fifteen including nominees of the queen, Herbert de Tucé her seneschal among them, found in the end that the areas in dispute had belonged to the counts of Maine since the days of Henry II and Bishop Guillaume Passavant. The queen's claims to revenues from these parishes were therefore legitimate, exception made only for those abbeys and other religious houses specifically exempted. This suggests that some of the privileges attached to the title were transferred to Berengaria, in her capacity as Lady of Le Mans.

The second interdict, in 1216-17, resulted from attempts by Julien Laurent, the queen's receiver or bailiff, to collect impost duties on the sale of animals within a fief belonging to the chapter of St Pierre, an action challenged by the cathedral authorities. The queen refused to hand over the money to the cathedral chapter, Julien and his family were excommunicated and the interdict was placed once again on all the churches within the city. These troubled events are brought to life in a document now extant only in a nineteenth-century handwritten copy[37] which contains an account of the enquiry which took place many years later, in 1245, at the request of the then papal delegate, into the jurisdiction of the cathedral chapter.[38]

The enquiry of 1245 was occasioned by precisely the same kind of demarcation disputes which had taken up so much time in Berengaria's day and whose origins went back almost half a century. These had consistently concerned the power of the cathedral chapter to administer secular justice and the conflicts engendered by the rights and obligations of other bodies and individuals, as well as the complaints and appeals provoked by the over-zealous imposition of suspensions, excommunications and interdicts on both laymen and clerics. The chapter at the time of the enquiry was a very powerful body consisting of 53 titles, nine '*dignités*' and 53 prebends, the former including the all-powerful dean, the cantor, an officer known as the '*scolastique*' who was responsible for overseeing the cathedral schools, the head archdeacon and the five regional archdeacons.[39]

Around one hundred witnesses were called, whose testimony covered a period of almost fifty years, and included the period of Berengaria's incumbency as Dame du Mans. Despite the uncertainty of some eye-witnesses in remembering dates – many of them, when asked how long ago such and such an event took place replied, understandably, in rather approximate terms – some of these testimonies demonstrate considerable attention to detail and capture vividly the atmosphere of uncertainty and tension at the time of the interdicts and excommunications, as well as the strong personality of the queen herself.

One of the more important witnesses in respect of the first interdict involving Berengaria, that of 1204-6, was a fifty-five year old canon named Clavel. He recalled at length the day sentence of excommunication was pronounced on Martin and Luke, the queen's officers, and how the queen then ordered the arrest and incarceration of André; 'afterwards it was said that the said queen seized and incarcerated in the tower of Le Mans, the same André and Fulk Benedict, men owing allegiance to the Cathedral chapter, and (as he thought) that the queen and her bailiff were warned concerning these men and, as I heard tell, because they refused to release them, the chapter put an interdict on the city.' He remembered the occasion quite clearly because he himself had been in church preparing for mass, robed and with attendants carrying candles and thuribles, when suddenly, as if from nowhere, a canon appeared, shouting at the choir 'Take it all away! Close the doors! The church is under the interdict.'[40] Several other witnesses gave accounts of the same event. The chapter of St Pierre resisted the interdict and pleaded with the papal legate to uphold their case. The legate instructed them to obey the decree and the chapter appealed to the Pope. In 1206 Innocent III pronounced judgement in the letter *Cum inter Vos:* he granted a concession which entitled the chapter of St Pierre to celebrate mass in a low voice, with doors closed, no bells and the exclusion of those who had been excommunicated. Nicolas, the dean at the time, read the letter out in French to the people assembled in the cathedral.[41]

These depositions refer to the first of the three interdicts placed on the city during Berengaria's time. On this occasion, according to the witness, 'Queen Berengaria had recently arrived to take up residence in the city of Le Mans.' The witness thought that the bishop, Hamelin, had not personally authorised the placing of the interdict and the excommunication of individuals, suggesting that it was the dean of the cathedral chapter who had been responsible.

The second occasion, in 1216-18, was even more dramatic in its impact and the interdict lasted about eighteen months. Several witnesses described how the church doors were closed and the bells were silent all over the city and recalled the day to day consequences of this cessation. Almost all of them described how the dead could not be buried, but were left in makeshift coffins propped up in trees in the cemetery or even lying as they were on the ground. Pestilence was an ever-present threat.[42]

The seventh witness, a man of seventy-odd years, who happened to be visiting Le Mans at the time, remembers the pressure which was put on the queen at this time to return the money allegedly owed to the cathedral chapter:

> Several other canons, acting on the authority and instructions of the Chapter, had warned Queen Berengaria to see that the money which her servants had taken in contravention of the rights of the Chapter was returned … It was, I think, a sum of five *denarii* of Tours. But she replied that she would not return the money because, as she said, this customary right was hers. They told her that the Chapter was ready to grant a hearing to her representatives and those of the man she had imprisoned and pass judgment. She replied that she would have none of it and after she had been warned several times about this by the Chapter and still refused to do anything about it, the Chapter placed the church and the city under the interdict.

The twelfth witness, Richard Tyoul, remembered the events because he was present in the church of La Couture when the bells stopped ringing, as they did in every other church in the city: '… the bodies of the dead were lying propped up in trees in the churchyard'. He added that he did not know who had ordered the interdict, nor could he remember how long it had lasted but it was certainly for a very long time.[43] He went on to comment on the effect of this: 'Because of the interdict, Queen Berengaria left Le Mans and moved to Thorée for the duration of the interdict and only returned once it was lifted,' but 'whether this was because of the lifting of the interdict or because of the favour she had obtained from the Pope, that neither her chapel nor her clerics nor her household should be subject to the interdict' he was unable to say.

The thirty-ninth witness, Scolastica, was the widow of the unfortunate Julian Laurent who was excommunicated in 1216/17. She recalled the occasion on which the whole family was excommunicated by the cathedral chapter and the obstinate response of the queen to the demands for money: 'The queen was strongly warned, it was said, but she refused to heed any of this.'

These and similar comments do not depict the queen as passive, fearful or compliant. On the contrary she appears robust and assertive, like her brother Sancho, whose bravery was never in question. Such qualities in a man were of course best demonstrated on the battlefield and it is as victor of the decisive battle of Las Navas de Tolosa in 1212, when the Christian kings of northern Spain sank their differences long enough to inflict a crushing defeat on the Muslims that Sancho El Fuerte will always be remembered. Blanca too, showed similar qualities in her willingness to pursue her enemies as aggressively as any man might have done. Theirs was a courage appropriate to the descendants of Garcia Ramirez, the kinsman of the Cid.

Two further references in the testimony of the witness Tyoul are of interest. One is the reference to Berengaria's temporary departure from the city to Thorée during the course of the interdict. It was at Thorée that she and Richard had jointly purchased land and built a house, possibly around 1195-6. Our only source of information about this purchase comes from a document issued at Le Mans and dated 1216, in which the queen states that 'trusting in the mercy of God and for the salvation of the soul of the aforesaid Richard and of our own soul', she has made over the property in *'puram et perpetuam elemosinam'* (freehold gift in perpetuity) to the brothers of the hospital of Jerusalem, so that chaplains might be installed there in perpetuity, to praise God and offer the divine offices.[44]

The document refers to the original vendors, Guillermus de Vallefrescu and Haimericus Lego, knights (about whom, unfortunately, nothing further is known) and others, from whom the royal couple purchased land with all present and future entitlements. They also built a house with an adjacent mill and mill-pond and these, together with 'woods, men, rents and tithes, vineyard, meadows, heaths, sheep-payments and oat-payments, quarterly tolls and other revenues' were included in the transaction.

The dating of the document 'sealed with our seal' to 1216 must mean that it was prepared before the queen left Le Mans at the time of the interdict. It is possible that it was prepared quickly to be taken with her, or even drawn up in her absence. It may possibly be a copy of an original deed which has not survived. In support of this possibility is the fact that the deed, though sealed, was not signed. Furthermore, the wording is terse and to the point: Berengaria styles herself simply as 'Berengaria by the grace of God Queen of England' rather than her usual 'humble former Queen of the English', and the references to Richard are equally brief. We can only guess the reasons for this decision. Perhaps the intention was to divest herself of a property in which she no longer intended to reside and, by putting it into the hands of a powerful order, to ensure a safer refuge for herself should the situation in Le Mans become untenable. She may also have had connections with the order of St John of Jerusalem in Spain and felt that the property would pass into suitable hands.

The present-day Thorée is a sleepy village set in attractive heath and woodland not far from Le Lude. It has a tiny twelfth-century church and a few houses but of Richard and Berengaria there is no trace. The memory of the Hospitallers is preserved in the name 'La Commanderie' which was retained when the property passed into private hands.[45] Although a house and chapel are listed in the *Dictionnaire topographique, historique et statistique de la Sarthe* of 1842,[46] no early buildings now stand on the presumed site west-north-west of the village, close to the road which runs between La Flèche and Le Lude, near a brook formerly known as the *'ruisseau des cartes'*.

The other reference in the testimony of the witness Tyoul is to the papal favour enjoyed by Berengaria which allowed her to escape the consequences of the interdict and saved her on more than one occasion from the hostilities of local enemies. In fact in the course of seven or eight years, Pope Honorius III had intervened nine times in the matter of the troubled relations between the cathedral chapter and the chapter of St Pierre de la Cour.[47] Many of the relevant letters, urging moderation, appointing independent arbitrators or safeguarding the rights of the chapter of St Pierre, expressly mention Berengaria. Several are addressed to her personally, assuring her of papal protection, granting her personal immunity from the interdicts, and praising her devotion to the Holy See. It was at this time too that Pope Honorius was urging the English king to honour the dower arrangements. Just as he had described the frequent acts of injury and theft which she had suffered, he also denounced her persecutors as 'moved more by hostility than by concern for what is right.'[48]

One letter, dated 9 April 1218, states that the Church 'does not protect the interests of all with equal zeal but greater care and respect is shown to those whom it finds most steadfast in devotion to itself'. The Pope declares that he is putting Berengaria under his special protection '... acknowledging the devotion you have shown both to the holy Roman church and to our own person, and because of the universal obligation of our pastoral office, which charges us to exercise our care and concern with special favour towards the orphan and the widow'.

No one was to put her or her chapel under any form of interdict.[49] The following month, the Pope wrote a stern letter to King Henry III reminding him of his solemn obligation to care for those whom God has promised to protect, especially widows.

These assurances of papal protection and support were only partly effective. The deadlock of 1218 was finally broken when some of Berengaria's supporters succeeded in persuading the cathedral chapter to lift the ban, with assurances that the queen was willing to pay up. Face-saving all round appears to have been the order of the day: the queen returned to a ceremonial welcome and the interdict was lifted. The process of arbitration, triggered by Berengaria's appeal to the Pope, took its customary length of time and when the money was finally handed over, in the queen's chamber, two years had elapsed. Pierre Prévost, her cantor and trusted advisor, handed the money to the papal delegate, who then gave it to the representatives of the cathedral chapter.[50]

Similar minor incidents continued to occur, however, over the course of the next four years because the basic problem of disputed revenues and taxes had never been clearly resolved. Berengaria was not the initiator of such problems. The enquiry of 1245 shows that similar incidents continued to take place even after her death, when agents of the king of France himself were compelled to make restitution to the chapter for alleged infringements of its privileges.

Several witnesses recall the frequent excommunication of individuals including that of Paulin Boutier, among whose duties was the supervision of weights and measures of wine.[51] His whole family was excommunicated on one particular occasion. Meanwhile, Bishop Maurice showed himself to be a strong supporter of the chapter and was quick to retaliate when he felt its interests and his own were not advanced by the result of independent adjudication. One final example from the letters of Pope Honorius, addressed in February 1223 to a panel consisting of the abbot of St Genevieve, G. Cornu, dean and G. Peverel, archdeacon of Paris, shows how long these disputes lasted. The letter urges the arbitrators to find a speedy solution to a range of matters in dispute between Berengaria and the bishop, including taxes and revenues, retaliatory over-use of the interdict, too many excommunications and a Palm Sunday procession which went wrong.

The Pope's letter carefully recounts the incidents as they had obviously been reported to him by eye-witness testimonies supplied by both parties:

> Our dear sons ... the Dean and Chapter of St Pierre de la Cour of Le Mans have reported to us in their petition that a dispute having arisen between our venerable brother Maurice, bishop of Le Mans and our dearest daughter in Christ, Berengaria, formerly illustrious queen of the English, concerning certain individuals caught in a brawl and other matters ... the Dean and Chapter of the aforementioned Church had gone in procession to the Cathedral, as had always been customary on certain feast days, and, with the full blessing of the Cathedral Chapter, were carrying the relics of St Scholastica into the Cathedral for the Palm Sunday observances. The queen herself accompanied by a large crowd, led the procession. The bishop and Chapter refused to admit them and shut the doors of the Church in their faces, to their utter confusion, creating scandal and dismay among the onlookers.[52]

Once more the accusations and counter-accusations flew backwards and forwards. The chapter of St Pierre protested the legitimacy of their actions on the grounds of the special indults and exemptions granted by the Pope, the bishop and chapter repeated their denunciations of those who sought to ignore their interdict. The chapter of St Pierre, backed by the queen, demanded the punishment of the bishop and the bishop's spokesmen demanded action against the queen.

The outcome of all this was presumably a stand-off, because there is no further word on this matter from the Pope and no record of further hostilities. Perhaps, as Henri Chardon suggests, the main protagonists were growing weary of it all. Once again, the documents portray Berengaria as a sturdy defender of her own rights and a loyal supporter of her chapter who also inspired loyalty in others, including the ordinary people who came to meet her when she returned from exile, and who followed her in crowds on that Palm Sunday and reacted with outrage at the insult to their lady.

Berengaria's popularity was derived from her reputation as a protector of the poor and sick, largely through her generous support of the religious orders, who were the only dispensers of welfare assistance. Despite all her differences with the cathedral chapter, she also donated money to the cathedral on more than one occasion. To the abbey of La Couture she gave both land and money, and to the brothers of the hospital of Coëffort she also made generous donations. She was quick to recognise the value of the newer orders, giving land in 1215 to the newly arrived Franciscans so that they could build their convent, and a few years later she gave a portion of land near the gallo-roman wall together with the chapel formerly known as Notre Dame des Marais (Our Lady of the Marshes) to the Dominicans. Gifts of money or land to religious orders were common at this time.

They were invariably associated with requests for memorial masses – not an entirely altruistic request, but certainly not one which is designed to procure an advantage for some which is thereby denied to others. In addition to dispensing 'welfare' – poverty relief, succour for the homeless and so on – the orders cared for the sick and dying and provided what education was available. The preaching orders also fulfilled a social need, as conduits for information and communication within the community.

Religious communities, then as now, were also thought of as powerhouses of prayer, whose intercession, self-denial and example might indeed move mountains. There is no indication that the revenues so jealously safeguarded by Berengaria during the period of conflict with the cathedral chapter were used for self-aggrandisement, for amassing wealth, patronising the arts or creating a courtly environment, in short, acquiring the kind of reputation associated not only with (rightly or wrongly) Eleanor of Aquitaine and Marie de Champagne but, to a lesser extent, Blanca/Blanche of Champagne her sister. Some of the criticisms levelled at Blanche by contemporary churchmen may have been inspired by the kind of prejudice attracted by women acting politically, but the theme of 'worldliness' is also present.

True to his pastoral obligation to protect the widow, Pope Honorius also extended his protection to Blanche, but there is a less than subtle difference in the wording of letters he addressed to the two sisters. Whereas Honorius praises Berengaria for her fortitude, offers her his permanent protection and does not hesitate to charge her enemies with malice, a letter written to Blanche in November 1219, urging her to settle her differences with the bishop of Troyes, sounds rather more like a warning from the school principal:

> ... in your territories the Church's censure is treated with contempt and episcopal authority overturned. Wherefore we have undertaken to warn you and exhort you, by apostolic precept ... not to make things worse, so that you may earn merit in the sight of God and a good name among men and that we may praise you for your devotion.'[53]

In Berengaria's case not even her worst enemies ever charged her with worldliness of this kind. Honorius's letters to John's widow, Isabella of Angoulême, also make interesting reading: in 1219 he was extending to her as a widow, the customary protection in recognition of her praiseworthy devotion; little over a year later, she was the recipient of two severely worded letters occasioned by her failure to behave appropriately towards her son, King Henry, and even worse, her liaison with her own prospective son-in-law! Berengaria, in contrast to these contemporaries, never once incurred papal censure and the criticisms levelled against her by some of her adversaries, including local churchmen, received no support from successive Popes.

This is probably yet another reason for the failure of modern novelists to find much to romanticise in Berengaria. While earlier novelists such as Nora Lofts and Margaret Campbell Barnes perpetuated the Victorian image of the self-sacrificing heroine, wronged but ever loyal, such qualities, it seems, hold little appeal for the readers of today's historical romances. Such readers are probably more readily attracted to figures like Eleanor who can be depicted in a more romantic light.

The most significant beneficiary of Berengaria's generosity was of course her own 'royal' chapter.[54] Unfortunately, many of these donations consisted of land and properties formerly owned by Jews. Some of these properties may have been properly purchased but it seems more likely, in the light of widespread practice, particularly in France, that they were confiscated without compensation. This has caused the local historian, André Bouton, to refer to Berengaria as a persecutor of the Jews,[55] a charge which casts something of a shadow over the reputation of the daughter of a king who not only protected his Jewish subjects, but employed them as his valued advisors, physicians and counsellors.

The history of Jewish-Christian relations in medieval Europe is long and complicated. Numerous studies have been devoted to the question and generalities are misleading and at times dangerous. Kenneth Stow is one scholar who has examined the theological basis of anti-Jewish policies in the Christian west.[56] While successive Popes, drawing on the Pauline metaphor of the regrafted olive tree, counselled Christians against harming or persecuting the Jews, urging at the least that they should be allowed to exist as a 'warning', one element in Christian thinking continued to stress the superiority of Christianity and to denigrate and vilify Judaism and the Jewish people. Some clerical writers like Guibert of Nogent were undoubtedly infected with a virulent and destructive anti-Semitism, and popular preachers all too often used the Jews as scapegoats.

The practice of lay lords was much more violent and predatory. Uninhibited by papal disapproval both of forced conversions and unwarranted plundering of Jewish property, they saw the ambivalent and marginalised position of Jewish communities in Christian society as an attractive excuse to enrich themselves further. Conditions varied over time and space. It appears that in the early Middle Ages, the situation of Jews still concentrated in the Mediterranean area was reasonably secure, but by the twelfth and thirteenth centuries this had changed.

In France in particular, things became rapidly worse after the accession of Philip Augustus.[57] Unlike the situation in Spain and Sicily, where Jews formed part of the landed classes and interacted freely with both Christians and Muslims, French Jews owned only small parcels of land, in or near cities, where they could cultivate small vineyards and develop their own schools, places of worship and ritual baths. In no country apart from Spain and Sicily did they ever constitute more than one per cent of the population and in no city did they exceed 1500.[58]

Prohibited by canon law from employing Christians as serfs or slaves,[59] they could not effectively develop large estates and were obliged to practise trades such as dyeing or metal work, as well as engaging in commerce. All loans made by Jews in France had to be recorded in writing and kings could and did find the taxing of Jews a lucrative and guaranteed source of revenue. Mid twelfth-century documents referring to '*Judaei nostri*' ('our Jews') point to the fact that kings and feudal magnates exercised control over 'their' Jews, restricting their movements, arresting them and holding them to ransom, releasing Christians from a part of their debt to Jewish money-lenders or traders and even expelling the Jews from their lands, as Philip Augustus did in 1182, but not before charging them fifteen thousand marks for their 'release'.

The Jewish community in Le Mans was quite large, partly as a consequence of expulsions from the French domain. Conditions under English rule in Maine and Anjou appear to have been relatively tolerable in comparison and many of those expelled from the royal domain had sought refuge there. Others had gone to Champagne, where successive counts, including Blanche, came to depend on their financial services. The Jews of Maine had enjoyed some measure of security up till the middle of the eleventh century, but after that time conditions changed: scare-mongering and accusations of ritual murder which originated in the French domain spread to Anjou, Touraine and Maine and Jewish horse-traders and pedlars, who sold spices, cloth, medicines and leather goods, were subjected to heavy tolls when crossing rivers or using the roads. As a result many of them preferred to remain in the towns where there was safety in numbers.

It is against this background that Berengaria's actions must be judged. She must have used the services of Jewish financiers in the past because the pipe roll for 1199, the last year of Richard's reign, records revenues from the tin mines of Devon and Cornwall assigned to cover the debts incurred by the queen to a certain Pontius Arnaldi, an Italian Jew.[60] There are three recorded instances on which she gave former Jewish property in Le Mans to individuals or institutions.

In 1207-8 she gave her sergeant Martin a house and vines belonging to a Jew named Désiré and vines belonging to a Jew named Copin. Martin sold these for 15 pounds local currency to the abbot of St Vincent. The following year he sold, with the queen's permission, an arpent (roughly one acre) of vines to the abbey of La Couture in return for annual memorial masses for Richard. In 1210 she gave a former Jewish school to her chapel. Conversion, not always totally voluntary, was a useful pretext for the acquisition of Jewish property, and around this same time a Jewish merchant named Cresson converted to Christianity, liquidated his goods and went off on a pilgrimage. Some of his land was sold to La Couture, perhaps under pressure, as was common after conversion, when there would presumably be no place in the tightly knit community for an apostate.

A similar procedure was followed in 1207 when, in the queen's presence, a whole family of converts sold to a cleric named Geoffrey their property located in the fief of Paulin Boutier, Berengaria's trusted liegeman.[61] Among the witnesses we find the name of Adam of Perseigne, suggesting that this was a high profile conversion. There is some suggestion that Berengaria's encouragement of the

Dominican order and gift of land to them in an area adjacent to the Jewish quarter was a recognition of their skill in converting Jews.

While some of the property acquired from Jews was purchased for a price, it appears that on many occasions it was confiscated without compensation, in defiance of papal rulings as recent as the bull *Sicut Judaeis Non* of 1120, which had stated that Jews should not be deprived of their property 'except by taxation and legal process.'[62] Records from Spain for the same period – the full and informative records from the cathedral archive of Tudela, for instance – show that land purchased by Christians from both Jews and 'Moors' was regularly acquired for prices no lower than that paid by Jews and Moors to Christians.[63] This is not an isolated example: an examination of documents in Hebrew and Arabic from the archives of Huesca, shows, in the words of J. Bosch Vila, 'Christians, Muslims and Jews, some of them important persons, importing, buying, selling, lending and exchanging' on a level playing field.[64] In this respect at least, we can only conclude that Berengaria's practice conformed more closely to that of her adopted land than that of her father and her brother. Whether this was driven by financial or ideological motives is impossible to say.

Almost nothing is known of her private life during these long years of widowhood. She appears to have had little contact with Navarre. Her younger brother Fernando, who had served as a hostage for the release of Richard, died in 1207 at the age of thirty after a fall from his horse during a jousting festival in Tudela. Her sister Costanza's death is nowhere recorded – not even in the Obituary of the Cathedral of Pamplona which records the death of every member of the immediate family and contains a good many other names of archival interest.[65] It cannot have happened before 1202 when King John issued a safe-conduct to her envoy Ysmael. We know nothing of the purpose of this mission or the identity of the envoy, who may have been a Muslim, although the name was also used by Christians. The employment by Spanish kings of Jews and Muslims as ambassadors was a practice which earned them a papal rebuke.[66]

At least one record suggests that Berengaria may have contemplated returning to Navarre. In 1219 King Henry III notified the seneschal of Poitou and Gascony, Guillaume de Neville, that a safe-conduct had been granted to 'Queen Berengaria and all whom she may take with her to travel, if she so wishes, through the territories of Poitou and Gascony to Spain, both departing and returning' and in the following year he is also to allow the messengers and representatives of the queen, 'going from her to the king of Navarre her brother and from that king to the queen, with messages, to travel safely through his territory'.[67] The Lord of Blaye was also warned against further attacks on her envoys.

No information is given as to the purpose of the request for a safe-conduct, and we do not know whether the journey was ever made. Was Berengaria simply homesick after these long years away from her native land? Or did she have a more practical purpose in mind, such as an attempt to enlist Sancho's support for her final appeal to Henry in respect of her still unpaid dower monies. The alliance between England and Navarre still held good, as attested a few years later when Sancho was repeating his assurances of loyalty to the old ally. The Navarrese monarch was also still in good standing at Rome, as evidenced by a letter written to him by the Pope around the same time – May 1219 – in which he put Sancho and his kingdom under the full protection of the Holy See, in appreciation for his participation in the crusade in Portugal.

The following year saw the return to Navarre as bishop of Pamplona of Remiro, illegitimate son of Sancho El Fuerte, who had gone to Champagne in 1211 to work for Blanche as her chancellor, after an education in Paris and Bologna. His appointment had been confirmed in 1218 by a special papal dispensation. It is also possible that Berengaria's projected visit was connected in some way with this appointment.

In 1224 Sancho contracted the illness which was to turn him into a recluse for the last years of his life and earn him the title of 'El Encerrado' – the Shut Away. Prince Jaume of Aragon was later to describe him as depressed and withdrawn, both because of his obesity and the varicose ulcer on his leg. Because he had no legitimate offspring from two failed marriages, he tried to make Prince Jaume his heir, but when he died in 1234 it was Blanche's son, Thibaut IV of Navarre, who succeeded him. Spanish historians have described Sancho as isolated and disillusioned, brooding in the tower of Tudela, a great hero who was to become the stuff of legend and the subject of a lost epic poem but one who had learned to put his trust in no man. Experience may well have led Berengaria to develop a similar reserve, but her brother's piety appears to have been more conventional than hers and he was apparently unable to find, as she did, the ultimate consolation of faith.

The closest contacts Berengaria enjoyed with a member of her own family were with her sister Blanche. It had been Berengaria who had escorted Blanca, as she then was, to her wedding in Chartres in 1199, had been present as a witness and perhaps had even been instrumental in arranging the marriage in the first place. Blanche in turn had sheltered her sister when she was alone and in need. Blanche too had been widowed, tragically, after barely two years of marriage, but, unlike Berengaria, Blanche had married a man who appears to have returned her affection. A baby girl was born during the first year of their marriage and a boy, the future Thibaut IV, shortly after his father's death. The protection of her children's interests, especially those of her infant son, became Blanche's first priority but her children also gave her a stake in the future and, to some extent, bargaining power. Thibaut, whether by inheritance or upbringing, turned out to be an accomplished musician and poet. This earned him a place in the history of French literature and – for those interested in such matters – a line of descent links him indirectly to the present Spanish monarchy.

The administrative records of the county of Champagne, one of the closest and most influential vassal states of France, have been relatively well preserved and the activities of Blanche as regent for twenty-one years are presented in much clearer detail than those of her sister in Le Mans. One particular set of accounts for the years 1217-19, preserved in a manuscript in the Bibliothèque Nationale, and published first by F. Bourquelot in 1862[68] and again by A. Lognon in 1914, testifies to contacts between the two sisters during a period which was particularly difficult for Berengaria, coinciding in part with one of the interdicts placed on the city, if the dating extrapolated from the somewhat approximate memory of the witnesses to the later enquiry is correct.

The court of Champagne and Brie was modelled closely on the royal court of France, with its seneschals, chancellors and other curial officials. The accounts published by Bourquelot represent expenditure incurred '*extra curias*', that is, in external matters. Many of the items involve missions to Rome or to the French court, in connection with Blanche's struggles with the relatives of her late husband's elder brother who were constantly challenging her legitimacy. There are also three and possibly four visits to Le Mans and at least one suggestion of multiple visits there in the same year.

Among the messengers are some familiar names: Remiro (Remi), chancellor of Champagne, soon to be bishop of Pamplona; Garsias, a Navarrese cleric, perhaps the same person employed by Berengaria as an envoy to England, who had also held the office of master cellarer of St Etienne de Troyes and who would later be referred to in terms of great affection by Thibaut IV; a lady named Julianeta Brodaresse (possibly also a Spaniard – the surname may be a professional designation); Girard de Waraie or Varaire and two envoys to Spain, 'Gaillard' and Brother John de Pruliaco.

Little if anything is indicated about the purpose of these trips. Girard was probably a banker or treasury official, and one of his visits to Le Mans was to buy horses, while another item lists his expenses as incurred '*pro domina regina*' – on behalf of the lady queen. An 'English' clerk, William, is also mentioned but without any details as to how his expenses were incurred.

This person may be the same William who acted as Berengaria's envoy to England on a previous occasion, and perhaps also the William designated as chaplain to the queen ('*Guillermo, capellán de la reina*') in the ecclesiastical archives of Tudela,[69] who bequeathed in his will, in 1227, monies to various Spanish monasteries, including significantly, the women's convents of Tulebras and Marcilla. He may have made these bequests during a visit to Navarre as Berengaria's envoy. This reference to the 'queen' is highly likely to be to Berengaria because she is referred to as 'Queen Berengaria' in some other adjacent entries in the Tudela archive and because at the time of these entries there was no official queen of Navarre, Sancho having outlived or divorced the only two women with whom he is thought to have contracted lawful matrimony.

After the death of Berengaria, the trusted cleric Garcia (Garsias) also returned to Navarre, because material from the same archives refers to his exchange, in 1235, of properties with the prior of St María, the collegiate church of Tudela, Miguel de Monzón. He is here described as 'Garcia de San Miguel, cleric of Queen Berengaria.'[70] There is also some evidence of a continuing connection with the order of St John of Jerusalem, the Hospitallers, who held properties in the vicinity of Monreal de Tudela, perhaps the territory of which Berengaria herself held the *tenencia* in 1185. Berengaria's father had, during his long reign, encouraged and supported the activities of the military orders, both international and local, and this practice was continued by his son.[71] Sancho El Fuerte was on close terms with the then prior of the Hospitallers in Navarre, don Jiméno de Morieta, and granted the order special privileges of various kinds. It was also to the Hospitallers, the knights of St John of Jerusalem, that Berengaria made over the property in Thorée some years previously: perhaps Garcia was instrumental in advising her in relation to that transaction.[72]

Also mentioned in the Champagne accounts are two Spanish archers, Sancius and Lupus (Sancho and Lobo), and a nephew of Lord Ferrando 'for his return to his homeland'. The identity of these three last mentioned people is obscure, but these references to frequent contact between Le Mans, Champagne and Navarre must surely be connected in some way with the safe conduct issued in 1219 by Henry III to Berengaria and her envoys to enable them to make the journey to Spain. Perhaps the imminent return of Remiro as bishop was connected in some way with concern about the succession. Berengaria would have been kept informed about any of these moves. The subsequent return to Spain of some of these important advisors and household chaplains shows that contact was never lost with Navarre.

Blanche's situation, though difficult at times, was not one of total isolation. At the time of her marriage she had obviously brought with her a small group of trusted Navarrese officials and companions. Her marriage though short-lived was apparently happy, and most importantly she had children to perpetuate her husband's name. Berengaria, by contrast, had left her homeland in most unusual circumstances and had been surrounded by Norman, Anglo-Norman or Angevin officials from the start. She had had to rebuild her contacts anew after Richard's death. That she should have sought to maintain contact with surviving members of her own family was entirely understandable. Why did she not return permanently to Navarre? We cannot be sure, but what we know of her character suggests that this might have seemed an admission of failure or an act of weakness. She had lived her life for better or for worse as Richard's queen: she would live and die as his widow and lady of Le Mans.

CHAPTER SIX

Shall These Stones Speak?

By the year 1228 Berengaria was approaching sixty – old by the standards of the day – her fighting spirit still undaunted, but tired perhaps, and feeling the weight of those long years alone. Her concern was now for the future, immediate and long-term. Much had changed since her arrival in Le Mans, as an uncertain beneficiary of the French king's ambiguous generosity. Many family members were already dead – Blanca would precede her in 1229 – and her remaining brother was already seriously ill. Old enmities were fading too, with the death of the principal protagonists. In 1223 Philip Augustus, chastened perhaps by the death 'of grief' in 1201 of Agnes of Merania and the long years of papal pressure, died 'peacefully and piously' at Mantes, ten years after taking back his queen, Ingeborg, who lived on for another thirteen years, surely the loneliest and most pitiable of all royal widows.

The young King Louis IX – 'St Louis' – succeeded his father Louis VIII, whose reign was cut short by sickness a mere three years after his accession. The young Louis was the son of Richard's niece Blanche of Castile, whom the old Queen Eleanor had brought from Spain to marry the son of Philip Augustus in May 1200. Although this marriage has been described by some as a shrewd piece of politics by Eleanor, designed to neutralise the effect of the Navarrese-Champenois alliance, its long-term effect was to prove advantageous to Berengaria. The young king and his mother regarded her as their friend and relative – Louis's charters refer to her as 'our dearest relative and liegewoman, Queen Berengaria' – all the more because Berengaria's nephew, the young Thibaut, had proved a reliable ally when Philippe Hurepel, the son of Agnes of Merania, tried to deprive Blanche of Castile, Louis's mother, of her regency.

St Louis and his mother were instrumental in assisting Berengaria to realise her last ambition, the foundation of the Cistercian abbey of the Pietas Dei, the Piété Dieu, of l'Epau. The foundation of this abbey makes a fitting conclusion to the story of her life.[1]

Berengaria's dower rights were strictly usufructuary – for life only – and thus any land she might wish to build on had to be purchased. The last years of her life were dedicated to carefully marshalling the resources to make a suitable purchase.

She was fortunate to receive in 1228 from the young king, her kinsman, a territory known as l'E (s)pau – referred to in Latin as 'Spallum' – which consisted of 46 acres of woodland, with seven meadows, two gardens and the right to some revenues. It was close to the river Huisne, with ready access to water and had been used as hunting and fishing grounds. It was said that the spot had been formerly inhabited by a hermit. Nothing further is known about this hermit, but the status of hermits as liminal holy men gave them a special standing in their relations with kings, as clearly seen in the documented lives of Henry II, Richard and John.[2]

From the start the Cistercian order took a close interest in the project. There were already a substantial number of Cistercian foundations in the diocese, of which Perseigne was the eldest, followed by Bellebranche. Berengaria's family had close connections with the Cistercians in Spain, and there had been significant links, too, between king Richard and the order. Two influential Cistercian abbots, Milo of St Marie du Pin and Adam of Perseigne, had been among his closest advisors and regular confessors. In 1219 the chapter general of the order initiated an anniversary memorial for Richard and in 1223 a similar decision was taken to commemorate Berengaria, perhaps at her own request: 'that after her death the anniversary of Berengaria queen of the English should be celebrated by the order'.[3] Adam in particular, with his compassionate nature and wealth of practical experience, was helpful to Berengaria in bringing her project to fruition.

Adam died in 1221 and so did not live to see Berengaria's dream take shape, but his successor, Abbot Gautier, became one of her most trusted advisors and negotiators. In 1229, the chapter general of the order, to whom the proposal had been referred, named two of their number, Richard of Louroux and Laurent of Clermont, to inspect the project and report back. Their inspection was to cover all aspects of the matter: suitability of the location, availability of resources, compatibility with the strict ideals of Citeaux, distance from other religious houses and so on.

A last-minute hitch was averted when the brothers of the hospital of Coëffort, who claimed to have been given the property by the young Prince Arthur during his brief tenure, agreed after mediation to surrender their deeds in return for one hundred pounds, to which the queen added a further twenty, to purchase neighbouring buildings, including the old hermitage.[4] They did so only because they recognised her as a generous benefactor and supporter of their work on past occasions. Berengaria also purchased land from local landowners, some of whose names have been recorded. These include: Hugues Haane and his son Herbert; Julienne, widow of Lambert le Taillandier; Hugues, her second husband and the children of her first marriage; Benevenua le Espallane; a certain Perret, and the knight Guillaume de Rivellon. She also purchased tithing rights and property in the vicinity, including vineyards, among which was one owned by the abbey of Fontevraud. The outlays were considerable.[5]

The archives of the Département de la Sarthe have preserved a number of the early documents recording these transactions, both purchases and donations. The sums involved are substantial, amounting to around four hundred *livres* (pounds) in the first instance. Many of the properties purchased carried the right to levy rents and other dues. Berengaria appointed a townsman (*bourgeois*), Thomas de Beaumont, as a lay administrator to assist with these and other matters. Louis and his mother Blanche of Castile visited Le Mans in May 1230 and confirmed their donations, assigning as a special gift fifty *livres* per annum from the royal revenues of Le Mans, one cartload of firewood regularly from the royal forest and a *bourgeois* in perpetuity so that the same services would continue to be provided after Berengaria's death.[6]

Two water mills which were purchased in June 1230 are the subject of a little anecdote or '*narratiuncula*' reproduced in

Bouquet's *Gallia Christiana*.[7] According to an early tradition, the
newly installed monks of l'Epau were irritated by the sound of the
water mills nearby, claiming that this distracted them from their
prayers. When Berengaria was told about this, she was advised by
a friend to buy the mills for the abbey, so that the sound would in
future be no longer a distraction but a reminder of their own good
fortune!

In May 1230 all these lengthy negotiations and transactions
were at last complete, and the monks moved in, under their first
abbot Jean. Berengaria died in December 1230, a month before the
bull of Pope Gregory IX which confirmed the foundation, and the
subsequent consecration of the abbey by Bishop Geoffrey de Laval.

The foundation charter of the abbey is conserved today in the
departmental archives at Le Mans.[8] The seal is missing and the only
description we have of it is from the eighteenth century:

> Seal in green wax, with attachment of yellow and red silk,
> the seal being oval in shape, figuring on each side a woman
> clothed in a long cloak holding in her left hand a cross sur-
> mounted by a dove, above her hand is a stem bearing several
> *fleur de lys* and in her right hand she holds a flower. Around
> it are written these words: on the one side, 'countess of the
> Normans and the Angevins' and on the other, 'Berengaria
> [by the grace] of God Queen of the English'. The same figure
> appears on the other side, in its right hand, a stem bearing
> similar flowers and on its left hand, a dove similar to the one
> on the other side.

Fragmentary as they are, these small pieces of parchment which
have survived for over seven and half centuries are the final tangi-
ble testimony to the faith which had sustained the queen throughout a long life lived largely at the bidding of others and represent
the culmination of so much patience, prayer and endeavour.

The name of the new abbey was probably chosen by the queen
herself, in keeping with the usual practice, whereby the name of a
monastery reflects the choice of its founder. According to one early
Cistercian tradition, more common in England than in France, the

name of God was frequently coupled with a mystical attribute. Berengaria or her advisors followed the same practice and her abbey was called the *Pietas Dei*, in line with other examples such as *Gratia Dei* (Grace of God) *Curia Dei* (House of God) *Claritas Dei* (Light of God) etc. It was also a common Cistercian custom to place their houses under the protection of Our Lady and the alternative designation, *Beata Maria de Pietate Dei*, (in the vernacular, *Notre Dame de la Piété-Dieu*), was quickly adopted. This is the name by which the abbey is known today, in keeping with the later medieval practice of dedicating all churches and shrines to the honour of the Mother of God.

The subsequent history of the abbey, with special reference to its architectural fortunes, has been described in some detail by J.M. Barrère.[9] After the death of its foundress, it flourished for over a hundred years and was further enriched by gifts, acquisitions and royal protection, some details of which are preserved in the local archives. In 1365, however, disaster struck. The abbey was burned to the ground, perhaps by the monks themselves, in order to prevent its falling into the hands of the lawless bands of mercenaries, *routiers*, or brigands who were swarming all over Maine and Anjou at the time. Some have suggested that these included English invaders posing as mercenaries. The monks took refuge in the town and only emerged later, around 1367, for the rebuilding.[10]

Barrère's history of the abbey gives a detailed account of its architectural evolution up till the eve of the Revolution, after which it passed into the hands of a family named Thoré, which owned it until 1924. During the German occupation of World War II, it was requisitioned by the occupying forces and after the liberation it became a public monument. The final restoration was only completed in the sixties. The abbey no longer functions as a religious building, although the Cistercian order took an official part in the ceremonies which marked its reopening in the sixties.

Berengaria's tomb is the focal point of the new abbey. The story of her 'return' to Notre Dame de l'Epau is a dramatic one. Berengaria was originally buried in the abbey, probably in the choir area, in accordance with special Cistercian dispensations of 1152 and 1158 which allowed for the burial of sovereigns in consecrated space. The whereabouts of her remains were for a long time the source of conjecture. The English antiquarian Charles Stothard visited the property in 1816, when it was in the hands of the Thoré family, and also visited the cathedral, where the reclining effigy had been relocated and sketched the statue, as reported by Agnes Strickland in her *Lives of the Queens of England*. Stothard also noted the existence of human remains from the vandalised tomb and heard eye-witness accounts from those who had demolished the mausoleum to convert its location into a barn. According to some of these accounts, the box had contained gold cloth.

No one is quite sure how and when the tomb came to be opened in the first place, but at least one local historian thinks that it occurred during the violent conflicts of the fourteenth century, when pillagers would have been attracted by valuable objects such as the crown. Others believe that it occurred earlier and that the monks themselves removed the crown and fine cloth as a form of insurance when they left the monastery. The removal of the crown was carried out hastily and violently, as evidenced by the post mortem trauma probably inflicted by a spade.

The tomb itself, with its beautiful reclining effigy, was removed and relocated in the cathedral of Le Mans in 1821. Almost a century and a half later, in 1960, a major discovery took place. The bones of a woman aged about sixty years old were discovered under the floor of the former chapter house of the then disused abbey and some local scholars were quick to claim that these were the remains of Berengaria. Not everyone was convinced, however, and for a while, a vigorous exchange of views took place, the course of which can be traced in the local journal *Vie Mancelle* and other regional publications over a period of years in the sixties and early seventies.[11] After some time, however, a majority of experts came to the conclusion that these were indeed the queen's remains. This conclusion was in part based on the detailed results of an examination carried out in the Faculty of Medicine in the University of Caen.[12]

The report, which is long and technical, can be summarised as follows: the skeleton is of a woman of about 157 cms in height, with a slight dislocation of the hip. The head is slightly larger than the average, suggesting, though not conclusively, an enlarged brain capacity. The cranium is damaged by a blow inflicted *post mortem*. Traces on the cranium clearly indicate the presence of metal, most likely a crown, the probable object of the vandalism (if such it was).

Dr Dastigue's report suggested that the face was narrow, with a well-defined, pointed chin, a broad, flat brow, a sharp nose and high, arched eyebrows. It belonged to 'no distinct racial type'. There were also present extra bones, belonging to one or more additional cadavers, which may have been thrown in when the original grave was pillaged. Intriguing is the suggestion that some of these scattered bones, in particular a femur, may have belonged to a young girl. It is also possible that these were added when the occupying German troops dug up the floor of the former chapter house, then in use as an improvised garage. The soldiers would presumably have reburied the bones they had disturbed.

The details of the skeleton, especially the traces of the crown, and the general configuration of the remains, suggest very strongly that these are indeed the mortal remains of Berengaria. This conclusion has now been accepted by the majority of scholars today. The remains were returned to the now restored chapter house of the abbey, beneath the relocated tomb with its striking effigy. Now at last the queen lies once more at rest amid the tranquillity of the abbey grounds, within earshot of the mill-race, and her name is once more linked in public association with the local and national heritage. France, the country of her former enemy, has honoured her final resting place, while England, which claims her as its queen, has all but forgotten her.

If circumstances had been different, Berengaria of Navarre might be known today as one of England's most successful queens, instead of the 'shadowy', 'colourless' and 'enigmatic' figure historians have made of her. Her courage, tenacity and loyalty would have equipped her well for the many roles a queen consort was called upon to play, both in public and in private.

But in the last resort, her fate was determined by her relationship with Richard and, as history has so often demonstrated, courage and tenacity are not enough to safeguard the position of a royal consort if her husband abandons or neglects her. Perhaps this justifies the assertion of David Herlihy and others that the institutionalisation of agnatic lineage and primogeniture has in the end disadvantaged and marginalised women.

If revisionist historians have succeeded in dismantling the nineteenth-century view of Richard as an irresponsible king, James Brundage's charge of emotional immaturity, which John Gillingham cites in distancing quote marks, is harder to shake off. If Richard as soldier and statesman can be seen to have planned his campaigns carefully and listened to the advice of a trusted circle of responsible advisors and officials, his private life, even after marriage, seems to have changed very little from that of his bachelor days. It was marriage and assumption of the responsibilities of a head of household which signalled the passage from youth to maturity, and there is now a general acceptance of Duby's view that the 'jeunes' – young males between puberty and marriage – enjoyed a great deal of license not allowed to their elders. Sexual experimentation or the sowing of 'wild oats' was one such liberty.

It is in this context that Richard's alleged homosexuality should be considered. Understandable though it is that gay people should wish today to reclaim their own history, long overshadowed by heterosexual orthodoxy, it does not follow that modern typologies of sexual orientation can appropriately be imposed on past societies, as the late John Boswell has often reminded us. Many aspects of male to male relations in the Middle Ages might be interpreted as homosexual today, whether we are talking about the affectionate language used by both laymen and monks, the references to kissing and other physical expressions of emotion or the textual expression of male beauty. The notion of beauty itself, today seen as a 'feminine' attribute, was for long periods of the past essentially applied to men.

Yet the medieval notion of sodomy as a sin is unambiguous. All the major authoritative studies of medieval sexuality based on extensive reading of the canons, penitentials and didactic writings confirm this fact. Whatever the original meaning of the biblical reference to Sodom, it is clear that in the medieval view, it was the 'unnatural' sex which brought about the fiery destruction of the cities of the plain.[13]

It does not follow however that in practice, every individual act was equally reprehensible. What medieval society appears to have found the least acceptable is the role of the catamite or passive male partner, precisely because, like the male cross-dresser, he plays the 'woman's' role. There is no medieval equivalent of today's artificial icon of glamorous femininity, the dazzling drag-queen. More representative of the medieval view is the humiliating portrayal of the unpopular chancellor of England, William Longchamps, who was groped by a fisherman on Dover beach when attempting to flee the country in women's clothing. Masculinity was both sacrosanct and fragile, it would seem: in the words of Vern Bullough, 'It is almost as if the 'superiority of the male' has to be demonstrated continually or else it will be lost.'[14]

The peccadilloes of a young unmarried man may well have been regarded more leniently. As one expert, J-L. Flandrin puts it:

> During the high middle ages, the penitentials refer to it (youthful sodomy) in very different terms from those reserved for adults: not only were the penalties much less serious, and often less than for debauchery (*stupre*) or heterosexual fornication, but it is clear that they are speaking of typically[15] juvenile behaviour, which was expected to cease upon marriage.

The significant word here is marriage, which makes it clear that the sense in which we should understand the term 'juvenile' is that proposed by Duby, i.e., unmarried. In a sense, the unmarried male is still a child: for a woman, however, the passage from virginity to marriage does not alter her status, in law and custom, as a minor, a dependant.

Even if this was so, some would argue that Richard himself did not behave in this way. While pointing to the ambiguous nature of the disputed passages in Howden and other chroniclers which describe Richard's intimacy with Philip Augustus of France in 1186 and the hermit's reference to Sodom in 1195, these scholars also make much of the fact that Richard fathered an illegitimate son and that he married in the full expectation of having legitimate issue.

These arguments are far from conclusive: as Boswell points out – active gay men can and do reproduce and many gay or bisexual men have camouflaged their orientation by marrying, particularly when they aspire to public life, or if their career would be jeopardised by any suggestion of sexual ambivalence. The strains imposed by such a double life have often resulted in tragedy, particularly if such men are part of a conservative and officially homophobic establishment.

Boswell, Duby, Flandrin and others are persuasive in the general argument that a different view was taken in past societies. In the medieval period, the same latitude which allowed young men to indulge in homosexual acts also allowed heterosexual experimentation. Pregnancies were an inevitable by-product. As Ralph Turner puts it:

> Most bastards acknowledged by monarchs or nobles resulted from youthful liaisons, usually with women of low rank, that predated the young man's marriage ... there was more tolerance for wild oats than children of adulterous relationships.

J.C. Parsons points out that, despite his homosexual relationship with Piers Gaveston – accepted by most scholars, though recently questioned by Pierre Chaplais[16] – Edward III fathered at least one ex-nuptial child and four legitimate ones.[17]

Neither is Richard's alleged reputation as a sexual predator a conclusive argument against his homosexual or bisexual inclinations. Many latter-day Don Juans have turned out to be sexually ambivalent or even predominantly homosexual. Such men are often incapable of forming mature relationships with women and their violence camouflages a deep-seated insecurity about their own masculinity. There is a great deal of circumstantial evidence in Richard's own life to support such an interpretation of his character and predilections.

Those who reject the notion that Richard was anything other than an uncomplicated heterosexual (who just happened to marry late and didn't fancy his wife) frequently claim that his alleged homosexuality is a twentieth-century invention and that neither his own contemporaries nor anyone else for several hundred years later had any such doubts.

Certainly, if he had been seen by his contemporaries as blatantly effeminate or a known paedophile this would not have passed without comment.

But is it true that no one prior to the twentieth century ever entertained doubts about Richard's sexual orientation? The discreet language of the chronicles sometimes suggests concern or, in the case of strongly partisan writing, appears to be overly defensive, insisting, for instance, on the permanent effect of absolution, as Roger of Howden does twice, in connection with Richard's acts of public penance.[18] There is also some evidence that later pre-twentieth-century scholars may have had their doubts. Bishop Stubbs makes a number of comments which could be interpreted in this way. On one occasion he compares Richard with William Rufus: 'there is a good deal of likeness between the worst points of Richard's character and that of William Rufus', only to add hastily that William '... seems to have been quite devoid of Richard's nobler traits'.[19] On another occasion, he concedes that Richard's vices were the 'normal' ones of the barrack-room, but qualifies this by saying that, however 'glaring in their foulness' these were, there was *probably* nothing more to it than that (my italics). A third comment also suggests a certain unease: 'As a knight errant, he might have fared better if the love of women had entered more into his adventures.'[20]

It is therefore in my view at least arguable that Richard's attitude to marriage and sex was problematic. He recognised the necessity of marriage and procreation and may have tried, especially at the beginning, to treat his wife correctly. He may even have been attracted to her in his youth, as some traditions suggest, and hoped that marriage to her would be successful. The reconciliation of 1195-6 may well have signalled a desire to start afresh. But old habits and more importantly his own temperament and inclination were increasingly urging him in another direction, and perhaps the enthusiasm with which he threw himself into tireless and at times almost reckless military activities provided an escape for such tensions.

It is important to avoid anachronistic judgements, too. Companionate marriage, though not entirely alien to medieval society, does not appear to have been widespread, and the sexes were segregated to a much greater extent than in western society today. But in as much as Richard enjoyed the company of others, and some chronicles speak of his affable and gregarious manner in private, he seems to have preferred the company of men, not only, of course, his official advisors and counsellors, but also his mercenaries and their captain, of whose baneful influence there can be little doubt. It was Mercadier who allegedly urged Richard to murder the saintly Hugh of Lincoln, whose advice on moral matters was clearly not always welcome. Mercadier was undoubtedly part of the 'bad company' Richard was accused by the clerics of keeping, and, if this story is true, it can only be because the mercenary recognised in the saintly but shrewd prelate a rival in the struggle for the king's soul.

Finally, many scholars have pointed out Richard's close emotional dependance on his mother, who, both as queen and confidante, left no place for Berengaria to grow into the role which should have been hers.

The lack of a child was a double blow for Berengaria. No doubt she was made to feel responsible for this by her husband's family and blamed by them, if not always by others. This charge, too, is not proven. Empress Matilda, for instance, had no children by her first husband but three by her second; Henry I of England had no children by his second wife Adeliza during fifteen years of marriage but she had sons by another husband.[21] Failure to conceive has many causes. It is also possible that Berengaria suffered miscarriages or still-births: deaths of children in extreme infancy were not always recorded, let alone miscarriages. In the judgement of history, however, it matters little: Berengaria has been labelled a 'barren' queen and judged accordingly.

If this reading of Richard's private life is correct, then Berengaria's situation would have been problematic from the start. Luis del Campo, whose work has been quoted previously, clearly agrees. Applying a psychocritical approach to the meagre historical evidence, he suggests that Richard's sexual ambivalence may have deprived him of satisfaction in his relations with women, including his wife, creating problems such as temporary impotence, frequent recourse to violence and perhaps deviant behaviour. Many contemporary witnesses testify to his violent temper, loud voice, furious face and so on, which contrasted with the affability and joviality which he displayed 'among intimates'.

Del Campo argues that Berengaria would have been unprepared for such a situation and found it hard to recover from this blow to her self-esteem. Because of this, he argues, she became, like her brother, inward-looking and mistrustful of others. Perhaps this is true, but whether or not this was the case, her pride and determination, coupled with a strong religious faith and an equally strong sense of duty ensured that she did not give in to despair. All her life and even after his death, she remained loyal to her husband and left no recorded word of reproach. Proudly and even defiantly she styled herself queen of the English and insisted on what was due to her rank and dignity. She gave no comfort by word or deed to her husband's enemies. Her silence and acceptance have been construed as passivity and timidity, and her private sorrows went unheeded and unassuaged, except perhaps by those who were close to her. And these, too, kept their counsel.

But all is not silence. The effigy of Berengaria in the chapter house at the abbey of l'Epau is striking by any standards. The figure of the queen, slightly larger than life-size, rests on a draped bier, with a pillow under her head. She is crowned: her hair is loosened and partly covered by a light veil. She is dressed in a long robe fastened at the waist by a girdle with a small purse attached to it, while the cloak which falls from her shoulders is caught up at the neck by an elaborate brooch. She holds in her hands a book, or possibly a reliquary in the form of a book, on the cover of which is her own image in miniature, on its bier with a large lighted candle on either side. Her feet rest on a lion, which holds pinned beneath it a small hound.

Very little attention has been paid to this effigy, except briefly in connection with the better known effigies of the Angevin monarchs at Fontevraud, with which it has been compared in respect of its general style and approximate dating (first half of the thirteenth century). These recumbent effigies were not common outside western France at this time and even after 1230 were far more numerous in England and areas of English influence. The Purbeck effigies in London are the best known examples of this later development.

In the early Middle Ages, sculpted tombs were largely the prerogative of saints and abbots, but in the twelfth century kings and nobles began to request that they too should be honoured in this way. Kings were usually depicted with their regalia of crown and sceptre just as they were when laid out on their death bed. Their eyes were usually depicted as closed and by the beginning of the thirteenth century serious efforts were being made to capture a likeness. Some of the heads may have been modelled on a death mask.

Alain Erlande-Brandenburg is the author of the most extensive studies of the Fontevraud effigies.[22] He concludes that the statues of Henry II and Richard were probably commissioned by Eleanor and executed by the same sculptor, a local man who knew the qualities of his material well. The statue of Eleanor, on the other hand, is by a very different artist: the moulding of the drapery is free and flowing and may have been modelled from her own living body at her own request, so that her effigy might lie beside those of her husband and her son and perhaps ensure that after her death, Philip Augustus or his agents would not allow her tomb to be dishonoured by neglect.

There are several important differences between the effigy of Berengaria and that of Eleanor, but in this respect at least they can be compared. Berengaria too, may have commissioned her own effigy and, if that is so, it is through this reposeful yet compelling stone portrait that she speaks to us today.

Unlike Eleanor, who wears a wimple and full veil beneath her crown, Berengaria's hair falls freely to her shoulders. Agnes Strickland was undoubtedly correct in seeing this as a representation of the queen as a virgin bride. Some recent studies of medieval queenship have seen in the liminal status of a queen the permanent tension between virginity and maternity, and this would have been enhanced in Christian art by its obvious Marian overtones. As a symbol of this rite of passage, a queen's hair was often worn loose on her wedding day. The wedding garment worn on the deathbed signifies another rite of passage and perhaps too prefigures the wedding garment of the parable, when the faithful are called to the marriage feast of the heavenly bridegroom.

Like those of her brother's effigy in the Colegio Real at Roncesvalles, Berengaria's eyes are not closed but look outward and upward, in a fixed gaze which compels us to look at her. Thus she both engages us as onlookers and looks beyond us in contemplation of something which we can as yet only see 'through a glass, darkly'.

Most striking of all is the book which she holds, not in a simulated reading position, as in Eleanor's case, but closed and close to her own heart, the all-important cover directed outwards to the attention of the onlooker. She holds it reverently and carefully, like a reliquary which contains a sacred object. The contents of the book, or reliquary, are hidden from us, but its cover provides a clue: it is the queen's own image, like a mirror within a mirror. We are reminded immediately of the practice of so many medieval artists, painters and sculptors, who depicted themselves or their benefactors in their works, kneeling among the shepherds at the Nativity, sheltering under the Virgin's cloak or holding a small model of the church or chapel they had helped to found. Berengaria here identifies herself as patron and founder of the abbey, associates herself with its offering of the perpetual sacrifice and asks to be remembered by those who will come to pray within its walls.

In a slightly different sense, we can say that she is offering her own story to the outside world, to a world which, as the Scriptures say, looks only on the outward show. Part of that story is her role as bride and queen, since it is as bride and queen that she has chosen to be remembered. In this light too, we may find some significance in the final detail of the sculpture, the ambiguous pose of the lion and the hound upon which the queen's feet are resting.

The use of a hound in this position is very common in such effigies in both England and France, and lions are not uncommon either. Occasionally a pair of animals, two dogs or two lions, is found in recumbent effigies, again, in both England and France. This particular combination is to my knowledge much more rare. But what is the lion doing to the dog? Some descriptions assume that the lion is attacking the dog, but this is questionable: the lion's claws are visible but not distended, its expression is watchful rather than aggressive. The dog lies submissively, in resignation perhaps; the head is turned sideways and its gaze, which betrays neither surprise, resistance nor distress, looks impassively out towards the onlooker, in unconscious imitation, it seems, of the queen herself. The lion looks away, watchfully, perhaps protectively or possessively. Its gaze does not engage with that of the onlooker, if he or she stands in the normal viewing position, at the feet of the statue. The intentions of this king of beasts are concealed. What does this pose suggest? Protection? Possession? Capture?

The medieval world was full of signs and symbols, often in incongruous and disturbing juxtaposition: the sublime and the grotesque, the banal and the lofty, the comic and the serious. Perhaps in this small detail the unknown sculptor has added his own playful postscript to the story of Coeur de Lion and his faithful queen.

Notes

1: WHY BERENGARIA?

1 The literature is now so extensive that it is not possible to summarise it in a single footnote. There are, however, a number of recent general overviews and review articles which trace the contribution of both 'women's history' and 'feminist history' to medieval studies. See G. Duby and M. Perrot, *Histoire des Femmes en Occident*, Paris 1991, vol. 2, *Le Moyen Age*, ed. Christiane Klapisch-Zuber, (translated into English as *A History of Women in the West*, Cambridge Mass. 1992-4) See also the excellent review article by Elizabeth Van Houts, 'The State of Research, Women in Medieval History and Literature', *Journal of Medieval History*, 20 (1994), pp. 272-92. The April 1993 issue of *Speculum* was entirely devoted to feminist approaches to medieval studies.

2 In his lively if somewhat partisan biography, *Richard the Lionheart*, London 1989.

3 M. Meade, *Eleanor of Aquitaine*, New York 1977. This is but one of a plethora of biographies of Eleanor, starting with the work of Amy Kelly, *Eleanor of Aquitaine and the Four Kings*, London 1952, which paint a somewhat romanticised portrait of Eleanor. An unsurpassed record was set in this respect by the French author Jean Markale, *Aliénor d'Aquitaine*, Paris 1979.

4 London 1900.

5 *Medieval Women and the Sources of Medieval History*, Athens, Ga and London 1990. See also 'Women and the Writing of History', in J.M. Ferrante, *To the Glory of Her Sex*, Indiana 1997, pp. 68-106.

6 J. Anderson and B. Zinsser, *A History of Their Own*, New York and London 1988, vol. 1, p. xvii.

7 Barbara Newman, 'Flaws in the Golden Bowl. Gender and Spiritual Formation in the Twelfth century', *Traditio* 45 (1989-90), pp. 111-46, reprinted in B. Newman, *From Virile Woman to Woman Christ*, Philadelphia 1995.

8 Peter Brown, *The Body and Society: Men, Women and Sexual Renunciation in Early Christianity*, New York 1988. Grace Jantzen, *Power, Gender and Christian Mysticism*, Cambridge and New York 1995.

9 David Herlihy, 'Did Women have a Renaissance?', *Medievalia et Humanistica*, 1985, pp. 1-22 (reprinted in *Women and Family in Medieval Europe*, ed. A.

Molho, *Providence* 1995, pp. 33-56); *Medieval Households*, Harvard 1985.

10 See, for instance, C. Richard, *Notice sur Richard Coeur de Lion*, Rouen 1839, who claimed that Richard 'lived, no doubt, in detestable times, but he was detestable even by those standards' or indeed, the disapproving tone which surfaces from time to time in A. Richard, *Histoire des comtes de Poitou*, Paris 1903. Régine Pernoud's popular biography, *Richard Coeur de Lion*, Paris 1988, attempts greater impartiality, but still contrasts noticeably with the enthusiastic partisanship of Bridge and the skilled advocacy of John Gillingham in *Richard the Lionheart*, London 1978, new edition 1989.

11 A useful general history of medieval Spain is Bernard Reilly, *The Medieval Spains*, Cambridge 1993 and see also Robert I. Burns, S.J., *The Worlds of Alfonso the Learned and James the Conqueror*, Princeton 1985. Spanish readers will be familiar with the multi-volume series by Ramón Menéndez Pidal, *Historia de España*, 18 vols, Madrid 1957 onwards.

12 Chris Given-Wilson and Alice Curteis, *The Royal Bastards of Medieval England*, London 1984.

13 'The Unromantic Death of Richard I', *Speculum*, 54 (1979), pp. 18-41, reprinted in *Richard Coeur de Lion*, London 1994. This volume is a selection of articles written by Gillingham on the subject of Richard, with updated bibliographical comment and an historiographical introduction.

14 See discussion of this in chapter 4, pp. 132-3 and references.

15 Wace was the official historiographer of Henry II and undertook two synthetic histories, the *Roman de Rou* (Romance of Rollo), a history of the dukes of Normandy and the *Roman de Brut*, the story of the British people, a vernacular adaptation of Geoffrey of Monmouth's *Historia Regum Britanniae*. In this work especially, however, he included elements of doubtful historicity such as the Round Table and a number of other motifs which were taken up by romance writers like Chrétien de Troyes. For this, as much as for his innovative use of the octosyllabic rhyming couplet and other stylistic features, he is seen as one of the originators of the Matter of Britain.

16 *Histoire de Guillaume le Maréchal*, ed. P. Meyer, 3 vols, Paris 1891. This text has not been translated into English, but there are two well-known secondary sources in English, and one in French, which provide both a synopsis and an analysis: S. Painter, *William Marshall*, Baltimore 1933; David Crouch, *William Marshal, Court, Career and Chivalry in the Angevin Empire*, New York and London 1990; G. Duby, *Guillaume le Maréchal*, Paris 1984.

17 *Mâle Moyen Age*, Paris 1988, English translation by J. Dunnett 1994, with the inadequate title *Love and Marriage in the Middle Ages*. Duby makes the point clearly in his contribution to the volume cited above, in the series *Histoire des Femmes:* '... the historian who seeks to examine the real situation of women at the time should not forget that courtly love (*la fine amour*), as he finds it represented, is a literary creation, a cultural construct which developed autonomously. In the final resort it is a literature

of escapism ...' from 'Le modèle courtois', *Histoire des Femmes en Occident*, pp. 261-6.

18 The so-called *cantigas de domna*, or *Frauenlieder* for instance: see Peter Dronke, *The Medieval Lyric*, 2nd ed., London 1978.

19 The life and work of this notorious figure is discussed by all the earlier authorities on the troubadour poetry, Jeanroy, Anglade, Mahn, and more recently by Kohler, Bec, Camproux, Riquer etc. The most recent comprehensive treatment in English of William of Aquitaine is that by Gerald Bond, *William VII Count of Poitiers: Poetry*, New York 1989. Much older but still extremely useful, in respect of the links between the troubadours and the Angevins is the short work by H.J. Chaytor, *The Troubadours and England*, Cambridge 1923.

20 William Paden, *The Voice of the Trobairitz*, Pennsylvania 1989; M.T. Bruckner et al., *Songs of the Women Troubadours*, New York 1995.

21 In Boccaccio and Chaucer, for instance, in the story of Griseldis. See also J. Wood, 'The Calumniated Wife in Medieval Welsh Literature', *Cambridge Medieval Celtic Studies*, 10 (1985), pp. 25-38. In a recent book, Andrew Breeze has made the controversial suggestion that the *Four Branches of the Mabinogi*, in which the stories of Rhiannon and Branwen are obvious examples of this tale type, were written by a woman: A. Breeze, *Medieval Welsh Literature*, Dublin 1996.

22 Some scholars, like Duby, have seen the literature of 'courtly love' as decidedly ambivalent, if not downright misogynistic: see for instance Howard Bloch;

Medieval Misogyny and the Invention of Western Romantic Love, Chicago 1991.

23 Agnes Strickland, *Lives of the Queens of England*, 1st ed., London 1840.

24 Mary Anne Everett Green, *Lives of the Princesses of England*, London 1849, vol. 1. Berengaria is described in the chapter on Joanna, her sister in law, in somewhat lush language: '... the lovely and gentle Berengaria, the spirited Joanna, equally beautiful though in a style strikingly dissimilar, with the melancholy dark-eyed Greek maiden reclining at their feet ...' (vol. 1, p. 357) The novelist Norah Lofts also wrote a popular history of the *Queens of Britain*, London 1977, with a very brief account of Berengaria (pp. 37-40) whose 'beauty and devotion were wasted on the homosexual Richard'.

25 *Berengaria: Enigmatic Queen of England*, Pook's Hill (UK) 1986.

26 *Histoire de la reine Bérengère, femme de Richard Coeur de Lion*, Le Mans 1866. Another early but still useful overview is found in Dom L. Piolin, 'Bérengère, reine d'Angleterre, Dame du Mans', *Revue des Questions Historiques*, 49 (1890), pp. 174-83.

27 Elizabeth Hallam, 'Bérengère de Navarre: les Plantagenêts et les Capétiens', *La Province du Maine*, 19 (1991), pp. 225-37.

28 The principal chronicles are: Roger of Howden, *Gesta Henrici II et Ricardi I*, ed. W. Stubbs, 2 vols, Rolls Series 49, 1867 (formerly attributed to 'Benedict of Peterborough'); *Chronica*, ed. W. Stubbs, 4 vols, Rolls Series 51, 1868-71 (English translation by Riley) (London 1853, 2 vols); Richard of Devizes, *Chronicle*, ed. J. Howlett, Rolls Series 1886, III and more recently, ed. tr. J.

Appleby, London 1963; Ralph of Diceto, *Opera*, ed. W. Stubbs, 2 vols Rolls Series 68, 1876; Ralph of Coggeshall, *Chronicon Anglicanum*, ed. J. Stevenson, Rolls Series 66, 1875; William of Newburgh, *Historia Regum Anglicarum*, 2 vols, *Chronicles of the Reigns of Stephen, Henry II and Richard I*, ed. R.G. Howlett, Rolls Series 82, 1884; Ranulph of Higden, *Polychronicon*, ed. J. Lumby, Rolls Series 41, 1882, Giraldus Cambrensis, *De Principis Instructione*, ed. G. Warner, Rolls Series 1891 and *De Rebus a Se Gestis*, ed. J. Brewer, Rolls Series 1861; *Oeuvres de Rigord et Guillaume le Breton*,ed. H.F. Delaborde, 2 vols, Paris 1882-5. For the crusade chronicles, see chapter 3. A general discussion of these and other contemporary writers is to be found in Antonia Gransden, *Historical Writing in England, c.550-c.1307*, London 1974.

29 Gillingham has written several books and a number of articles on Richard himself and on the so-called Angevin Empire. Among the most important are: *Richard the Lionheart* London 1978, 1989; *The Life and Times of Richard I*, London 1973; *Richard Coeur de Lion* London 1994 (see note 13); 'Richard I and Berengaria of Navarre', *Bulletin of the Institute of Historical Research*, 53 (1980), pp. 157-73; *The Angevin Empire*, London 1984; 'The Art of Kingship: Richard I, 1189-99', *History Today*, 35 (April 1985), pp. 17-23; 'Conquering Kings: Some Reflections on Henry II and Richard I', in *Warriors and Churchmen in the High Middle Ages*, ed. T. Reuter, London, 1992, pp. 163-78. A recent overview of the period is the

useful and succinct Richard Mortimer, *Angevin England*, Oxford 1994.

30 There are several older biographies of Richard, of which Kate Norgate, *Richard the Lionheart*, London 1924 is still useful. Among more recent works is the biography by Anthony Bridge, cited above, and James Brundage *Richard Lionheart*, New York 1974. Brundage's view of Richard is more critical than that of the two English biographers and he supports the view that Richard was probably bisexual. Richard's itineraries have been traced by Lionel Landon, in his useful compilation *The Itinerary of King Richard I*, London 1935. Recent biographies in languages other han English include: Régine Pernoud, *Richard Coeur de Lion*, Paris 1988 and U. Kessler, *Richard I Löwenherz*, Graz 1995.

31 Bradford B. Broughton, *The Legends of King Richard I Coeur de Lion*, The Hague 1966; *Riccardo Cuor di Leone nella storia e nella leggenda*, Academia Nazionale dei Lincei, Anno CCCLXXVIII, Colloquio italo-britannico, Rome 1981; Janet Nelson, ed., *Richard Coeur de Lion in History and Myth*, London 1992. Also useful, though only for the earlier period, is G.H. Needler, *Richard Coeur de Lion in Literature*, Leipzig 1890.

32 John Carmi Parsons, *Medieval Queenship*, New York 1993. The essays in this volume build on such important earlier studies as those by M. Facinger, 'A Study of Medieval Queenship, Capetian France 987-1237', *Studies in Medieval and Renaissance History*, 5 (1968), pp. 3-48, Lois L. Huneycutt, 'Images of Queenship in the High Middle

Ages', *Haskins Society Journal:
Studies in Medieval History*, 1
(1989) pp. 61-72 and Pauline
Stafford, *Queens, Concubines
and Dowagers*, London 1983.
Edward Black, *Royal Brides and
Queens of England in the Middle
Ages*, London 1987 is descriptive
rather than analytical, in the
tradition of the earlier studies by
Agnes Strickland, Nora Lofts and
others. See also 'Never Better
Ruled by Any Man: Women as
Consorts, Regents and Rulers' in
A. Echols and M.N. Williams,
Between Pit and Pedestal, New
York 1994, chapter 3. A recent
collection of essays entitled
*Queens and Queenship in
Medieval Europe*, ed. A. Duggan,
Boydell Press, Woodbridge 1997,
further extends the discussion and
contains some excellent chapters.
Among recent full length biogra-
phies of individual queens, M.
Chibnall's excellent biography of
Empress Matilda must be singled
out as a model example. This
model can only be emulated
where there is an abundance of
primary sources, and sufficient
sustained narrative among them.

2: DAUGHTER

1 Jaime del Burgo, *Navarra*,
Madrid 1972.
2 Rachel Bard, *Navarre, the
Durable Kingdom*, Reno 1982.
3 For the history of Navarre in the
early years of its independence,
see, in the first instance, J.M.
Lacarra, *Historia Política del
Reino de Navarra*, 3 vols,
Pamplona 1971 and B. Leroy, *La
Navarre au moyen âge*, Paris
1984.
4 Susana Hereros Lopetegui, 'Las
Territorios Ultrapirinaicos y su
evolución historica' (kindly lent

by the author in proof copy only).
5 Robert I. Burns, S.J., *The Worlds
of Alfonso the Learned and James
the Conqueror*, Princeton 1988.
6 *Fuero General de Navarra*, ed.
Juan Utrilla Utrilla, Pamplona
1987, vol. II, p. 153 'De levantar
rey'.
7 J.M. Lacarra, *Guía del Archivo
General de Navarra*, Pamplona,
Madrid 1954.
8 A comprehensive and analytical
treatment of medieval Spanish
historical writing is found in Peter
Linehan, *History and the
Historians of Medieval Spain*,
Oxford 1993. See also E. Procter,
Alfonso X of Castile, Oxford
1951, chapter 5, 'Historical
works' and Linehan's brief but
informative article entitled '
History in a Changing World: the
case of Medieval Spain' in *Past
and Present in Medieval Spain*,
New York 1992.
9 Ed. L. Cooper, Zaragoza 1960.
10 Ed. R. Menéndez Pidal, Madrid
1955.
11 Ed. Josefa F. Martínez, Valencia
1968.
12 Ed. L. Cooper, Bogotá 1979.
13 Ed. Carmen Orcastegui Gros,
Pamplona 1977.
14 Ed. Carmen Orcastegui Gros,
Pamplona 1978.
15 On 18 December, almost a fort-
night after incurring his fatal
injuries. The date given by
Carlos, Príncipe de Viana, 1201,
does not tally with the evidence
from other sources, which give
the year as 1207.
16 P. Laslett ed., *Family and Illicit
Love in earlier generations*,
Cambridge 1977. See also R.
Turner, 'The Children of Anglo-
Norman Royalty and their
upbringing', *Medieval Prosopography*, 11 (1990), 2, pp. 17-52.
17 Jaume I, El Conqueridor, *Llibre
dels feyts del rey En Jaume*, in

Les Quatre Grans Cròniques ed.
F. Soldevila, Barcelona 1971.
18 Rodericus Ximenius de Rada,
Opera, ed. F. de Lorenzana,
Madrid 1793, reprint Valencia
1968, *De Rebus Hispaniae*, lib. v,
cap. XXIV, p. 114.
19 See the letters of Innocent III in
J.P. Migne, *Patrologiae latinae
cursus completus*, Paris 1858
(hereafter Migne); book 214, col.
509, letter 556.
20 T. Rymer, *Foedera, Conventiones,
Literae etc*, 1816-69, vol. I, p. 86.
21 Luis del Campo, *Dos Esculturas
de Sancho El Fuerte*, Pamplona
1976
22 On Rodrigo Jiménez as a
historian, see Linehan, op. cit.,
pp. 316ff.
23 Moret, *Anales*, vol. IV, p. 114
(see below note 25).
24 *Crónica* of Don Gonzalo de la
Hinojosa, in *Colección de
documentos inéditos para la
historia de España*, El Marqués
de la Fuensanta del Valle, Madrid
1893.
25 J. Moret y Mendi, *Anales del
Reino de Navarra* (Pamplona
1684-1704) published Tolosa
1890: a more recent edition by
Susana Hereros Lopetegui was in
preparation at the time of
writing.
26 Jose Goñi Gaztambide, *Historia
de los Obispos de Pamplona,
s.IV-XIII*, Pamplona 1979,
Ricardo García Villoslada,
'Leyendo la 'Historia de los
Obispos de Pamplona', *Hispania
Sacra*, XXXIV (1982), vol. 69,
pp. 255-88.
27 Carmen Orcastegui Gros, 'Tudela
durante los reinos de Sancho El
Fuerte y Teobaldo I', *Estudios de
Edad Media de la Corona de
Aragon*, X (1975), pp. 63ff and
'Tudela' in *Sedes Reales de
Navarra*, Gobierno de Navarra,
Pamplona 1990, pp. 106-28.

28 The most up to date and comprehensive biography of this king is
by Juan Francisco Elizari Huarte,
*Sancho VI El Sabio, Rey de
Navarra*, Reyes Pirinaicos, Iruña
1991. See also the relevant
summary of his reign in J.M.
Lacarra, *Historia Politica del
Reino de Navarra*, (see above n.
3). Unfortunately, neither of these
works is to my knowledge,
available in English translation.
29 The use of Basque, Hispano-
romance and Occitan in medieval
Navarre has been examined by
Ricardo Cierbide Martinena in
'Estado actual de los estudios de
la lengua occitana en Navarra,
línea de investigación', *Principe
de Viana* XLIX (1988), pp. 365-
76 and in 'La scripta administrativa en la Navarra medieval en
lengua occitana', *Zeitschrift für
Romanische Philologie*, 105
(1989), 3-4, pp. 276-312.
30 C. Sánchez-Albornoz, *Vascos y
Navarras en su primera historia*,
Madrid 1976; id. *La trayectoria
histórica de Vasconia. El destino
de Navarra*, Madrid 1977; J.M.
Lacarra, *Vasconia Medieval*, San
Sebastian 1957; Jose Orlandis,
'Sobre las minorias cristianas
como sujetos de la historia' in *El
método historico*, ed. W. Laslett,
Pamplona 1977, pp. 165-71. A
succinct account in English is
found in Roger Collins, *Early
Medieval Spain*, 2nd edition, New
York 1995, pp. 246ff.
31 See note 5 above and, by the
same author, 'Muslims in 13th
century Aragon' in *Muslims
under Latin Rule*, ed. T. Powell,
Princeton 1990, pp. 57-102.
32 B. Leroy, 'Les juifs de Navarre du
XIIe au XVe siècle', *Revue des
Etudes Juives*, 138 (1979) pp.
491-3, and particularly, by the
same author, *The Jews of Navarre
in the Late Middle Ages*,

Jerusalem 1985. See also M. García Arenal and B. Leroy, *Moros y judios en Navarra en la baja edad media*, Madrid 1984.

33 *Fuero General de Navarra*, ed. Juan Utrilla Utrilla, Pamplona 1987, vol. II, p. 100, 'de iudio muerto'.

34 F. Pérez Castro 'España y los judios españoles,' in *The Sephardi Heritage*, ed. R. Barnett, London 1971, vol. I, pp. 275-322.

35 See E. Taitz, *The Jews of Medieval France*, Westport, Connecticut 1994. On the other hand, Leroy, (*The Jews of Navarre in the Late Middle Ages*, pp. 138-9) argues that the situation began to deteriorate in the last years of the reign of Sancho El Fuerte, when the king's condition had begun to deteriorate.

36 Kenneth R. Stow, 'Hatred of the Jews or Love of the Church: Papal policy towards the Jews in the Middle Ages' in *Antisemitism through the Ages*, ed. S. Almog, Pergamon Press UK1988 pp. 71-87.

37 M. Dufourneaux, *Les Français en Espagne aux XI et XII siècles*, Paris 1949; J.M. Lacarra 'A propos de la colonisation 'franca' en Navarre et en Aragon', *Annales du Midi* LXV (1953) pp. 330-42. Lacarra points out that during the later waves of repopulation in Navarre, in the Ebro Valley for instance, the communities were not segregated as they were in earlier stages (as indicated by early *fueros* such as that of Jaca) and in the final stages, in Navarre proper and the Basque province of Guipúzcoa, which took place between 1180 and 1190, new 'mixed' suburbs were added to old ones in the city of Pamplona itself.

38 See the 1966 reprint of the classic *De los trovadores en España*, of

M. Mila y Fontanals, ed. C Martínez and F.R. Manrique, Barcelona 1966, pp. 222ff. and Carlos Alvar, *La poesía trovadoresca en España y Portugal*, Barcelona 1977.

39 John Harvey, 'Political and Cultural Exchange between England and the Iberian Peninsula in the Middle Ages' in *Literature, Culture and Society of the Middle Ages*, M.M. López ed., Barcelona 1989.

40 *Le Guide des Pélerins*, ed. J. Vieillard, Macon 1968.

41 Sancho El Fuerte is the subject of a large part of the poem by the late troubadour, Guilhem Anelier de Toulouse: see his *Histoire de la guerre de Navarre*, ed. F. Michel, Paris 1856 and Mila y Fontanals, op. cit., pp. 224ff. The poet calls Sancho '... bolder than a lion'.

42 And, in this respect, perhaps, unusual in the Spanish context: probably because of the demands of *repoblación*, the policy of settling Christians in areas where they had formerly been thin on the ground, rules such as consanguinity and indissolubility appear to have been observed less frequently. As Peter Linehan succinctly puts it, 'In the contest between the two 'models' of marriage, the 'lay' and the 'ecclesiastical' ... it is clear which side the peninsular episcopate was on.' (op. cit., p. 256).

43 Moret, *Anales*, IV, Bk XIX, p. 55.

44 Aziz Ahmad, *A History of Islamic Sicily*, Edinburgh 1975, pp. 58ff.

45 Luis del Campo, 'Cuatro Infantas Navarras' in *Navarra: Temas de Cultura Popular*, 120 (1971), pp. 4-31.

46 The most comprehensive recent biography of this king is that by Luis Javier Fortun Perez de Ciriza, in the series *Reyes de*

Navarra, Iruña 1987. See also the relevant summary in J.M. Lacarra, *Historia Política del Reino de Navarra*. Neither of these works is, to my knowledge, available in English translation. There is no comparable treatment of this monarch available in English.

47 Jaume I, El Conqueridor, *Llibre dels feyts*, ch. 138, p. 66ff.

48 As is well known, Jaume was Sancho's first preference as his successor, but the plan, mooted at the time of a treaty of 2 February 1231, pledging mutual assistance, was abandoned, allegedly due to unfavourable public opinion. On the life and times of this larger than life prince, see Robert I. Burns, S.J., 'The Spiritual Life of James the Conqueror, king of Arago-Catalonia 1208-1276: Portrait and Self-Portrait' in *Jaime I y su Epoca*, Congreso de Historia de la Corona de Aragon, Zaragoza 1980, pp. 323-57.

49 Little attention is paid to girls, for instance in N. Orme, *From Childhood to Chivalry*, London 1984 or Antonia Gransden, 'Childhood and Youth in Medieval England', *Nottingham Medieval Studies*, 16 (1972), pp. 3-19. More information is provided in the two works by Shulamit Shahar, *Childhood in the Middle Ages*, London 1990 and *The Fourth Estate*, London and New York 1983. See also, R.B. Tobin, 'Vincent de Beauvais on the Education of Women', *Journal of the History of Ideas*, 35 (1974), pp. 485-9 and the many additional references in Klapisch-Zuber cited above, chapter 1, note 1.

50 Anderson and Zinsser, op. cit., p. xv.

51 Available in English translation in David Staines, ed. tr. *Chrétien de Troyes, the Complete Romances*, or D.D.R. Owen, in the recent updated Everyman Classics translation. The Old French text has been edited several times, most recently by W. Roach and by F. Lecoy.

52 See for instance, the scene in the tent where a courtly lady is thrown off guard by the unexpected arrival of the blundering Perceval, and the far from chivalrous reaction of her knightly lover: Owen, op. cit., pp. 382-5.

53 See chapter 1, n. 1, Klapisch-Zuber, op. cit.

54 See, for instance, the proceedings of the conference held in 1981 entitled *La Condición de la mujer en la edad media*, Coloquio Hispano-Francés, Madrid 1986.

55 *Daughters of the Reconquest*, Cambridge 1984.

56 *Fuero General de Navarra*, Book 4; 1, 2.

57 See n. 45 above.

58 F. López Estrada, 'Las mujeres escritores en la Edad Media castellana' in *La condición de la mujer en la edad media* (n. 54 above). See also *Las Siete Partidas del rey don Alfonso el Sabio*, Madrid 1807.

59 Santos A. García Larragueta, *El Gran Priorado de Navarra de la Orden de San Juan de Jerusalén*, Institución Príncipe de Viana, Pamplona 1957, vol. 2, p. 60, Colección diplomatica, document 54. It is also possible that the reference may be to the town of Monreal, some thirty kilometres south east of Pamplona.

60 A. Ubieto Arteta, 'Aportación al estudio de la 'tenencia' medieval; la mujer 'tenente', *Estudios de Edad Media de la Corona de Aragon*, X (1975), pp. 47-61.

61 The letters of Adam of Perseigne have been edited by Canon J.

Bouvet, *Adam de Perseigne, Lettres*, Paris 1960 and also in *Archives Historiques du Maine* XIII, vols 1-10, 1951-1962. They are also available in Migne's *Patrologia Latina*. English text in Grace Perigo, Adam of Perseigne, *Letters*, Kalamazoo 1970.

3: BRIDE

1 Such was certainly the view of the influential Bishop W. Stubbs, who edited a number of the early chronicles and set out his judgements on men and events in the lengthy prefaces to these editions. An interesting study of Stubbs's attitudes – many of which today seem pompous, judgemental and complacently ethnocentric, if not racist, – can be found in G.O. Sayles, 'The Changed Concept of History: Stubbs and Renan' in *Scripta Diversa*, London 1982, pp. 133-50. As the author dryly observes, '... his approach was not that of the enquiring and objective spirit.'

2 See notes 28-31, chapter one.

3 The question of homosexual behaviour – not to say, homosexuality as a condition – in the Middle Ages is a vexed one, despite the existence of a large secondary literature. See: W. Johansson and W.A. Percy 'Homosexuality' in *A Handbook of Medieval* Sexuality, eds V.L. Bullough and James Brundage, New York 1996, pp. 155-89. Many scholars argue that the main difference between the modern and the medieval viewpoints is that, in medieval times, individual actions did not define a person's status as homosexual and that such acts were regarded differently in different circumstances. For a comprehensive

summary of the debate, and the primary sources on which conflicting theories are based, see Anne Gilmour-Bryson, 'Sodomy and the Knights Templar', *Journal of the History of Sexuality*, 7, no. 2 (1996), pp. 151-83. This study complements and brings up to date the earlier survey in H.J. Kuster and R.J. Cormier, 'Old and New Trends. Observations on the Problem of Homosexuality in the Middle Ages', *Studi Medievali*, 25 (1984), pp. 587-610. Several English kings have been identified as homosexual, but, it has been pointed out, the language of male affection, used by lay as well as monastic writers, may be interpreted quite differently. Pierre Chaplais's recent book on Piers Gaveston uses similar arguments to attack the common view that Gaveston was Edward II's homosexual lover. Some of the evidence adduced in such discussions seems to suggest that in the Middle Ages, as today, according to Kinsey and subsequent researchers, many men who would not describe themselves as gay have at one time or another had sex with men, and a number of these men are or have been married.

4 Giraldus Cambrensis, *De Principis Instructione*, (*Opera*) ed. G. Warner, London, Rolls Series 1891, 8 vols.

5 William of Tyre, *A History of Deeds Done beyond the Sea*, ed. E. Babcock and A.C. Krey, New York 1943, vol. 2, p. 186.

6 E.R. Labande, 'Les filles d'Aliénor d'Aquitaine: étude comparative', *Cahiers de Civilisation Médiévale*, 29 (1986), 101-12.

7 See the often cited article by E.R. Labande, 'Pour une image

véridique d'Aliénor d'Aquitaine', *Bulletin de la Société des Antiquaires de l'ouest*, II, série 4, Poitiers 1952, and F.M. Chambers, 'Some Legends Concerning Eleanor of Aquitaine', *Speculum*, 16 (1944), 459-68. J. Richardson in 'The Letters and Charters of Eleanor of Aquitaine', *English Historical Review* 74 (1959), pp. 193-219, takes a very much more sceptical view: 'The impression conveyed by modern writers that Eleanor kept continuous court at Poitiers until her flight and capture in 1173 – 'the presiding genius in a society of troubadours and knights' – cannot be correct. She certainly travelled outside Poitou from time to time during those years and was perhaps more often absent than present.' (p. 198)

8 See M.D. Legge, 'Beaumont Palace' in *Etudes de Civilisation Médiévale*, Mélanges offerts à E.R. Labande, Poitiers 1990, pp. 491-5.

9 A. Richard, *Histoire des Comtes de Poitou, 778-1204*, Paris 1903.

10 Richard's nickname, Oc-e-No, has been interpreted in different ways. While some argue that it means a vacillating person (which does not appear to fit the Richard of the chronicles) others have explained it as meaning ' a person whose Yes is Yes and whose No is No'. Is there any evidence that Richard was familiar with Abelard's influential philosophical tract *Sic et Non*, which was written shortly after his official condemnation by the Council of Soissons in 1121? The tract became well-known among theologians like Peter Lombard and even Aquinas was influenced by its methodology. It seems unlikely, given what we know of Richard's character and tastes

and in the absence of any logical explanation it seems best to adopt the position stated by K. Lewent in his article 'The Pseudonym Oc-e-No', *Modern Language Review*, 38 (1943) p. 113ff, which is outlined above.

11 The classic exposition of this idea is found in the article written by the late Georges Duby entitled, 'Au XIIe siècle: les 'jeunes' dans la société aristocratique', *Annales*, 19 (1964), pp. 835-46. See also J.A. Burrow, *The Ages of Man*, Oxford 1986.

12 J.K. Beitsche, ' "As the twig is bent" – children and their parents in an aristocratic society', *Journal of Medieval History*, 2 (1976), pp. 181-92; Ralph V. Turner 'Eleanor of Aquitaine and her children: an enquiry into medieval family attachment', ibid, vol. 14 (1988), pp. 321-36; and 'The Children of Anglo-Norman Royalty and their upbringing' in *Medieval Prosopography*, (1990), 2, pp. 17-32.

13 For a concise overview of the external policies of Henry II, see John Gillingham, *The Angevin Empire*, 1984.

14 W. Paden, ed. *The poems of the troubadour Bertran de Born*, no. 35, p. 381, 'S'ieu fos aissi segner' C.A.F. Mahn, *Werke der Trobadors*, I, Berlin 1846, pp. 299.

15 See Mila y Fontanals, op. cit. In the *tenso* (debate poem) beginning 'S'ie us qier cosseil, bel-l'ami Alamanda ...' the troubadour Giraut de Borneil asks a lady, the possibly fictitious Alamanda, for advice on love matters and protests at one point that better advice had been given him by 'Lady Berenguera' (Ruth Verity Sharman, *The Cansos and Sirventes of the Troubadour Giraut de Borneil*, Cambridge

1989, p. 384ff) Giraut spent some time in Spain, probably at the Court of Alfonso II of Aragon, and mentions King Sancho El Sabio of Navarre, but it would be drawing a very long bow indeed to suggest that this is a reference to the Infanta of Navarre, given that the name Berenguela/Berenguera was extremely common at the time.

16 Broughton, op. cit., pp. 132-6.

17 J.L. Flandrin, 'Mariage tardif et vie sexuelle', *Annales*, 27 (1972), pp. 135-75.

18 Lacarra, *Historia*, vol. III, p. 80; Elizari, *Sancho El Sabio*, pp. 188-9. At this meeting the troubadour Guilhem de Berguedà was also present: Martin de Riquer, *Los Trovadores*, Barcelona 1975, vol. I, p. 520.

19 Moret, *Anales*, IV, Bk. XIX, p. 55ff, suggests that the negotiations began in 1186, the year after the meeting at Najac.

20 The role of the medieval mercenary is well analysed by Stephen Brown, 'The Mercenary and his Master; Military Service and Monetary Reward in the 11th and 12th centuries', *History*, 74 (1989) pp. 20-38. On the sinister Mercadier, see H. Géraud, 'Mercadier; les routiers au treizième siècle', *Bibliothèque de l'Ecole des Chartes*, 1842, 3, pp. 417-43.

21 A comprehensive overview of his reign, in English, is J.R. Baldwin, *The Government of Philip Augustus*, Berkeley 1986.

22 J. Boswell, *Christianity, Social Tolerance and Homosexuality*, Chicago 1980 pp. 231-2. Some of Boswell's key ideas have been challenged by Johanssen and Perey in the *Handbook of Medieval Sexuality* (ed. Bullough and Brundage), pp. 155-89 at pp. 178-9.

23 See John Baldwin, 'Five discourses on desire: Sexuality and Gender in Northern France, c.1200', *Speculum* 66 (1991), pp. 797-819, especially pp. 808ff and 814ff.

24 in 'L'Amour des Rois: structure sociale d'une forme de sensibilité aristocratique', *Annales* 46, 3 (1991), pp. 547-71.

25 It is curious that, despite the progression from 'women's studies', through 'feminist studies' to 'gender studies' in other areas of history, the concept of masculinity in the Middle Ages has been all but ignored. Whether this is due to the supposed conservatism of medievalists, some of whom may have assumed that masculinity was the norm, is difficult to say. See Clare A. Lees, ed., *Medieval Masculinities*, Minnesota 1994.

26 The French on the other hand, see him as one of their greatest kings: representative in this respect is the view of R.H. Bautier in 'Philippe Auguste, la personnalité du roi' in *Etudes sur la France capétienne*, New York 1992. It was inevitable that a revisionist view of this king would appear in English: see J. Bradbury, *Philip Augustus*, London and New York 1998.

27 J. Misrahi and W. Henderson, 'Roland and Oliver: Prowess and Wisdom, the Ideal of the Epic Hero', *Romance Philology*, XXXIII (1980), pp. 357-72. Bradbury, on the other hand, refers to Richard as a 'kind of maniac'! (op. cit., p. 333)

28 Ralph of Diceto, *Opera Historica*, ed. W. Stubbs, Rolls Series 68, London 1876, II, 50ff.

29 *Itinerarium Peregrinorum et Gesta Regis Ricardi*, ed. W. Stubbs, Rolls Series, London 1864. There are modern English versions by K. Fenwick, *The*

Third Crusade, London 1968,
and Helen Nicholson, *Chronicle
of the Third Crusade*, Aldershot,
1997.

30 ed. Gaston Paris, Paris 1897;
English version in *The Crusade of
Richard Lion-heart*, by M.J.
Hubert and J.L. La Monte, New
York 1976 (1941), (free verse
translation) and in E.N. Stone,
*Three Old French Chronicles of
the Crusades*, Washington 1939
(prose translation). I am not concerned here with the complex
question of the relationship
between these texts, or the multiple authorship of the *Itinerarium*.

31 M.W. Labarge, *Medieval
Travellers*, London 1982; N.
Ohler, *The Medieval Traveller*, tr.
J. Hillier, Suffolk 1989.

32 The account which follows, of
Richard's movements during the
crusade, is based on Lionel
Landon, *The Itinerary of Richard
I*, Pipe Roll Society 51 (1935) and
the principal primary sources
from which it is is drawn.
Landon's chronology may be
inaccurate in minor respects, and
the authenticity of some of the
charters he has used has been
questioned, but such questions
properly concern Richard's
biographers and do not throw
light on the activities of
Berengaria, which are not well
documented by Landon. See also
J.C. Holt and R. Mortimer, eds
Acta of Henry II and Richard I,
Gateshead 1986.

33 Similar instances of national prejudices abound in both Ambroise
and the *Itinerarium*: see
Itinerarium, Bk. 5, ch. 20, where
the author lambastes the French
for 'hanging about' (*vacabant*) in
taverns, dressing effeminately and
smashing their way into brothels.

34 H.F. Delaborde, *Recueil des Actes
de Philippe Auguste*, vol. I, Paris

1916, p. 464, no. 376. As part of
the settlement, Richard gave
Tancred Arthur's sword,
Excalibur (Howden, *Chronica*, 3,
p. 97). As to how he came by
such an item, see Emma Mason,
'The Hero's Invincible Weapon:
an Aspect of Angevin Propaganda' in *The Ideals and Practice
of Medieval Knighthood* III, eds
C. Harper-Bill and R. Harvey,
Woodbridge 1989, pp. 121–36.

35 Howden, *Gesta* vol. II, pp. 140-1.

36 Howden, *Chronica* III, p. 74.

37 Ambroise, *Estoire de la guerre
sainte*, ed. G. Paris, Paris 1897, ll.
1138ff.

38 *De rebus Anglicis*, Book IV, p. 24,
in Bouquet, *Recueil des
Historiens de la Gaule et de la
France*, 1878, vol. XVIII. William
of Newburgh suggests that
Richard married Berengaria as a
remedy against the 'great dangers
of fornication'.

39 Ranulph of Higden,
Polychronicon, ed. J. Lumby,
Rolls Series 41, VIII, p. 106.

40 Karl Brunner, ed., *Der mittelenglische Versroman über
Richard Löwenherz*, Vienna
1913. This romance is thought to
have been an adaptation of a lost
Anglo-Norman original: 'In
Frenssche bookys this rym is
wrought: Lewede men ne knowe
it nought/ Lewede men canne
Ffrenshe non ...' The Prose text
known as *The Crusade and
Death of Richard I*, ed. R.C.
Johnston, Oxford 1961, does not
discuss Richard's marriage.

41 Ed. Brunner, ll.204off (variant
version).

42 Richard of Devizes, *Chronicle*,
ed. Howlett, Rolls Series, 1886,
III, p. 422 or in Appleby's modern
edition, pp. 26 ff.

43 'Of all the writers, the original
author of the *Itinerarium
Peregrinorum* was presumably

the only one who ever saw Berengaria.' J. Ramsay, *Angevin England*, London 1903, p. 175. To this we must probably add Roger of Howden and Ambroise.

44 *The Chronicle of Pierre de Langtoft*, ed. Wright, Rolls Series 47, London 1866, II, pp. 47ff.

45 P.W. Edbury, *The Kingdom of Cyprus and the Crusades, 1191–1374*, Cambridge 1991.

46 Ambroise, *Estoire*, II, p. 1735ff; cf. *Itinerarium*, Bk 2, ch. 35 (p. 195) The marriage is briefly reported in Howden, *Gesta*, II, p. 166 and *Chronica*, III, p. 110. The Middle English romance also reports the wedding in celebratory terms: 'There Kyng Ric spoused Beringer,/the kynges doughter of Nauuer,/ and made ther the richest spousyng/ That euer maked any kyng,/And corouned himself emperour,/ and her emperice with honoure;' (ed. Brunner, line 2456ff, variant version). The references to Berengaria occur only in Brunner's version 'b', represented by five of the eight MSS: see the stemma in Brunner's edition, page 14 and comments on page 18, where the references to Eleanor, Berengaria and Joanna in version 'b' are attributed to a reviser who 'believed he had to fill in historical facts.'

47 E. Makowski, 'The Conjugal Debt and Medieval Canon Law' in *Women in the Middle Ages: Equally in God's Image*, ed. J.B. Holloway et al., New York 1990. Against this view, see: Dyan Elliott, 'Bernardino of Siena vs. the Marriage Debt' in *Desire and Discipline: Sex and Sexuality in the Pre-Modern West*, ed. J. Murray and K. Eisenbichler, Toronto 1996, pp. 168-200.

48 *The Medieval Idea of Marriage*, Oxford 1989. Duby has discussed this topic in a number of his best-known publications, in particular, *Medieval Marriage*, Baltimore 1978.

49 My translation from the edition by Bartina H. Wind, *Les fragments du Tristan de Thomas*, Paris 1960. An excellent English version is that by A.T. Hatto, appended to his translation of the *Tristan* of Gottfried von Strassburg in the Penguin Classics series (1960).

50 '*Fin'amors*' is the term used by the troubadours. It has sometimes been equated with the more general 'courtly love' but there are significant differences in the treatment of love by the southern troubadours and the romance-writers of northern France, the most significant one being that, with the exception of the Tristan and Lancelot stories, the latter favoured traditional love situations which led to marriage, rather than adulterous affairs.

51 Namely, M. Hewlett, *The Life and Times of Richard Yea and Nay*. The Tristan story has many associations with the House of Anjou, see R.S. Loomis, 'Tristram and the House of Anjou', *Modern Language Review*, XLVII (1922), pp. 24-30. I have pointed out the similarities between the situation of Berengaria and the bride of Tristan in 'Nouvelles perspectives sur le personnage d'Iseut aux Blanches Mains', *Tristan-Tristrant*, Mélanges en l'honneur de Danielle Buschinger, eds A. Crépin and W. Spiewok, Greifswald 1996.

52 Martène and Durand, *Veterum Scriptorum et Monumentorum historicorum dogmaticorum moralium amplissima collectio*, vol. I, 1724: 33, col. 995.

53 Susana Hereros Lopetegui, 'El Castillo de Rocabruna en

Ultrapuertos: una nueva teoria sobre su localización', paper presented to the second *Congreso General de Historia de Navarra*, Pamplona-Estella, 25-29 September 1990 (details of subsequent publication not known to me.)

54 W. Rudt de Collenberg, 'L'Empereur Isaac de Chypre et sa fille (1155-1207)', *Byzantion*, 38 (1968), pp. 123-79.

55 See Helen Nicholson, 'Women on the Third Crusade', *Journal of Medieval History*, 23 (4) (1997), p. 339ff. This article barely mentions Berengaria.

56 Régine Pernoud, *La Femme au Temps des Croisades*, Paris 1989.

57 The narrative which follows is based mainly on the three principal crusade sources, Howden, Ambroise and the *Itinerarium*.

58 E.N. Stone, *Three Old French Chronicles of the Crusades*, Washington 1939, pp. 40-1

59 *Itinerarium*, Bk 4, ch. 4, p. 243, Ambroise, ll. 5513-42. Both authors seek to place the action in as favourable a light as possible. This may perhaps be an indication that others, even on the Christian side, did not.

60 On Richard's 'tough and versatile men' and the loyalty which he inspired in them, see J.O. Prestwich 'Richard Coeur de Lion: Rex Bellicosus' in *Riccardo Cuor di Leone nella storia e nella leggenda* (note 31, chapter 1, above).

61 Some credence might be lent to this possibility in view of the fact that still-births and miscarriages were not normally recorded officially and early miscarriages are not always recognised as such.

62 Jean Mouzat, ed., *Les poèmes de Gaucelm Faidit*, Geneva 1989 (reprint) pp. 415ff. The author of

the *Histoire de Guillaume le Maréchal* was even more extravagant in his eulogy: 'Dead was the noble king, Richard the brave and the courtly, the generous giver, the daring, the conquering, who would have carried off the prize of this whole world if he had lived, even the sovereignty and the dominion and the lordship and the honour of Muslims and Christians and of all mankind on earth.' (*Histoire*, ed. Meyer, lines 11819-11828). Richard was seen by the writer of the *Itinerarium* and by Ambroise as the quintessential martial hero: see *Itinerarium*, Bk. 6, ch. 23, pp. 366-7 where he is compared to the classical heroes Antaeus, Achilles and Alexander, the biblical Judas Maccabaeus and the Frankish Roland.

63 Giraut de Borneil; this troubadour also laments the death of Richard in the poem 'Si per mon sobre-totz non fos'; see Ruth Verity Sharman, *The Cansos and Sirventes of the Troubadour Giraut de Borneil: A Critical Edition*, Cambridge 1989, p. 473ff.

4: QUEEN

1 S. Shahar, *Childhood in the Middle Ages*, London 1990, p. 371: 'A woman who did not take the veil but never gave birth had failed in the central function assigned to her by nature according to the Divine will ...'

2 See Broughton, op. cit., pp. 70-1.

3 The story of Richard's captivity and of the negotiations which secured his release, which are not covered in detail here, can be read in John Gillingham's biography of Richard, cited above, at pp. 217-40.

4 Mahn, *Die Werke der Trobadors*, Paris & Berlin 1846-86.

5 J.H. Round, *Calendar of Documents present in France, illustrative of the History of Great Britain and Ireland*, vol. I, 918-1206, London HMSO 1899, p. 94.

6 Howden, *Chronica*, III, p. 133.

7 Howden, *Chronica*, III, p. 228.

8 So called because of the derivation of the Old French word for 'Yes' which is *Oïl* (from Latin *hoc ille*) 'That's it'.

9 Howden, *Chronica*, III, p. 216ff.

10 Howden, *Chronica*, III, p. 247ff.

11 See R. Heiser, 'The Royal Familiares of King Richard I', *Medieval Prosopography*, 10 (1989), pp. 227-50 for an interesting analysis of the importance of Richard's regular advisors, based on the charter witness evidence.

12 See for instance, the description of the coronation of King Arthur and his queen in Wace's *Romance of Brut*, ed. I. Arnold, Paris 1938-40, lines 10301-10542. In this passage, probably based on a similar one in Geoffrey of Monmouth's *Historia Regum Britanniae*, the king and queen are escorted separately to their coronation and eat separately with their respective retinues. Although the subject matter is fictitious, the practice described may reflect contemporary custom.

13 Rigord, *Gesta Philippi Augusti* in *Oeuvres de Rigord et de Guillaume le Breton*, ed. H.F. Delaborde, Paris 1882-5, vol. 1, pp. 124-5. Ingeborg's tragic story has been discussed by many commentators, and various solutions proposed to the riddle of the wedding night. The latest discussion is that by George Conklin in the volume *Queens and Queenship in Medieval Europe*, edited by A. Duggan (see above, note 32, chapter 1) pp. 39-52. In keeping with his revisionist view of Philip, Jim Bradbury plays down Philip's responsibility in the matter, while admitting that he treated his queen 'harshly' (op. cit., p. 183).

14 Régine Pernoud, *Isambour, la Reine Captive*, Paris 1987. Philip also treated his first wife Isabelle, in an inconsiderate way. He tried to repudiate her in 1184, after four years of marriage but popular sympathy and Church pressure forced him to back down. Isabelle (Elizabeth) died in childbirth in 1190.

15 From Nature's Confession, in the *Romance of the Rose*, ed. tr. C. Dahlberg, Princeton 1995, p. 280.

16 *Histoire de Guillaume le Maréchal*, ed. Meyer, lines 11596ff. This outburst was provoked by what Richard saw as inappropriate support for a cleric who had forfeited the respect which was due to his office. Prior to this, Richard had demonstrated moderation and a willingness to compromise, especially when the nuncio appealed for peace between England and France for the sake of the Holy Land. That Richard may still have hoped to return is suggested by Howden, *Chronica*, III, p. 233.

17 *Chronique des Eglises d'Anjou*, ed. Marchegay and Salmon, Paris 1869, pp. 49ff.

18 The Spanish sources differ on this point: see Elizari, *Sancho El Sabio*, pp. 205-7.

19 J. Boase, 'Fontevraud and the Plantagenets', *Journal of the British Archaeological Association*, 3rd series, 34 (1971), p. 1; J.M. Bienvenu, 'Aliénor

d'Aquitaine et Fontevraud', *Cahiers de Civilisation Médiévale*, 29 (1986), pp. 15-27.

20 Howden, *Chronica* III, p. 288ff. My translation. (Another English version in Riley's translation, pp. 356-7).

21 Coggeshall, for instance, in his *Chronicon Anglicanum*, pp. 90 ff.

22 Adam of Eynsham, *Magna Vita Sancti Hugonis*, ed. tr. D.L. Douie and D.H. Farmer, Oxford 1985. The other contemporary biography of St Hugh, by Gerald of Wales, is much less specific: it speaks merely of 'certain serious and irregular excesses' ('... *super excessibus quibusdam gravibus et enormibus ...') Vita Sancti Hugonis*, ed. R.M. Loomis, New York and London 1985, pp. 28-9.

23 Translated into English by A. Fedrick, Penguin 1970. The Old French text was edited, with notes in English by Alfred Ewert in 1957.

24 Dom J. Leclercq has discussed this motif in 'Monks and Hermits in Medieval Love Stories', *Journal of Medieval History*, 18, 2 (1992), pp. 341-56.

25 M. Goodich, *The Unmentionable Vice: Homosexuality in the Later Medieval Period*, Santa Barbara & Oxford 1979. An indispensable guide to the canonical literature in which Church teaching was expressed is James Brundage, *Law, Sex and Christian Society in Medieval Europe*, Chicago 1987. See also Brundage, 'Sex and Canon Law' in *Handbook of Medieval Sexuality*, pp. 33-50.

26 K.J. Leyser, 'The Angevin Kings and the Holy Man,' in *St Hugh of Lincoln*, ed. H. Mayr-Harting, Oxford 1987 and D. H. Farmer, 'Hugh of Lincoln, Carthusian Saint' in *De Cella in Seculum*, Cambridge 1989, pp. 9-15. Richard was not the only king to

be reproved by a hermit. His brother John received similar warnings, but with very different results: Roger of Wendover, *Flores Historiarum*, ed. H.G. Hewlett, Rolls Series, London 1887, II, p. 203ff.

27 Very similar words are put into the mouth of Richard himself in the latin verse narrative of Guillaume le Breton: 'And now am I joined in the marriage bed with Berengaria, daughter of the king of Navarre; the sacred union has been consummated, we have become one flesh. There is no cause for me to dismiss her since she is united with me in the flesh and by law ...' *Philippidos*, ed. H.F. Delaborde, Paris 1885, Book IV, p. 101. As the editor points out, Richard could not possibly have uttered these words at Messina, to Philip Augustus, since he was not married to Berengaria until several months later, in Cyprus.

28 'Roger of Howden on Crusade' in *Medieval Historical Writing in the Christian and Islamic Worlds*, ed. D.O. Morgan, London 1982, pp. 60-76; see also David Corner, 'The *Gesta Regis Henrici Secundi* and *Chronica* of Roger, Parson of Howden', *Bulletin of the Institute of Historical Research* 1983, pp. 126-44, and Jane Sayers, 'English Charters from the Third Crusade' in *Law and Records in Medieval England*, London 1988, pp. 195-213. On what exactly constituted the marriage bond, see Penny S. Gold, 'The Marriage of Mary and Joseph in the Twelfth Century Ideology of Marriage' in *Sexual Practices and the Medieval Church*, ed. V. Bullough and J. Brundage, Buffalo 1982, pp. 102-7; J. Brundage, 'Concubinage and Marriage in Medieval Canon Law', ibid., pp. 118-28; M.

Pacaut, 'Sur quelques données du droit matrimonial de la seconde moitié du XIIe siècle', *Mélanges offerts à Georges Duby*, vol. I: *Le couple, l'ami et le prochain*, Aix en Provence 1992, pp. 31-41.

29 'Fort chausa es que tot lo major dan ...' see note 62, chapter 3.

30 J.C. Holt, in the Italo-British Colloquium cited above, says of this period that 'Richard behaved, and can be seen to have behaved, very much like the medieval monarch of the textbook' (op. cit., p. 22). See also V.H. Galbraith, 'Good Kings and Bad Kings in Medieval English History' in *Essays in Medieval English History*, London 1982, and Karl Leyser, Some Reflections on Twelfth Century Kings and Kingship' in *Medieval Germany and its Neighbours 900-1250*, London 1982, p. 246ff.

31 A frequently occurring topos: see *Gesta Stephani*, ed. Potter, p. 115.

32 See J. F. Elizari, *Sancho El Sabio*, pp. 196-205

33 See n. 53, chapter 3.

34 See J.A. Brutails, *Documents des archives de la chambre des comptes de Navarre*, Bibliothèque de l'Ecole des Hautes Etudes, Paris 1890. John Gillingham sees the reference in this text to a difference between the king of England and Arnaldo Ramón de Tartás as a possible indication of a change in relations between Richard and Sancho. See also C. Marichalar, *Colección diplomatica del rey don Sancho VIII (El Fuerte) de Navarra*, Pamplona 1936, doc. 7, 28.

35 R. Champollion Figeac, *Lettres de rois, reines et autres personnages des cours de France et d'Angleterre*, Documents inédits de l'histoire de France, v. I, Paris 1839, p. 34.

36 Migne, ccxiv, 509.

37 Rymer, *Foedera*, I, 70; Migne, ccxiv,182, Marichalar, doc. 15.

38 D. Mansilla, *La documentación pontificia de Honorius III, 1216-1227*, Monumenta Hispanica Vaticana, sección: Registros, vol. II, Rome 1965, docs. 223 (p. 170) and 227 (p. 173).

39 M. Powicke, *The Loss of Normandy*, Manchester 1913, describes Richard as isolated and 'Titanic'.

40 '... Richard I himself looked back in time for his ideals; to the crusade, to the troubadours or the Languedoc and to international chivalry. These all turned out to be lost causes ... and so he became a hero of romance.' M.T. Clanchy *England and its Rulers 1066-1272*, p. 141.

41 *De Rebus a se Gestis* (Giraldus Cambrensis, *Opera*, ed. J.S. Brewer, J.F. Dimock and G.F. Warner, Rolls Series, London 1861-91, 8 vols, at vol. 8, p. 109).

42 See note 13, chapter 1, above. For the traditional French view, see C. Richard, *Notice sur Richard Coeur de Lion*, Rouen 1839, where Richard's reckless character is seen as the cause of his own downfall.

43 *Chronicon*, pp. 94ff.

44 I was reminded recently of the secrecy which still surrounds the sickness and especially a terminal condition, of heads of state. The death of President Mitterand of France is an obvious example as were the terminal conditions of King George V and his son George VI.

45 Walter of Guiseborough, *Chronicle*, ed. H. Rothwell, Camden Society LXXXIX, London 1957, p. 142. See also the *Philippidos*, lines 600-5, *Oeuvres de Rigord et Guillaume le Breton*, ed. H.F. Delaborde, Paris 1882-5, vol. 2.

46 Kuno Meyer, ed., *The Death Tales of the Ulster* Heroes, Todd Lecture Series XIV, Dublin 1906, *Aided Chonchobuir*, at pp. 4-10.
47 *Layettes du Trésor des Chartes*, ed. A. Teulet, Paris 1863, vol. I, doc. 489, p. 200.
48 Ibid., doc. 497, p. 204.

5: WIDOW

1 R. Grégoire, OSB, 'Il matrimonio mistico' in *Il matrimonio nella società altomedievale*, 2 vols, Spoleto 1977, pp. 701-94. Widows, as a class, have until recently not attracted much attention from medievalists; see Mirrer, (note 5); M. Sheehan, ed. *Aging and the Aged in Medieval Europe*, Toronto 1990 and S.S. Walker, *Wife and Widow in Medieval England*, Ann Arbor 1993.
2 Guibert's autobiography has been edited, with French translation, by E.R. Labande (Paris 1981). The most recent English edition is by Paul J. Archambault, *A Monk's Confession*, Penn State UP 1996: the relevant chapters are Book 1, sections 12 and 13 (English version, pp. 34-47).
3 Peter of Blois, letters, in Migne 207, 536A.
4 Christine de Pisan, *Livre des Trois Vertus*, ed. C.C. Willard and E. Hicks, Paris 1989; English version, *The Medieval Woman's Mirror of Honor: the Treasury of the City of Ladies*, translated C.C. Willard, New York 1989.
5 See James Brundage, 'Legal Aid for the Poor and the Professionalization of Law in the Middle Ages', *Journal of Legal History*, 9 (1988), pp. 169-79; 'Widows as Disadvantaged Persons in Medieval Canon Law' in *Upon my Husband's Death*, ed. L. Mirrer, Michigan, 1992,

pp. 193-206; *Medieval Canon Law*, London 1995; and also B. Tierney, *Medieval Poor Law*, Berkeley and L.A. 1959.
6 Chardon, op. cit.
7 See note 17, chapter 4.
8 L. Delisle, ed., *Catalogue des Actes de Philippe Auguste*, Paris 1856, n. 805; Delaborde, *Recueil*, II, p. 416, no. 837.
9 This official belonged to a distinguished local family, whose existence is attested from the eleventh century. He continued as seneschal after the death of the queen for another fifteen years or so. Descendants of the same family are attested as recently as 1888. On the duties assigned to these curial officials in the Province of Maine, see: A. Bouton, *Le Maine. Histoire économique et sociale*, vol. I, Le Mans 1962, pp. 150ff.
10 Round, *Calendar of Documents*, p. 392.
11 Marchegay, *Archives d'Anjou*, no. 82.
12 Rymer, *Foedera* I, 84.
13 See Richardson, op. cit. (note 7, chapter 3)
14 Rymer, *Foedera*, I, 141.
15 There have been attempts this century to rehabilitate the reputation of John, who has gone down in popular tradition as a 'bad' king. Not withstanding these attempts, John Gillingham, influential in promoting the revisionist view of Richard, does not hesitate to condemn the revisionist view of John, calling him the 'most over-rated king in English history' (*Richard the Lionheart*, 2nd edition, p. 278). Even in popular tradition, John had a bad press: the popular Anglo-Norman romance of *Fouke le Fitz Waryn*, for instance, has John as a bad-tempered child who could not play with others with-

out throwing a tantrum. When he did so, even his father King Henry unhesitatingly sided with his victims: *Fouke le Fitz Waryn*, ed. Hathaway, Ricketts, Robson and Wiltshire, Oxford 1976, pp. 22ff. A new English version has become available recently: G.S. Burgess, ed., *Two Medieval Outlaws*, Cambridge, 1997.

16 The letters of Pope Innocent are reproduced in Migne, ccxiv-ccxvii, and in A. Potthast, ed., *Regesta pontificum romanorum inde ab anno post Christum natum MCXCVIII ad annum MCCCIV*, 2 vols, Berlin 1873-79, nos. 996-9, 2081, 2345,3171, 3618-9; 4000; 5141 and 5148. For a synopsis, see also the calendars edited by W.H. Bliss, *Calendar of Entries in Papal Registers relating to Great Britain and Ireland*, London 1893 and by C.R. Cheney and M.G. Cheney, *The Letters of Pope Innocent III concerning England and Wales*, Oxford 1967; (C.R. Cheney and W.P. Semple, *Selected Letters of Pope Innocent III concerning England*, London 1953 omits the letters relating to Berengaria's dower problems). For a discussion of Innocent's political stance in respect of English affairs, see Cheney, *Innocent III and England*, Stuttgart 1976. Cheney sees the relationship between Richard and Innocent as as clash of strong personalities: when Innocent was first elevated to the see of St Peter, Richard sent him a letter (now lost) urging him to show rectitude in his high office. Innocent was offended by this unsolicited advice but relations improved later. His relations with John were less cordial. John's letters to Berengaria are reproduced in Rymer, *Foedera*, I: 84, 94, 126,138,141.

17 London 1846. This volume contains a facsimile of Berengaria's first letter, to the bishop of Winchester, in 1220, one of the earliest original extant letters of a queen.

18 *Letters of the Queens of England*, Stroud, 1994, pp. 43ff.

19 *Honorii III Romani Pontificis Opera Omnia*, ed. Horoy, 4 vols Paris 1879-80; vol. I, letter CXVI, col. 149.

20 Ibid., Book II, letter CXC, col. 696.

21 *Rotuli Litterarum Clausarum*, 1204-1216, ed. T. Duffus Hardy, London 1833-44, vols I & II, Patent Rolls of Henry III, PRO (Kraus reprint 1971) vol. I (1216-1225) pages 73, 179, 243-5, 253, 265, 292, 319, vol. II (1225-1232) pages 39, 381.

22 On Innocent's relations with Philip and with John, see Brenda M. Bolton, *Innocent III: Studies on Papal Authority and Pastoral Care*, New York, Variorum 1995, especially chapter v 'Philip Augustus and John: Two Sons in Innocent III's Vineyard,' pp. 113-34. Compare with Cheney's remarks on Innocent's relationship with Richard, above note 53, chapter 3. Innocent's dealings with France are discussed in detail in R. Foreville, *Le Pape Innocent III et la France*, Stuttgart 1992. See also Jane Sayers, *Innocent III, Leader of Europe 1198-1216*, Harlow 1994.

23 *Corpus Iuris Canonici*, ed. E. Friedberg, 2 vols, Leipzig 1879-81: Decretals, X 2.2.15. Potthast, *Regesta* no.7744; Horoy *Honorii III Romani Pontificis Opera Omnia*, Book II, letter VI, col. 478

24 Teulet, *Layettes du Trésor des Chartes*, vol. I, doc. 745, p. 281

25 P. Marchegay, *Archives d'Anjou*, Angers 1843, p. 70ff.

26 Bliss, op. cit., vol. ix p. 48.

27 Innocent IV, *Apparatus toto urbe celebrandus super V libris decretalium*, Frankfurt am Main 1570, reprinted 1968; X 1.29.38 § 4, fol. 142va.

28 Bouton, *Le Maine*, vol. I, p. 535.

29 For details of the episcopates of these bishops and other aspects of Church history, see the invaluable Dom L. Piolin, *Histoire de l'Eglise du Mans*, 6 vols, Paris 1858.

30 *Raoul de Cambrai*, ed. P. Meyer and A. Lognon, Paris 1882, lines1477ff. Outside literary texts, too, examples abound: see *Gesta Stephani*, ed. Potter, p. 113.

31 *Recueil des Actes de Philippe Auguste*, vol. IV, 1215-23, ed. M. Nortier, Paris 1979, doc. 1505, pp. 130-1.

32 Vicomte Menjot d'Elbenne and Abbé L. Denis, *Cartulaire du Chapitre Royale de St Pierre de la Cour, Archives Historiques du Maine*, IV (1907) and X (1910); vol. IV, pp. 49-50, document xxxix.

33 Ibid., pp. 54-5; Piolin, op. cit., IV, 579. Prévost subsequently became Dean of the Chapter of St Pierre, an office he held from 1228 to 1237.

34 Ibid., p. 61.

35 Piolin, op. cit., IV, 228.

36 Horoy, *Honorii Opera*, Book II, CXCIII.

37 *Cartulaire de l'Eglise du Mans: Livre Blanc du Chapitre*, MS 259 Archives départementales de la Sarthe. Copied by Lottin in 1848 from the original (fonds Gaignières no. 2737)18th century copy by G. Savaré.

38 J. Chappée, A. Ledru and L.J. Denis, *Enquête de 1245 relative aux droits du chapitre de St Julien du Mans*, Paris 1922; Menjot d'Elbenne, *Cartulaire* (n. 145)

39 Chappée et al. *Enquête*, p. lxxix. At the time of its foundation there had been a mere eighteen prebendary canons, including the dean and the cantor, and four honourary canons.

40 Testimony of the witness Raginaldus Clavel, a 55-year-old canon of Le Mans, *Livre Blanc*, p. 40ff; Chappée et al., *Enquête*, cxxxiiff.

41 Chappée et al., *Enquête*, loc. cit.; Menjot d'Elbenne, *Cartulaire*, p. 40ff.

42 *Livre Blanc*, pp. 123ff.

43 Ibid., p. 149.

44 J. Delaville le Roulx, *Cartulaire général de l'Ordre de St Jean de Jerusalem*, 1110-1310, Paris 1894-1906, 4 vols: vol. II, 1201-1260, p. 179, document 1451.

45 L. Calendrini, 'La commanderie de Thorée', *Annales Fléchoises*, 1910, pp. 300-10.

46 Ed. J.R. Perche, Paris 1842, reprinted Paris 1974, vol. VI, p. 30.

47 Menjot d'Elbenne, *Cartulaire*, pp. 53, 56ff. Honorius's successor, Gregory IX issued bulls dated 6.2.1230 and 7.2.1230 on the same matter and it is clear from later entries in the collection that the controversies continued long after the death of Berengaria.

48 Horoy, *Honorii Romani Pontificis Opera Omnia*, Book II, letter CXCV, col. 701.

49 Horoy, ibid., Book II, letter CXC, col. 696.

50 Chappée et al., *Enquête*, cxxxiiff. The sum of money owed was negligible – about FF 1, 30 in the 'old' currency.

51 *Livre Blanc*, pp. 46-7, 69, 89, 119; Paulin Boutier's excommunication appears to have taken place around the time of the second interdict, i.e. 1216-18, but this is not entirely clear from the testimonies. He may

have been excommunicated more than once. He was loyal to the queen for the whole of his career.

52 *Cartulaire de St Pierre de la Cour*, ed. Menjot d'Elbenne, Supplément, pp. 299-301 (document CCXIII).

53 Horoy, *Honorii Romani Pontificis Opera Omnia*, Book IV, letter XLVII, col. 341.

54 Piolin, op. cit., IV, 231.

55 A. Bouton, 'La vie tourmentée de la reine Bérengère,' *Vie Mancelle*, 45 (1964), pp. 26-7; *Le Maine*, pp. 249ff.

56 See note 36, chapter 2, above and note 58, following.

57 Robert Chazan, *Medieval Jewry in Northern France*, Johns Hopkins 1983; M. Yardeni, *Les Juifs dans l'Histoire de France*, Leiden 1980; E. Taitz, *The Jews of Medieval France*, Westport Ct. 1994.

58 Kenneth Stow, *Alienated Minority: The Jews of Medieval Latin Europe*, Cambridge Mass. 1992; N. Jordan, *The French Monarchy and the Jews*, Philadelphia 1989.

59 By Canon 26, issued at the Third Lateran Council in 1179. This instruction was however, not always observed and many Jews in France and elsewhere did employ Christian servants.

60 *Pipe Roll of Richard I*, 43 NS, vol. VIII, 1931 p. 8. See also H.G. Richards, *The English Jewry under the Angevin Kings*, London 1960, p. 57.

61 Bouton, *Le Maine*, vol. I, p. 764. Parents and five children all changed their names, symbolising a rejection of both their community and their own past.

62 Reiterated on six different occasions during the twelfth century and finally extended to cover all Jews in the Christian West. In

practice, however, the papal command could easily be subverted: Taitz, *The Jews of Medieval France*, pp. 139ff.

63 F. Fuentes, *Catálogo de los Archivos Eclesiasticos de Tudela*, Tudela 1944, *passim*.

64 J. Bosch Vila, 'Los documentos arabes y hebreos de Aragon y Navarra', *Estudios de Edad Media de la Corona de Aragon*, V (1952), 407-16.

65 *Obituario de la Catedral de Pamplona*, ed. A. Ubieto Arteta, Pamplona 1954.

66 Horoy, *Honorii Opera*, Book V. Letters LXXXI & CCCL urge the king of Leon and the archbishop of Bordeaux respectively not to use Jews in positions of responsibility: the same caution had been expressed by Pope Innocent III in respect of Muslims.

67 *The Patent Rolls of Henry III*, vol. I, AD.1216-1225, London 1901, pp. 189, 228-9.

68 F. Bourquelot, 'Fragments des comptes du XIII siècle', *Bibliothèque de l'Ecole des Chartes*, 5e série, vol. IV (1863), pp. 51-79.

69 Fuentes, op. cit., document 215, p. 59.

70 Ibid., document 233, p. 63.

71 García Larragueta, op. cit., II, doc. 30 (p. 35), doc. 43 (p. 44).

72 On the presence of the Order in Tudela, see García Larragueta, ibid., docs 85-90; Carmen Orcástegui Gros, 'Tudela durante los reinados de Sancho El Fuerte y Teobaldo I', *Estudios de Edad Media de la Corona de Aragon*, X (1975), at p. 74ff; J. Delaville Le Roulx, 'Les archives de l'ordre de l'hôpital dans la péninsule ibérique', *Rapport publié par les Nouvelles Archives des Missions Scientifiques*, IV, ed F. Leroux, Paris (1893). On the general question of the military orders in northern Spain, see P.G. Caucci

von Saucken, 'Gli Ordini Militari e Ospedalieri sul Camino de Santiago' in *Militia Sacra*, eds E. Coli, M. de Marco and F. Tommasi, Perugia 1994, pp. 85-100; D.W. Lomax, *Las órdenes militares en la peninsula ibérica durante la edad media*, Salamanca 1976; 'El carácter de los prímeros Establecímientos de la orden de S. Juan en el Reino de Navara', *Annales de l'ordre souverain et militaire de Malte*, 1961 (I) pp. 18-22.

6: SHALL THESE STONES SPEAK?

1 In this respect too, the lives of Berengaria and her sister Blanca followed a similar pattern: Blanca (Blanche) retired in 1922 and founded a convent at Argensolles on land she had purchased: *Gallia Christiana*, ix, instr. 132-3, no. 53.

2 Hermits and 'sylvans' were particularly numerous in the province of Maine. Their relationship with the regular orders varied: Piolin (IV, 242) cites a document in which the (Benedictine) monks of Loulay gave a church and a piece of land to a company of hermits, in the year 1213, on the specific understanding that if they ever gave up the eremitical life they would not give the land to the Cistercians. Presumably, the hermits stuck to their bargain because the land was finally taken over by the Premonstratian order for the foundation of the abbey of Belle-Etoile.

3 Details in J.M. Canivez, *Statuta Capitulorum Generalium Ordinis Cisterciensis*, 3 vols, Louvain 1933-6.

4 Piolin, op. cit., IV, 583; original charter of agreement in the

Archives départementales de la Sarthe, Série H, Abbaye de l'Epau, no. 833.

5 Original documents in the *Archives de la Sarthe*, above, loc. cit.

6 *Cartulaire de l'abbaye de l'Epau*, Archives départementales de la Sarthe, no. 941 (copy of 1847 from MS Gaignières BN 205). On the custom of donating the services of a 'bourgeois' to assist in the running of monasteries, see Bouton, *Le Maine*, I, 218ff and Piolin, op. cit., iv, 586.

7 *Gallia Christiana*, (Paris, 1715-1865) vol. XIV col. 536, *Archives ... Sarthe*, nos 925, 933.

8 *Cartulaire de l'abbaye de l'Epau*, doc. 941, Archives départementales de la Sarthe.

9 *La Piété-Dieu de l'Epau: construction et aménagement d'une abbaye cistercienne*, 1230-1365, Collection Archives Historiques du Maine, no. XV, Le Mans 1968. See also, L. Froger, 'L'abbaye de l'Epau du XIIIe au XVe', *Revue historique et archéologique du Maine* 34 (1893), pp. 253-313.

10 Piolin, op. cit., Book V, p. 28, Froger, op. cit., 297ff.

11 A. Bouton, 'Quelle est cette dame de l'Epau?', *Vie Mancelle*, 41 (1963), pp. 8-10; 'La Reine perdue' 43 (1964), 6-8; 'La Reine Bérengère perdue et retrouvée', 100 (1969), pp. 5-8; 'La Reine Bérengère perdue et retrouvée', *Bulletin de la Société d'Agriculture, Sciences et Arts de la Sarthe*, 439, Mémoires IV série, t. VII, 1969-70, pp. 15-25; P. Térouane, 'A la quête d'une tombe sans nom,' ibid., 27-44.

12 Cited in some detail in Térouane.

13 M. Goodich, *The Unmentionable Vice: Homosexuality in the Late Medieval Period*, Santa Barbara and Oxford 1979, p. 29, citing

Peter Damian's *Liber Gomorrhianus* (Migne, 145, 160-90). Pierre Payer, *Sex and the Penitentials*, Toronto 1984 agrees, see Appendix D: 'Homosexuality and the Penitentials,' p. 135ff.

14 Vern L. Bullough, 'One Being a Male in the Middle Ages' in *Medieval Masculinities*, ed. Clare A. Lees, chapter 2. As Bullough demonstrates, women's attempts 'to gains status by becoming more masculine were condoned and encouraged' though not when they challenged the male in the privileged area of political power. Perceived 'femininity' in men, however, was never anything other than undesirable and even seen as a sickness. Since sexual performance, in the most basic sense, was crucial to proving masculinity, the fear of impotence lent force to the fear of 'malevolent feminine forces' which might express themselves in sorcery and spells. This lends weight to Régine Pernoud's suggestion that Philip Augustus's rejection of his Queen Ingeborg and his accusation of sorcery may have been motivated by humiliation and performance anxieties.

15 J. Flandrin, *Un temps pour embrasser*, Paris 1983 (not available in English). But see the caveat expressed by Pierre Payer, 'Confession and the Study of Sex in the Middle Ages' in Bullough and Brundage, *Handbook of Medieval Sexuality*, pp. 3-31.

16 Pierre Chaplais, *Piers Gaveston*, Oxford 1995.

17 Parsons, in: *Medieval Queenship*, p. 67, 'Mothers, Daughters, Marriage, Power: Some Plantagenet Evidence, 1150-1500'.

18 One scholar has suggested that a similar defensiveness prompted the inclusion in the Middle English *Romance of Richard Coer de Lyon* of the king of Almain's daughter, with whom Richard falls in love: '... possibly to answer implicitly rumours about Richard's sexual inclinations generated by Roger of Howden's report of the hermit ...' J. Finlayson, 'Richard Coer de Lyon: Romance, History or Something In Between?', *Studies in Philology* 87, 2 (1990), pp. 156-80.

19 *Chronicles and Memorials of the Reign of Richard I*, vol. I, ed. W. Stubbs, 1864, Introduction, p. xviii.

20 Ibid., p. xxxii.

21 Even the subsequently fertile Eleanor of Aquitaine only produced her first child after eight years of marriage.

22 Alain Erlande-Brandenburg, 'Le cimitière des rois à Fontevrault', *Congrès archéologique de France*, Anjou,1964, CXXII (1966), p. 484; *Les rois de Fontevrault*, Centre Culturel de l'Ouest, 1979 and *Le Roi est Mort*, Geneva 1975. See also the recent article by John Carmi Parsons, 'The Burials and Posthumous Commemorations of English Queens to 1500' in *Queens and Queenship in Medieval Europe*, ed. Duggan, pp. 317-37. Parsons makes a only a passing reference to the tomb of Berengaria (foot-noted to the inadequate and unreliable biography of Berengaria by Mitchell) but his article appears to lend support to Erlande-Brandenburg's belief that Eleanor commissioned her own effigy and by extension, my own view that Berengaria did the same.

Bibliography

PRIMARY SOURCES

Abelard, *Historia Calamitatum*, ed. Muckle, J., *Medieval Studies* 1950.
—, *The Letters of Abelard and Heloise*, ed. Radice, B., London, 1974.
Acta of Henry II and Richard I, eds Holt, J.C. and Mortimer, R. Gateshead, 1986.
Adam of Eynsham, *Magna Vita Sancti Hugonis*, eds Douie, D.L. and Farmer, D.H., Oxford, 1985
Adam of Perseigne, *Lettres*, ed. Bouvet, J., Paris, 1960. Also in: *Archives Historiques du Maine*, XIII, 1-10, 1951-1962 (English version: *Letters*, ed. Perigo, Grace, Kalamazoo, 1970).
Aimeric Picaud, *Guide des Pèlerins*, ed. Vieillard, J., Macon, 1968.
Ambroise, *Estoire de la Guerre Sainte*, ed. Paris, G., Paris, 1897; (English versions: *The Crusade of Richard Lion-heart*, ed. Hubert, M.J. and La Monte, J.L., New York, 1976; *Three Old French Chronicles of the Crusades*, ed. Stone, E.N., Washington, 1939.
Archives d'Anjou, ed. Marchegay, P., Angers, 1843.
(Les) *Archives de l'ordre de l'hôpital dans la péninsule ibérique*, rapport publié par les Nouvelles Archives des Missions Scientifiques, IV, ed. Leroux, F., Paris, 1893.
Archives Départementales de la Sarthe, série H: abbaye de l'Epau; *varia: Docs*: 833, 925, 933, 941.
Béroul, *The Romance of Tristram*, ed. Ewert, A., Oxford, 1957, 2 vols.
—, (English version: tr. Fedrick, A., London, 1970).
Bertran de Born, *The Poems of the Troubadour Bertran de Born*, ed. Paden, W. et al., Berkeley, 1986.
Calendar of Documents preserved in France, illustrative of the History of Great Britain and Ireland, ed. Round, J.H., vol. I, 918-1206, London, H.M.S.O., 1899.
Calendar of Entries in Papal Registers relating to Great Britain and Ireland, ed. Bliss, W.H., London, 1893.
Carlos, Príncipe de Viana, *Crónica de los reyes de Navarra*, ed. Orcastegui Gros, Carmen, Pamplona, 1978.
Cartulaire de l'abbaye de l'Epau, Archives Départementales de la Sarthe, doc. no. 941.

Cartulaire du Chapitre Royale de St. Pierre de la Cour, ed. Menjot d'Elbenne, Vicomte, et Denis, abbé L., *Archives Historiques du Maine*, IV (1907) and X (1910).

Cartulaire de l'Eglise du Mans: Livre Blanc du Chapitre, Archives Départementales de la Sarthe, MS. 259.

Cartulaire général de l'ordre de St. Jean de Jérusalem, 1110-1310, 4 vols, ed. Delaville le Roulx, J., Paris, 1894-1906.

Catálogo de los Archivos Eclesiásticos de Tudela, ed. Fuentes, F., Tudela, 1944.

Catalogue des Actes de Philippe Auguste, ed. Delisle, L., Paris, 1856.

Chevalier de la Tour Landry, *The Book of the Knight of La Tour-Landry*, ed. Wright, T., Early English Texts Society (OS 1906), reprint New York, 1969.

Chrétien de Troyes, Arthurian Romances, tr. Owen, D.D.R., London, 1987.

—, *The Complete Romances*, tr. Staines, David, Bloomington, 1990.

Christine de Pisan, *Livre des Trois Vertus*, ed. Willard, C.C. and Hicks, E., Paris, 1989.

Chronique des Eglises d'Anjou, ed. Marchegay, P. and Salmon, A., Paris, 1869.

Colección diplomatica del rey don Sancho VII (El Fuerte), ed. Marichalar, C., Pamplona, 1936.

Corpus Iuris Canonici, ed. Friedberg, E., 2 vols, Leipzig, 1879-81

Corpus Iuris Canonici una cum glossis, 4 vols, Venezia, 1605.

(The) Crusade and Death of Richard I, ed. Johnston, R.C., Oxford, 1961.

Death Tales of the Ulster Heroes, ed. Meyer, K., Todd Lecture Series XIV, Dublin, 1906.

Der mittelenglische Versroman über Richard Löwenherz, ed. Brunner, K., Vienna, 1913.

Documents des archives de la chambre des comptes de Navarre, ed. Brutails, J., *Bibliothèque de l'Ecole des Hautes Etudes*, Paris, 1890.

Enquête de 1245 relative aux droits du chapitre de St. Julien du Mans, ed. Chappée, J., Ledru, A. et Denis, L.J., Paris, 1922.

Foedera, Conventiones, Literae etc. ed. Rymer, T., London, Record Commission, 4 vols, 1816-69.

Fouke le Fitz Warin, ed. Hathaway, P. et al., Oxford, 1976.

Fragments des comptes du xiii siècle, ed. Bourquelot, F., *Bibliothèque de l'Ecole des Chartes*, 5e série, vol. iv (1863), 51-79.

Fuero general de Navarra, ed. Utrilla Utrilla, J., Pamplona, 1987.

Gallia Christiana, ed. Bouquet, J., Paris, 1715-1865.

Garcí Lopez de Roncesvalles, *Crónica*, ed. Orcastegui Gros, Carmen, Pamplona, 1977.

Gaucelm Faidit, *Les poèmes de Gaucelm Faidit*, ed. Mouzat, J., Geneva 1989 (reprint).

Gesta Stephani, ed. Potter, K.R., Oxford, 1955.

Geoffrey of Monmouth, *History of the Kings of Britain*, tr. Thorpe, L., Harmondsworth, 1966.

Giraldus Cambrensis, *Opera*, eds. Brewer, J.S., Dimock, J.F. and Warner, G.F., Rolls Series 21, London, 1861-91, 8 vols.

—, *Vita Sancti Hugonis*, ed. Loomis, R.M., New York and London, 1985.

Giraut de Borneil, *The Cansos and Sirventes of the Troubadour Giraut de Borneil*, ed. Sharman, Ruth V., Cambridge, 1989.

Gonzalo de la Hinojosa, *Crónica*, Colección de documentos inéditos para la historia de España, por el Marquis de la Fuensanta del Valle, Madrid, 1893.

BIBLIOGRAPHY

Gottfried von Strassburg, *Tristan*, tr. Hatto, A.T., London, 1960.

El Gran Conquista de Ultramar, ed. Cooper, L., Bogotá, 1979.

Guibert de Nogent, *Autobiographie*, ed. Labande, E.R., Paris, 1981

—, (English: *A Monk's Confession*, tr. Archambault, P., Philadelphia, 1996.)

Guilhem Anelier de Toulouse, *Histoire de la guerre de Navarre*, ed. Michel, F., Paris, 1856.

Guillaume Le Breton, *Philippidos*, ed. Delaborde, H.F., Paris, 1882-5 (*Oeuvres de Rigord (q.v.) et de Guillaume le Breton*).

Guillaume de Lorris and Jean de Meung, *Romance of the Rose*, ed. & tr. Dahlberg, C., Princeton, 1995.

Histoire de Guillaume le Maréchal, ed. Meyer, P., 3 vols, Paris, 1891.

Honorius III, Pope, *Honorii III Romani Pontificis Opera Omnia*, ed. Horoy, J., 4 vols, Paris, 1879-80.

—, *Honorius iii, Acta*, ed. Tautu, A., Rome, 1950.

—, *La documentación pontífica de Honorio III, 1216-1227*, Monumenta Hispanica Vaticana; sección: registros, vol. 2, ed. Mansilla, D., Rome, 1965.

Innocent III, Pope, *Letters of Pope Innocent III concerning England and Wales*, ed. Cheney, C.R. and Cheney, M.G., Oxford, 1967.

Innocent IV, Pope, *Apparatus tote urbe celebrandus super V libris decretalium* (1570) Frankfurt am Main; reprint 1968.

Itinerarium Peregrinorum et Gesta Regis Ricardi, ed. Stubbs, W., *Chronicles and Memorials of the Reign of Richard I*, Rolls Series, 38, London, 1864-5. (English: *The Third Crusade*, tr. Fenwick, K., London, 1968; *Chronicle of the Third Crusade*, tr. Nicholson, H., Aldershot, 1997.)

Jaume I, El Conqueridor, *Llibre dels feyts del rey En Jaume*, in *Les Quatre Grans Cróniques*, ed. Soldevila, F., Barcelona, 1971.

Landon, L., *The Itinerary of King Richard I*, Pipe Roll Society 51, London, 1935.

Layettes du Trésor des Chartes, ed. Teulet, A., vol. I, Paris, 1863.

Letters of Royal and Other Illustrious Ladies of Great Britain, ed. Wood, M.A.E., 3 vols, London, 1846.

Letters of the Queens of England, 1100-1547, ed. Crawford, A., Stroud, 1994.

Lettres de rois, reines et autres personnages des cours de France et d'Angleterre, ed. Champollion Figeac, R., Documents inédits de l'histoire de France, vol. I, Paris, 1839.

Liber Regum, ed. Cooper, L., Zaragoza, 1960.

Libro de las generaciones, ed. Martínez, J.F., Valencia, 1968.

Moret y Mendi, J., *Anales del Reino de Navarra*, Pamplona, 1684-1704, Tolosa, 1890.

Obituario de la Catedral de Pamplona, ed. Ubieto Arteta, A., Pamplona, 1954.

Patent Rolls of Henry III, vol. I, AD 1216-1225, London, PRO, 1901, Kraus reprint 1971.

Patrologiae Latinae Cursus Completus, ed. Migne, J.P., Paris, 1858.

Peter of Blois, *Letters*, in Migne, ed., op. cit., 207, 536.

Peter Damian, *Liber Gomorrhianus*, in Migne, op. cit., 145, 160-190.

Pierre de Langtoft, *The Chronicle*, ed. Wright, J., London, Rolls Series 47, 2 vols, 1866-8.

The Great Pipe Roll for the Ninth Year of the Reign of King Richard the First, Michaelmas, 1197, ed. Stenton, D.M., Pipe Roll 43, PRS, NS, 8, London, 1931.

BIBLIOGRAPHY

Primera Crónica General de España, ed. Menéndez-Pidal, R., Madrid, 1955.
Ralph of Coggeshall, *Chronicum Anglicanum*, ed. Stevenson, J., London, Rolls Series 66, 1875.
Ralph of Diceto, *Opera Historica*, ed. Stubbs, W., London, Rolls Series 68, 2 vols, 1876.
Ranulph of Higden, *Polychronicon*, ed. Lumby, J. , London, Rolls Series 41, 9 vols, 1865-86.
Raoul de Cambrai, ed. Meyer, P. and Lognon, A., Paris, 1882.
Recueil des Actes de Philippe Auguste, vol. I, ed. Delaborde, H.F., Paris, 1916; Vol. IV, ed. Nortier, M., Paris, 1979.
Recueil des Historiens des Gaules et de la France, ed. Bouquet, J., vol. XVIII, Paris, 1878.
Regesta pontificum romanorum inde ab anno post Christum natum MCXCVIII ad annum MCCCIV, ed. Potthast, A., 2 vols, Berlin, 1871-9.
Richard of Devizes, *Chronicle*, ed. Appleby, J., London, 1963.
Rigord, *Gesta Philippi Augusti* in *Oeuvres de Rigord et de Guillaume le Breton*, ed. Delaborde, H.F., Paris 1882-5.
Rodericus Ximenius de Rada, *De Rebus Hispaniae*, in *Opera*, ed. de Lorenzana, F., Madrid, 1793, reprint, Valencia, 1968.
Roger of Howden, *Gesta Henrici II et Ricardi I*, ed. Stubbs, W., London, Rolls Series 49, 2 vols, 1867.
—, *Chronica*, ed. Stubbs, W., London, Rolls Series 51, 4 vols, 1868-71.
Roger of Wendover, *Flores Historiarum*, ed. Hewlett, H.G., London, Rolls Series 84, 1887.
Rotuli Litterarum Clausarum 1204-1216, 1216-27, ed. Duffus Hardy, T., London, Record Commission, 1833-44.
(Las) Siete Partidas del rey don Alfonso el Sabio, colegadas con varios códices antiguos por la Real Academia de la Historia, 3 vols, reprint 1972.
Statuta Capitulorum Generalium Ordinis Cisterciensis, ed. Canivez, J., 3 vols, Louvain, 1933-6.
Veterum scriptorum et monumentorum historicorum dogmaticorum moralium amplissima collectio, ed Martène et Durand, vol. I , Paris, 1724.
Wace, *Le Roman de Brut*, ed. Arnold, I., Paris, 1938-40.
—, *Le Roman de Rou*, ed. Holden, A.J., 3 vols, Paris, 1970-1973.
Walter of Guiseborough, *Chronicle*, ed. Rothwell, H., Camden Society LXXXIX, London, 1957.
William of Newburgh, *Historia Rerum Anglicarum*, 2 vols, in *Chronicles and Memorials of The Reigns of Stephen, Henry II and Richard I*, ed. Howlett, R.G., London, Rolls Series 82, 1884-5
William of Tyre, *A History of Deeds Done Beyond the Sea*, ed. tr. Babcock, E. and Krey, A.C., New York, 1943.

SECONDARY SOURCES

Ahmad, Aziz, *A History of Islamic Sicily*, Edinburgh, 1975.
Alvar, Carlos, *La poesia trovadoresca en España y Portugal*, Barcelona, 1977.
Anderson, J. and Zinsser, B., *A History of Their Own*, New York and London, 1988, vol. I.
Baldwin, J.R., *The Government of Philip Augustus*, Berkeley, 1986.

—, 'Five Discourses on Desire: Sexuality and Gender in Northern France, *c.*1200', *Speculum* 66 (1991), 797-819.

Bard, Rachel, *Navarre, the Durable Kingdom*, Reno, 1982.

Barrère, J.M., *La Piété-Dieu de l'Epau: construction et amènagement d'une abbaye cistercienne 1230-1365. Collection archéologique et historique du Mans*, no. XV, Le Mans, 1968.

Bautier, R., 'Philippe Auguste, la personnalité du roi' in *Etudes sur la France capétienne*, New York, 1992.

Beitsche, J.K., 'As the twig is bent: children and their parents in an aristocratic society', *Journal of Medieval History* 2 (1976), 181-92.

Bienvenu, J.M., 'Aliénor d'Aquitaine et Fontevraud', *Cahiers de Civilisation Médiévale*, 29 (1986), 15-27.

Black, Edward, *Royal Brides and Queens of England in the Middle Ages*, London, 1987.

Blamires, Alcuin, *The Case for Women in Medieval Culture*, Oxford, 1997.

Bloch, R. Howard, *Medieval Misogyny and the Invention of Western Romantic Love*, Chicago, 1991.

Boase, J., 'Fontevraud and the Plantagenets', *Journal of the British Archaeological Association*, 3rd series, vol. 34 (1971) 1-10.

Bolton, Brenda M., *Innocent III: Studies on Papal Authority and Pastoral Care*, New York, 1995.

Bond, Gerald, *William VII, Count of Poitiers: Poetry*, New York, 1989.

Bosch Vila, J., 'Los documentos árabes y ebreos de Aragon y Navarra', *Estudios de Edad Media de la Corona de Aragon* V (1952), 407-16.

Boswell, John, *Christianity, Social Tolerance and Homosexuality*, Chicago, 1980.

Bouton, André, *Le Maine. Histoire économique et sociale*, Le Mans, 1962

—, 'Quelle est cette dame de l'Epau?' *Vie Mancelle*, 41 (1963), 8-10

—, 'La Reine perdue', ibid. 43 (1964), 6-8;

—, 'La vie tourmentée de la reine Bérengère', ibid., 45 (1965), 26-7.

—, 'La Reine Bérengère perdue et retrouvée', ibid., 100 (1969), 5-8.

—, 'La Reine Bérengère perdue et retrouvée', *Bulletin de la Société d'Agriculture, Sciences et Arts de la Sarthe, Mémoires*, IVe série, t. VII, 1969-70

Bradbury, J., *Philip Augustus*, London and New York, 1998.

Breeze, A., *Medieval Welsh Literature*, Dublin, 1996.

Bridge, A., *Richard the Lionheart*, London, 1989

Brooke, Christopher, *The Medieval Idea of Marriage*, Oxford, 1989.

Broughton, B.B., *The Legends of King Richard I, Coeur de Lion*. The Hague, 1966.

Brown, Peter, *The Body and Society: Men, Women and Sexual Renunciation in Early Christianity*, New York, 1988.

Brown, Stephen, 'The Mercenary and his Master: Military Service and Monetary Reward in the 11th and 12th centuries', *History* 74 (1989), 20-38.

Bruckner, M.T. et al., *Songs of the Women Troubadours*, New York, 1995.

Brundage, James, *Richard Lionheart*, New York, 1974.

—, *Law, Sex and Christian Society in Medieval Europe*, Chicago, 1987.

—, 'Legal Aid for the Poor and the Professionalistion of Law in the Middle Ages', *Journal of Legal History* 9 (1988), 169-79.

—, 'The Merry Widow's Serious Sister: Marriage in Classical Canon Law' in *The Power of the Weak*, ed. Carpenter, J. and MacLean, S.B. (q.v.), pp. 33-48.

—, 'Sex and Canon Law' in *Handbook of Medieval Sexuality*, ed. Bullough and Brundage, New York, 1996.
—, 'Widows as Disadvantaged Persons in Medieval Canon Law' in Mirrer, *Upon my Husband's Death* (q.v.).
—, *Sex, Law and Marriage in the Middle Ages*, London 1993.
—, *Medieval Canon Law*, London, 1995.
Bullough, V., 'On Being a Male in the Middle Ages' in *Medieval Masculinities* (q.v.) pp. 31-45.
— and Brundage, J., *Sexual Practices and the Medieval Church*, Buffalo, 1982
— and Brundage, J., *A Handbook of Medieval Sexuality*, New York, 1996.
Burns, Robert I., S.J., 'The Spiritual Life of James the Conqueror, King of Arago-Catalonia 1208-1276; Portrait and Self-Portrait' in *Jaime I y su Epoca*, Zaragoza, 1980.
—, *The Worlds of Alfonso the Learned and James the Conqueror*, Princeton, 1985.
Burrow, J.A., *The Ages of Man*, Oxford, 1986.
Bynum, Caroline Walker, *Jesus as Mother: Studies in the Spirituality of the High Middle Ages*, Berkeley and Los Angeles, 1982
Calendini, L., 'La commanderie de Thorée', *Annales Flêchoises*, 1910, pp. 300-10.
Caucci von Saucken, P.G., 'Gli Ordini Militari e Ospedalieri sul Camino di Santiago', *Militia Sacra*, ed. Coli, C. et al., Perugia, 1994.
Chambers, F.M., 'Some Legends Concerning Eleanor of Aquitaine', *Speculum* 16 (1944), 459-68.
Chaplais, P., *Piers Gaveston*, Oxford, 1995.
Chardon, Henri, *Histoire de la reine Bérengère, femme de Richard Coeur de Lion*, Le Mans, 1866.
Chaytor, H.C., *The Troubadours and England*, Cambridge, 1923.
Chazan, Robert, *Medieval Jewry in Northern France*, Johns Hopkins, 1983.
Cheney, C.R., *Innocent III and England*, Stuttgart, 1976.
Chibnall, M., *The Empress Matilda*, Oxford, 1991.
Cierbide Martinena, Ricardo, 'Estado actual de los estudios de la lengua occitana en Navarra, línea de investigación', *Príncipe de Viana* XLIX (1988), 365-76.
—, 'La scripta administrativa de la Navarra medieval en lengua occitana', *Zeitschrift für romanische Philologie* 105 (1989), 276-312.
Clanchy, M.T., *England and its Rulers 1066-1272*, London, 1983.
—, *From Memory to Written Record*, 2nd edition, Oxford, 1993.
Collins, Roger, *Early Medieval Spain*, 2nd edition, New York, 1995.
La Condición de la mujer en la baja edad media, Coloquio Hispano-Francés, Madrid, 1986.
Corner, D., 'The Gesta Regis Henrici Secundi and Chronica of Roger, Parson of Howden', *Bulletin of the Institute of Historical Research 1983*, pp. 126-44.
Coss, Peter, *The Lady in Medieval England*, Stroud, 1998.
Crouch, D., *William Marshal: Court, Career and Chivalry in the Angevin Empire*, New York and London, 1990.
Del Burgo, Jaime, *Navarra*, Madrid, 1972.
Del Campo, Luis, *Dos Esculturas de Sancho El Fuerte*, Pamplona, 1976.
—, 'Cuatro Infantas Navarras', in *Navarra: Temas de Cultura Popular* 120 (1971), 4-31.

Dillard, Heath, *Daughters of the Reconquest*, Cambridge, 1984.

Dronke, Peter, *The Medieval Lyric*, 2nd edition, London, 1978.

Duby, Georges, 'Au XII siècle: les "jeunes" dans la société aristocratique', *Annales* 19 (1964), 835-46.

—, *Medieval Marriage: Two Models from Twelfth Century France*, Baltimore, 1978.

—, *Le Chevalier, la femme et le prêtre: le mariage dans la France féodale*, Paris, 1981.

—, *Guillaume le Maréchal*, Paris, 1984.

—, *Mâle Moyen Age*, Paris 1988, *see also* Dunnett.

Dunnett, J., *Love and Marriage in the Middle Ages*, London, 1994.

Duby, G. and Perrot, M., *Histoire des Femmes en Occident*, Paris, 1991, vol. 2, ed. Klapisch-Zuber, C., *Les Silences du Moyen Age*. (English: *A History of Women in the West*, Cambridge Mass. 1992-4, vol. 2, *The Silences of the Middle Ages*.)

Dufourneaux, M., *Les Français en Espagne aux XI et XII siècles*, Paris, 1949.

Duggan, A. ed., *Queens and Queenship in Medieval Europe*, Woodbridge, 1997.

Echols, A. and Willliams, M., *Between Pit and Pedestal*, New York, 1991.

Edbury, P.W., *The Kingdom of Cyprus and the Crusades 1191-1374*, Cambridge, 1991.

Edwards, R. and Ziegler, V., *Matrons and Marginal Women in Medieval Society*, Woodbridge, UK and Rochester, NJ, 1995.

Elizari Huarte, Juan F., *Sancho VI El Sabio*, Rey de Navarra, Iruña, 1991.

Elliott, Dyan, *Spiritual Marriage: Sexual Abstinence in Medieval Wedlock*, Princeton, 1993.

—, 'Bernardino of Siena vs. the Marriage Debt' in *Desire and Discipline. Sex and Sexuality in the Pre-Modern West*, ed. Murray, J. and Eisenbichler, K., Toronto, 1996, pp. 168-200.

Erlande-Brandenburg, A., 'Le cimitière des rois à Fontevraud', *Congrès archéologique de France*, Anjou, 1964, CXXII (1966) 484 ff.

—, *Le Roi est Mort*, Geneva, 1975.

—, *Les Rois de Fontevraud*, Centre culturel de l'ouest, 1979.

Facinger, M., 'A Study of Medieval Queenship, Capetian France 987-1237', *Studies in Medieval and Renaissance History* 5 (1968), 3-48.

Farmer, D.H., 'Hugh of Lincoln, Carthusian Saint' in *De Cella in Saeculum*, ed. Vale, M., Cambridge, 1989, pp. 1-15.

Ferrante, Joan M., *To the Glory of Her Sex*, Indiana, 1997.

Finlayson, J., 'Richard Coer de Lyon: Romance, History or Something in Between?' *Studies in Philology* 87, 2 (1990), 156-80.

Flandrin, J.L., 'Mariage tardif et vie sexuelle', *Annales* 27 (1972), 1351-78.

—, *Un Temps pour Embrasser*, Paris, 1983.

Foreville, R., *Le Pape Innocent III et la France*, Stuttgart, 1992.

Fortun Pérez de Ciriza, Luis J., *El Rey Sancho VII: El Fuerte*, Iruña, 1987.

Froger, abbé L., 'L'abbaye de l'Epau du XIII au XV siècle', *Revue historique et archéologique du Maine*, 34 (1893), 353-93.

Galbraith, V.H., 'Good Kings and Bad Kings in Medieval English History' in *Kings and Chroniclers: Essays in Medieval English History*, London, 1982.

García Arenal, M. and Leroy, B., *Moros y Judios en Navarra en la baja edad media*, Madrid, 1984.

García Villoslada, Ricardo, 'Leyendo la Historia de los Obispos de Pamplona', *Hispania Sacra* XXXIV (1982) 69, 255-88.

Gaudemet, J., *Le Mariage en Occident*, Paris, 1987.

Géraud, H., Mercadier: les routiers au treizième siècle', *Bibliothèque de l'Ecole des Chartes* 1842, (3) 417-43.

Gillingham, J., 'The Unromantic Death of Richard I', *Speculum* 54 (1979), 18-41.

—, 'Richard I and Berengaria of Navarre', *Bulletin of the Institute of Historical Research* 53 (1980), 157-73.

—, *The Angevin Empire*, London, 1984.

—, *Richard the Lionheart*, London (1978), 2nd edition 1989

—, 'Roger of Howden on Crusade' in Morgan, D.O. ed. *Medieval Historical Writing in the Christian and Islamic Worlds*, London 1982, pp. 60-76.

—, 'The Art of Kingship: Richard I 1189-99', *History Today* 35 (1985), 17-23.

—, 'Conquering Kings: Some Reflections on Henry II and Richard I' in *Warriors and the Church*, ed. Reuter, T. ed., London, 1992.

—, *Richard Coeur de Lion*, London, 1994.

Gilmour-Bryson, A., 'Sodomy and the Knights Templar', *Journal of the History of Sexuality* 7 (2) (1996), 151-83.

Given-Wilson, C. and Curteis, A., *The Royal Bastards of Medieval England*, London, 1984.

Goñi Gaztambide, J., *Historia de los Obispos de Pamplona*, s.IV-XIII, Pamplona, 1970.

Goodich, M., *The Unmentionable Vice: Homosexuality in the later Medieval Period*, Sta. Barbara and Oxford, 1979.

Gransden, A., 'Childhood and Youth in Medieval England', *Nottingham Medieval Studies* 16 (1972), 3-19.

—, *Historical Writing in England c.550-1307*, London, 1974.

Green, M.A.E., *Lives of the Princesses of England from the Norman Conquest*, vol. I, London, 1849.

Grégoire, R., O.S.B., 'Il matrimonio mistico' in *Il matrimonio nella società altomedievale*, 2 vols, Spoleto, 1977, pp. 701-94.

Hallam, E., *Bérengère de Navarre: les Plantagenêts et les Capétiens'*, *La Province du Maine* 19 (1991), 225-34.

Harvey, J., 'Political and Cultural Exchanges between England and the Iberian Peninsula in the Middle Ages', *Literature, Culture and Society of the Middle Ages*, ed. López, M.M., Barcelona, 1989.

Hassall, Arthur, *Historical introductions to the Rolls series by William Stubbs*, London, New York, 1902.

Heiser, R., 'The Royal Familiares of King Richard I', *Medieval Prosopography* 10 (1989), 227-50.

Helmholz, R., *Marriage Litigation in Medieval England*, Cambridge, 1974.

Hereros Lopetegui, Susana, 'Las Territorias Ultrapirinaicos y su evolución historica', date unknown.

—, 'El castillo de Rocabruna en Ultrapuertos: una nueva teoria sobre su locación', paper presented to the 2nd Congreso General de Historia de Navarra, Pamplona-Estella, 1990.

Herlihy, David, 'Did Women have a Renaissance?' *Medievalia et Humanistica* 1985, 1-22.

—, *Medieval Households*, Harvard, 1985.

—, *Women and Family in Medieval Europe*, Providence 1995. (ed. A. Molho).

Hewlett, M., *The Life and Death of Richard Yea and Nay*, London, 1900.

Howell, M., *Eleanor of Provence: Queenship in Thirteenth-Century England*, Oxford, 1997.

Huneycutt, L., 'Images of Queenship in the High Middle Ages', *Haskins Society Journal: Studies in Medieval History*, 1 (1989), 61-72.

Jaeger, S., 'L'amour des rois: structure sociale d'une forme de sensibilité aristocratique', *Annales* 46, 3 (1991), 547-71.

Jantzen, Grace, *Power, Gender and Christian Mysticism*, Cambridge and New York, 1995.

Johansson, W. and Percy, W.A., 'Homosexuality' in *A Handbook of Medieval Sexuality*, ed. Burrough, V.L. and Brundage, J., New York, 1996, pp. 155-89.

Jordan, N., *The French Monarchy and the Jews*, Philadelphia, 1989

Kelly, Amy, *Eleanor of Aquitaine and the Four Kings*, London, 1952.

Kessler, U., *Richard I Löwenherz*, Graz, 1995.

Kuster, H.J. and Cormier, R., 'Old and New Trends. Observations on the Problem of Homosexuality in the Middle Ages', *Studi Medievali*, 25 (1984), 587-610.

Labande, E.R., 'Pour une image véridique d'Aliénor d'Aquitaine', *Bulletin de la société des antiquiaires de l'ouest*, II, série 4, Poitiers, 1952.

—, 'Les filles d'Aliénor d'Aquitaine: étude comparative', *Cahiers de Civilisation Médiévale*, 29 (1986), 101-12.

Labarge, M.W., *Medieval Travellers*, London, 1982.

Lacarra, J.M., 'A propos de la colonisation "franca" en Navarre at Aragon', *Annales du Midi* LXV (1953), 330-42.

—, *Guia del Archivo General de Navarra*, Pamplona, 1954.

—, *Vasconia Medieval*, San Sebastian, 1957.

—, *Historia Politica del Reino de Navarra*, 3 vols, Pamplona, 1971.

Larragueta, S.A. García, *El Gran Priorado de Navarra de la Orden de San Juan de Jerusalen*, 2 vols, Pamplona 1957.

Laslett, P., ed., *Family and Illicit Love in Earlier Generations*, Cambridge, 1977.

Laslett, P., ed., *El método historico*, Pamplona, 1977.

Leclercq, Dom J., *La femme et les femmes dans l'oeuvre de St. Bernard*, Paris, 1982.

—, 'Monks and Hermits in Medieval Love Stories', *Journal of Medieval History* 18, 2 (1992), 341-56.

—, *Monks and Love in Twelfth Century France*, Oxford, 1979.

Lees, Clare A., ed., *Medieval Masculinities*, Minnesota, 1994.

Legge, M.Dominica, 'Beaumont Palace', *Etudes de Civilisation Médiévale: Mélanges offerts à E.R. Labande*, Poitiers, 1990, pp. 491-5.

Leroy, B., 'Les Juifs de Navarre du XII au XV siècle', *Revue des Etudes Juives* 138 (1979), 491-3.

—, *La Navarre au Moyen Age*, Paris, 1984

—, *The Jews of Navarre in the Later Middle Ages*, Jerusalem, 1985.

Lewent, K., 'The Pseudonym Oc-e-No', *Modern Language Review* 38 (1943), 113 ff.

Leyser, K.J., 'Some Reflections on Twelfth Century Kings and Kingship' in *Medieval Germany and its Neighbours 900-1250*, London, 1982, pp. 246 ff.

—, 'The Angevin Kings and the Holy Men' in *St Hugh of Lincoln*, ed. Mayr-Harting, H., Oxford, 1987.

Linehan, P., 'History in a Changing World: the Case of Medieval Spain' in *Past and Present in Medieval Spain*, New York, 1992.

—, *History and the Historians of Medieval Spain*, Oxford, 1993.

Lofts, Norah, *Queens of Britain*, London, 1977.

Lomax, D.W., 'El carácter de los primeros establicímientos de la Orden de San Juan de Jerusalen en el Reino de Navarra', *Annales de l'ordre souverain et militaire de Malte* 1961, 1, 18-22.

—, *Las órdenes militares en la península ibérica durante la edad media*, Salamanca, 1976.

Loomis, R.S., 'Tristram and the House of Anjou', *Modern Language Review* XXVII (1922), 24-30.

López Estrada, F., 'Las mujeres escritores en la Edad Media castellana' in *La condición de la mujer en la baja edad media* (q.v.).

Mahn, C., *Werke der Trobadors*, Paris and Berlin, 1846-86.

Makowski, E., 'The Conjugal Debt and Canon Law' in *Equally in God's Image: Women in the Middle Ages*, ed. Holloway, J.B. et al. New York, 1990.

Markale, J., *Aliénor d'Aquitaine*, Paris, 1990.

Mason, E., 'The Hero's Invincible Weapon: an Aspect of Angevin Propaganda' in *The Ideals and Practice of Medieval Knighthood III*, ed. Harper-Bill, C. and Harvey, R., Woodbridge, 1989, pp. 121-36.

Meade, M., *Eleanor of Aquitaine*, New York, 1977.

Menéndez-Pidal, R., *Historia de España*, 18 vols, Madrid, 1957-.

Mila y Fontanals, M. , *De los Trovadores en España*, ed. Martínez, C. and Manrique, F.R., Barcelona, 1966.

Mirrer, L., *Upon My Husband's Death*, Michigan, 1992.

Misrahi, J. and Henderson, W., 'Roland and Oliver: Prowess and Wisdom, the Ideal of the Epic Hero', *Romance Philology* XXXIII (1980), 357-72.

Mitchell, M., *Berengaria: Enigmatic Queen of England*, Pook's Hill, 1986.

Mortimer, R., *Angevin England*, Oxford, 1994.

Needler, G.H., *Richard Coeur de Lion in Literature*, Leipzig, 1890.

Nelson, Janet, *Richard Coeur de Lion in History and Myth*, London, 1992.

Newman, B., *From Virile Woman to Woman Christ*, Philadelphia, 1995.

Nicholson, Helen, 'Women on the Third Crusade', *Journal of Medieval History* 23, 4 (1997), 339 ff.

Norgate, K., *Richard the Lionheart*, London, 1924.

Ohler, N., *The Medieval Traveller*, tr. Hillier, J., Woodbridge, 1989.

Orcastegui Gros, Carmen, 'Tudela durante los reinos de Sancho El Fuerte y Teobaldo I', *Estudios de Edad Media de la Corona de Aragon x* (1975), 63 ff.

—, 'Tudela' in *Sedes Reales de Navarra*, Gobierno de Navarra, Pamplona, 1990, pp. 106-28.

Orme, N., *From Childhood to Chivalry*, London 1984.

Pacaut, M., 'Sur quelques données du droit matrimonial de la seconde moitié du XIIe siècle', *Mélanges offerts à Georges Duby*, vol. I: *Le couple, l'ami et le prochain*, Aix-en-Provence, 1992, pp. 31-41.

Paden, W., *The Voice of the Trobairitz*, Pennsylvania, 1989.

Painter, S., *William Marshall*, Baltimore, 1933.

Parsons, J.C., *Medieval Queenship*, New York, 1993.

—, 'The Queen's Intercession in Thirteenth-Century Europe' in *The Power of the Weak* (q.v.) pp. 147-77.

—, 'The Burials and Posthumous Commemoration of English Queens to 1500' in *Queens and Queenship in Medieval Europe* (q.v.).

Payer, P., *Sex and the Penitentials*, Toronto, 1984.
—, 'Confession and the Study of Sex in the Middle Ages' in *Handbook of Medieval Sexuality*, Bullough and Brundage, eds (q.v.).
Perche, J.R., *Dictionnaire topographique et statistique de la Sarthe*, Paris, 1842, reprint 1974.
Pérez Castro, F., 'España y los judios españoles' in *Sephardic Heritage*, ed. Barnett, R., London, 1971, vol. I, 275-322.
Pernoud, R., *Isambour, La Reine Captive*, Paris, 1987.
—, *Richard Coeur de Lion*, Paris, 1988.
—, *La Femme au Temps des Croisades*, Paris, 1989.
Piolin, Dom L., *Histoire de l'Eglise du Mans*, 6 vols, Paris, 1858
—, 'Bérengère, reine d'Angleterre, Dame du Mans', *Revue des Questions Historiques* 49 (1890), 174-83.
Powell, T., ed., *Muslims under Latin Rule*, Oxford, 1951.
Powicke, F.M., *The Loss of Normandy*, Manchester, 1913.
Procter, E., *Alfonso X of Castile*, Oxford, 1951.
Ramsay, J., *Angevin England*, London, 1903.
Reilly, B., *The Medieval Spains*, Cambridge, 1993.
Riccardo Cuor di Leone nella Storia e nella Leggenda, Academia Nazionale dei Lincei, anno CCCLXXVIII, colloquio italo-britannico, Rome, 1981.
Richard, A., *Histoire des Comtes de Poitou 778-1204*, Paris, 1903.
Richard, C., *Notice sur Richard Coeur de Lion*, Rouen, 1839.
Richards, H.G., *The English Jewry under the Angevin Kings*, London, 1960.
Richardson, J., 'The Letters and Charters of Eleanor of Aquitaine', *English Historical Review* 74 (1959), 193-213.
de Riquer, M., *Los Trovadores*, 3 vols, Barcelona, 1975.
Rosenthal, J., *Medieval Women and the Sources of Medieval History*, Athens, GA. and London, 1990.
Rudt de Collenburg, W., 'L'Empereur Isaac de Chypre et sa fille', *Byzantion* 38 (1968), 123-79.
Sánchez-Albornoz, C., *Vascos y Navarros en su primera historia*, Madrid, 1976.
—, *La trayectoria histórica de Vasconia. El destino de Navarra*, Madrid, 1977.
Sayles, G.O., 'The Changed Concept of History: Stubbs and Renan', *Scripta Diversa*, London, 1982, pp. 133-50.
Sayers, J., 'English Charters from the Third Crusade', *Law and Records in Medieval England*, London, 1988, pp. 195-213.
—, *Innocent III, Leader of Europe 1198-1216*, Harlow 1994.
Shahar, S., *The Fourth Estate*, London and New York, 1983.
—, *Childhood in the Middle Ages*, London, 1990.
Sheehan, M., *Aging and the Aged in Medieval Europe*, Toronto, 1990.
Stafford, P., *Queens, Concubines and Dowagers*, London, 1983.
—, *Queen Emma and Queen Edith: Queenship and Women's Power in 11th Century England*, Oxford, 1997.
Stow, K., 'Hatred of the Jews of Love of the Church: Papal Policy towards the Jews in the Middle Ages' in *Antisemitism through the Ages*, ed. Almog, S., London, 1988
—, *Alienated Minority: the Jews of Medieval Latin Europe*, Cambridge, Mass., 1992.
Strickland, Agnes, *Lives of the Queens of England*, 1st edition, London, 1840, vol. 1, 2nd (revised) edition, 1851.

Stubbs. W., *Introduction to the Chronicles and Memorials of the Reign of Richard i*, London, 1864.

Taitz, E., *The Jews of Medieval France*, Westport, Conn. 1994.

Térouane, P., 'A la quête d'une tombe sans nom', *Bulletin de la Société d'Agriculture, Sciences et Arts de la Sarthe, Mémoires*, IVe série, t. VII, 1969-79, pp. 27-44.

Tierney, B., *Medieval Poor Law*, Berkeley and Los Angeles, 1959.

Tobin, R.B., 'Vincent de Beauvais on the Education of Women', *Journal of the History of Ideas* 35 (1974), 485-9.

Trindade, W.A., 'Nouvelles perspectives sur le personnage d'Iseut aux Blanches Mains', in *Tristan-Tristrant*. Mélanges en l'honneur de Danielle Buschinger, ed. Crépin, A. and Spiewok, W., Greifswald, 1996.

Turner, R., 'Eleanor of Aquitaine and her children: an enquiry into medieval family attachment', *Journal of Medieval History* 14 (1988), 321-36.

—, 'The Children of Anglo-Norman Royalty and their Upbringing', *Medieval Prosopography* 11 (1990), 2, 17-32.

Ubieto Arteta, A., 'Aportación al estudio de la "tenencia" medieval: la mujer "tenente"', *Estudios de Edad Media de la Corona de Aragon* X (1975), 47-61.

Van Houts, E., 'The State of Research: Women in Medieval History and Literature', *Journal of Medieval History* 20 (1994), 272-92.

Walker, S.S., *Wife and Widow in Medieval England*, Ann Arbor, 1993.

Warren, W.L., *King John*, London, 1961.

Wood, J., 'The Calumniated Wife in Medieval Welsh Literature', *Cambridge Medieval Celtic Studies* 10 (1985), 25-38.

Yardeni, M., *Les Juifs dans l'histoire de France*, Leiden, 1980.

Index

Abelard 154, 208 n. 10
Acre 97; siege of 97-8; massacre of
    prisoners 98-101, 102, 104-5, 108
Adam of Eynsham 121-2, 134, 214
    n. 22
Adam of Perseigne 55, 153-5, 176,
    184, 206-7 n. 61
Adela of Champagne 70
Adémar of Angoulême 118
Aélis (Alice, Aloysia) of France 64,
    69, 74, 78, 79, 108, 111
Agnes of Merania 72, 114-15, 183,
    184
Aimeric Picaud 44
'al-Adil 103
Alfonso II of Aragon 69, 111, 129,
    208-9 n. 15
Alfonso X of Aragon 53, 206 n. 58
Alfonso VIII of Castile 55, 56
Alfonso El Batallador of Navarre 38,
    41
Alix of Blois 62,110
Ambroise 67, 82-3, 91, 95, 97, 101-3,
    105, 210 n. 33, 210 n. 37, n. 43,
    211 n. 46, 212 n. 59, n. 62
Amiens 45, 114
Anales del Reino de Navarra 36, 70
Anderson, J. 16, 199 n. 6, 206 n. 50
Angers 118, 142
Angevin dynasty 9
Anjou 19, 22, 64, 70, 91, 110, 111,
    112, 118, 143, 144, 146, 187
Aquitaine 62, 105
Aragon 30, 37, 67, 127, 128
Amaldo Ramón de Tartás 128

Arsuf 97, 102
Arthur of Brittany 63, 143, 159, 185
Ascalon 97, 104
Audita Tremendi 73
Austria 19, 108

Baha al-Din 100
Bani Qasi 38, 45
Barfleur 118
Barnes, Margaret Campbell 14, 174
Barrère, J.M. 187
Basque (language) 37-8, 44, 204 n. 29
Basques 30, 38, 40, 44
Basque provinces 128-9, 205 n. 37
Bautier, R. 70, 209 n. 26
Bayonne 30, 87, 128
Beata (Sancha), queen of Navarre 34,
    47
Beaufort en Vallée 118-9, 134-5,
    142, 149
Benjamin of Tudela 42
Berengaria of Navarre (Berenguela,
    Bérengère) 12-15, 18, 22, 23, 24,
    27, 34, 35; youth in Navarre 29;
    possible birthplace 37; language
    spoken 38; ancestry 39; family ties
    46-7; early contacts with Richard
    54, 66, 69; in Sicily 81-5;
    descriptions of 82-4; wedding day
    86-7; dower 90, 150-6; dowry 90,
    128-9, 150; in Palestine 98-9, 101-
    2, 104-5; in Rome 110-11;
    reconciliation with Richard 122-6;
    absence at Richard's death 132-4;
    as destitute widow 141, 145; as

'Dame du Mans' 146-9, 157-62; character of 148, 157, 168, 189, 195; clashes with Cathedral Chapter 163-72; relations with Jews 42, 174-7; later contacts with Navarre 177-82; founds Abbey of l'Epau 184-6; tomb 11, 187-8; remains of 188-9; effigy 10, 196-8
Bernard of Clairvaux 62, 96
Bertram de Verdun 91, 99
Bertran de Born 66, 208 n. 14
Bezzola, R. 109
Bibiano de Agramont 129
Bigorre 128
Blanca (Blanche) of Navarre, countess of Champagne 21, 32, 33, 34, 35, 47, 48-9, 55, 135, 145, 154, 168, 173, 178-82, 183, 220 n. 1
Blanche of Castile 183-5
Blondel 14, 59, 108
Bohadin 104
Bonport, Abbey 160
Book of the Three Virtues 140
Bordeaux 30, 76, 128, 129
Bosch Vila, J. 177
Boswell, John 68, 71-2, 190, 192, 209 n. 22
Bourquelot, F. 179
Bouton, A. 174, 218 n. 28, 219 n. 55, 220 n. 11
Bridge, A. 14, 64, 71, 84, 101, 202 n. 30
Brindisi 110
Brooke, C. 88, 89
Broughton, B.B. 59, 202 n. 31, 209 n. 16, 212 n. 2
Brundage, J. 140, 190, 202 n. 30, 207 n. 3, 214 n. 25, 214-15 n. 28
Bullough, V. 191, 214 n. 28, 221 n. 14
Burns, R., S.J. 40, 200 n. 11, 203 n. 5, 206 n. 48

Caen 118
Canterbury 43
Carlos, Principe de Viana 33, 203 n. 15
Castile 30, 37, 67, 127, 129
Cathedral Chapter of St Julien du Mans 158, 162, 218 n. 37-8

Celestine III, pope 108, 114
Chalus-Chabrol 19, 131
Champagne 32, 73, 149, 179, 180
Chaplais, P. 192, 207 n. 3, 221 n. 16
Chardon, H. 27, 143, 150, 172
Chartres 135, 179
Château-Gaillard 126, 131
Chaytor, H.J. 65
Chinon 118, 131, 142, 145, 155
Chipia, Martín 128
Chizé 69
Chrétien de Troyes 25, 52, 113, 149, 200 n. 15, 206 n. 51
Christine de Pisan 140, 216 n. 4
Chronica of Roger of Howden 76, 80, 119, 121, 124, 125, 130, 201 n. 28
Chronicle of St Aubin 118, 144
Cisa 128
Cistercian Order in France 10; in Maine 184-5; in Spain 43, 45
Clavel, Canon 165
Clemencia of Toulouse 35
Clifford, Rosamund 143
Coëffort, hospital of 159, 172, 185
Compiègne 114
Compostella 20, 43, 94
Conrad of Montferrat 96
Constance of Brittany 63, 143
Constance of Castile 70
Constanza (Costanza, Constancia), Infanta of Navarre 32-5, 129, 145, 177
Corfu 108
Corpus Iuris Canonici 156, 217 n. 23
Crawford, Anne 153
Crónica de los reyes de Navarra 33
Crónica of Garci Lopez de Roncesvalles 33
Cyprus 18, 19, 33, 54, 56, 85-6, 110, 113, 158, 211 n. 45; princess of 91, 112, 145, 212 n. 54

Danube 108
Daroca 32, 146
Darun 104
Dax 128
Decretals of Gregory IX 156
Delaborde, H.F. 79, 210 n. 34, 214 n. 27, 215 n. 45

Del Campo, L. 53, 148, 194-5, 204 n. 21, 205 n. 45
De Rebus Hispaniae 34, 139, see also Rodrigo Jiménez de Rada
Dictionnaire topographique, historique et statistique de la Sarthe 169
Dillard, H. 52-3
Dominican Order 159, 172, 177
Dreu de Mello 155
Duby, G. 17, 24, 45, 68, 75, 88, 116, 190, 191, 192, 199 n. 1, 200 n. 17
Dürnstein, castle 108

Ebro, river 38, 45, 128, 205 n. 37
Egypt 104
Eilhart von Oberg 89
Eleanor (Aliénor) of Aquitaine 9, 10, 14, 18, 22, 33, 46, 49, 60-4, 74, 75, 78, 84, 94, 107, 112, 113, 117, 118-9, 125, 134-5, 143, 150, 173, 183, 199 n. 3, 207-8 n. 6-7, 208 n. 12
Eleanor Plantagenet, queen of Castile 55, 66, 110
Elizabeth (Isabelle, Isabella) of Hainault, queen of France 72, 114, 115
Elizari, J. 46, 204 n. 28, 209 n. 18, 213 n. 18, 215 n. 32
Enquête de 1245 165-72, 218 n. 38-41
Epau (Spallum) 159, 184
Erlande-Brandenburg, A. 196, 221 n. 22
Estella 30, 37, 41, 77
Estoire de la Guerre Sainte 66, 76, 82, see also under Ambroise

Fernando (Ferrando) Infante of Navarre 32-5, 112, 127, 146, 177
Flanders 73
Flandrin, L. 68, 191, 192, 209 n. 17
Fontevraud 9, 10, 117, 118-9, 135, 144, 149, 185, 195, 196-7, 213 n. 19, 221 n. 22
Fortun Pérez, L.X. 127, 205 n. 46
Fortun Rodrigo de Bazton 128
Franciscan Order 159, 172
Friedrich Barbarossa 73

Fueros 39
Fuero General de Navarra 31, 39, 41, 53, 206 n. 56
Fuenterrabía 128

Gallia Christiana 186, 220 n. 1
García (Garsia, Garsias), clerk 149, 152, 153, 180, 181
Garcia Ramirez, El Restaurador 31, 37, 127, 146, 168
Gascony 56, 62, 67, 69, 75, 111, 127-8, 145, 151
Gaucelm Faidit 101, 124, 212 n. 62
Gaveston, Piers 192
Genoa 77, 111
Geoffrey of Anjou 60
Geoffrey of Brittany 62, 70, 143
Geoffrey of Rancon 118
Geoffrey, archbishop of York 60, 119
Geoffrey de Laval 186
Gervaise de Cogners 161
Gesta of Roger of Howden 71, 76, 79, 124, 125, 201 n. 28
Gillingham, John 22, 64, 67, 71, 75, 101, 116, 119, 124, 128, 131, 200 n. 10, n. 13, 202 n. 29, 208 n. 13, 215 n. 34, 216 n. 15
Giraldus Cambrensis (Gerald of Wales) 60, 66, 68, 121, 131, 201 n. 28, 207 n. 4, 214 n. 22, 215 n. 41
Giraut de Borneil 208 n. 15, 212 n. 63
Gisors 73
Gonzalo de la Hinojosa 36
Green, M.A.E. 26, 201 n. 23, see also Wood)
Gregory VIII, pope 73, 95
Gregory IX, pope 186, 218 n. 47
Guibert de Nogent 139-40, 174, 216 n. 2
Guide des Pèlerins 44
Guillaume de la Guierche 156
Guillaume des Barres 101
Guillaume des Roches 141, 143, 144, 146, 164
Guillaume Passavant, bishop of Le Mans 158, 164
Guyenne 56, 62, 67

Hallam, E. 27, 201 n. 27
Hamelin, bishop of Le Mans 158, 166

Hattin 73, 95
Heloise 61
Henry II, king of England 9, 10, 46,
   59-60, 67, 73, 74, 80, 107, 111,
   157, 159, 164, 208 n. 13
Henry III, king of England 153, 170,
   173, 177, 217 n. 21, 219 n. 67
Henry, the 'Young King' 62, 65
Henry, count of Champagne 96
Henry, emperor of Germany 108
Herbert de Tucé 146, 164
Hereros Lopetegui, Susana 67, 90,
   128, 203 n. 4, 212 n. 53
Herlihy, D. 17, 91, 190, 199 n. 9
Hewlett, M. 14, 103, 211 n. 51
Holt, J.C. 116
Honorius III, pope 153, 169, 171,
   173, 215 n. 38, 217 n. 19, n. 23,
   218 n. 48-9, 219 n. 66
Hugh of Avalon, bishop of Lincoln
   19, 121, 134-5, 194, 214 n. 26
Huisne, river 10, 184
Huneycutt, L. 91, 113

Ingeborg of Denmark, queen of
   France 26, 114-16, 151, 155, 183,
   213 n. 13, 221 n. 14
Iñigo Arista 38
Innocent III, pope 22, 35, 114, 129,
   135, 151-3, 155, 166, 204 n. 19,
   217 n. 16, 217 n. 22
Innocent IV, pope 42, 156, 218 n. 27
Isaac Comnenos, ruler of Cyprus 86
Isabella of Angoulême 9, 173
Itinerarium Peregrinorum et Gesta
   Regis Ricardi 66, 76, 82, 86, 87,
   95, 101, 105, 210 n. 29-30, 210 n.
   43, 212 n. 57, 212 n. 59, 212 n.
   62

Jaeger, S. 72
Jaffa 97, 102, 104, 105
Jaume (Jaime) prince of Aragon 33,
   49, 50, 178, 203 n. 17, 206 n. 47-
   8
Jerusalem 58, 101, 104, 105
Jews in Navarre 30, 41-2; in Spain
   177; in France 119, 175; in Le
   Mans 42, 174-7
Jiménez dynasty 31, 146

Joanna Plantagenet, queen of Sicily
   19, 48, 78, 82, 84, 85, 99, 102,
   103, 104, 110, 126, 144-5, 149
John, king of England 9, 23, 35, 91,
   108, 129-30, 135, 141, 145, 149;
   prevarications over dower of
   Berengaria 151-6; 177, 216 n. 15;
   217 n. 16, n. 22
Juhel de Maine 160
Julianeta Brodaresse 149, 180
Julien Laurent 164, 167

Kelly, Amy 199 n. 3
Kyrenia 91

La Couture, abbey 160, 172, 176,
   abbot of 164
La Flèche 169
La Oliva, abbey 45
La Réole 75
Labarge, M.W. 76, 210 n. 31
Lacarra, J.M. 38, 69, 77, 127, 129,
   203 n. 3, n. 7, 205 n. 37, 209 n.
   18
Lancelot 75
Landon, L. 126, 210 n. 32
langue d'oïl 62, 111
Las Huelgas, abbey 44, 45, 55, 56
Las Navas de Tolosa 31, 40, 168
Latrun 104
Leclercq, Dom J. 214 n. 24
Le Goff, J. 45
Le Lude 90, 169
Le Mans 10, 27, 36, 74, 142-4, 150,
   158-9, 185, 218 n. 29
Leon 30
Leopold, duke of Austria 98, 108,
   119
Les Andelys 126
Letters of Queens and Other Royal
   Ladies 153
Liber Regum 32
Libro de las generaciones 32
Lieu-Dieu, abbey 160
Limassol 18, 33, 86
Llibre dels feyts 33, 206 n. 47
Loches 118, 155
Lofts, N. 14, 174, 201 n. 24
Loire, river 20
Lombardy 76

Lopez Estrada, F. 53, 206 n. 58
Louis VII, king of France 49, 56, 60, 62, 94, 105, 113
Louis VIII, king of France 72
Louis IX, king of France 183, 185
Lyons 77

Magna Vita Sancti Hugonis 121-3
Maine, county of 22, 119, 122, 143, 146, 151, 158, 164, 187, 216 n. 9, 218 n. 28
Maine, diocese of 10, 159, 160, 218 n. 29, 220 n. 2, n. 6
Marcilla, abbey 47, 55, 56, 180
Marfan's syndrome 50
Margarita of Navarre, queen of Sicily 48
Markale, J. 199 n. 3
Marguerite of France 74
Marie de Champagne 62, 63, 109, 110, 173
Marriage in the Middle Ages 87-8, 211 n. 48
Marseilles 77, 107, 111
Martin, sergeant 149, 176
Matilda, 'empress' of England 60
Matilda, duchess of Saxony 110
Meade, M. 14, 199 n. 3
Melior, Cardinal 111
Mercadier 70, 132, 194, 209 n. 20
Messina 77, 78, 79, 125
Miguel de Monzón 181
Milo, abbot of Ste. Marie du Pin 184
miserabiles personae 140, 156
Mitchell, M. 27
Monreal 54, 206 n. 59
Moret y Mendi, J. 36, 127, 204 n. 23, n. 25, 205 n. 43, 209 n. 19
muladies 30, 38
Muslims 31; in Navarre 40-1

Najac 69, 75
Nájera 41
Naples 77-9, 110
Navarre 20, 29-30, 67; social organisation 39; Muslims in 40-1; Jews in 41-2; French influence in 42-3, 44-5; music and the arts 44; languages in 44, 177
Navarrese 38, 44, 77, 111

Nicolas, royal chaplain 86; as bishop of Le Mans 158, 164
Niort 61
Norgate, K. 69
Normandy 9, 64, 70, 113, 118, 121, 143, 146, 151, 215 n. 39
Notre Dame de la Piété-Dieu de l'Epau, abbey 10, 27, 184; foundation charter 186; name of 187; later history 187-195; *Cartulaire* of 220 n. 6, n. 8, n. 9

Obituario of the Cathedral of Pamplona 177
Occitan (language) 42, 44, 62, 77, 109, 111, 204 n. 29
Occitania 76
Ohler, N. 76, 210 n. 31
Olite 37
Order of St John of Jerusalem (Hospitallers) 104, 126, 168, 169, 181, 218n. 44, 219 n. 72
Otto of Brunswick 43
Oxford 64, 121

Palestine 56, 86, 92, 94, 97, 101, 103, 107, 108
Pamplona 30, 31, 32, 35, 37, 43, 77, 118, 127; bishops of 45
Parsons, J.C. 113, 202 n. 32, 221 n. 17, n. 22
Paulin Boutier 149, 160, 170, 176
Pernoud, R. 95, 115, 200 n. 10, 212 n. 56, 213 n. 14
Peter II of Aragon 129, 145
Peter of Blois 139
Peter the Chanter 71
Philip Augustus, king of France 9, 22, 67; birth and character 70-1; intimacy with Richard I 70-3, 191; in Sicily 78-9, 98, 108, 112, 113; marriage to Ingeborg 114-16; 126, 146-7, 155, 164, 175, 183, 209 n. 21, n. 26, 216 n. 8, 217 n. 22
Philip of Cognac 68, 110, 132
Pierre, sergeant 149
Pierre de Langtoft 83, 85, 211 n. 44
Pierre Prévôt (Prévost) 141, 161, 170
Piolin, Dom. L. 135, 160, 164, 201 n. 26, 218 n. 29, 220 n. 2, 220 n. 4

Pipe Roll 176
Pisa 76, 111
Plaidy, J. 14
Poitiers 131, 135
Poitou 57, 58, 62, 67, 70, 91, 178
Pradillas 32, 146
Primera Crónica General 32
Provins 149
Puente la Reina 30, 34

Queenship in the Middle Ages 13, 48, 93, 106-7, 113

Ragusa 108
Ralph of Coggeshall 132-3, 201 n. 28, 214 n. 21
Ranulph of Higden 83, 201 n. 28, 210 n. 39
Raoul de Cambrai 158-9, 218 n. 30
Raymond of Poitiers 62, 94
Raymond VI of Toulouse 85, 126, 144
Reggio di Calabria 77
Remiro, bishop of Pamplona 33, 178, 180-1
Richard I, king of England, 'Lionheart' 9-11, 18, 19, 20, 44, 91; illegitimate son 21,68; biographies of 27, 57-8; ancestry and upbringing 59, 64-6; pre-nuptial contacts with Berengaria 67; wedding 31, 32, 86-7; on Crusade 73, 94-5, 97-105; marital relationship 56, 75, 122-5; sexual orientation 59, 68, 71-2, 122-5, 130, 190-3; early relationship with Philip Augustus 70-3; in Sicily 77-84; in Cyprus 86-92; recurrent illnesses 21, 95, 97-8; public penances 79-81, 120-2; Arab view of 100; poems attributed to 102, 109-10; captivity and release 107, 112-13; character and reputation 116-17; military activities in France 117-18; death 22, 131-4, 150-1, 184
Richard of Devizes 27, 71, 84, 94, 201 n. 28, 210 n. 42
Richard Tyoul 167, 169
de Riquer, M. 109, 209 n. 18
Robert d'Arbrissel 9

Robert of Alençon 164
Robert of Turnham 91
Rocabruna, castle 90, 128, 150, 211 n. 53
Rodrigo Jiménez de Rada 33-6, 46, 49, 55
Roger of Howden 27, 31, 36, 67, 71, 72, 76, 79, 96, 105, 111-12, 119-26, 127, 130, 191, 193, 201 n. 28, 210 n. 35-6, 213 n. 6-7, n. 9-10, 214 n. 20, n. 28
Romance of Richard Coeur De Lion 83-4, 221 n. 18
Romance of the Rose 116
Rome 76
Roncesvalles 30, 35, 40, 50, 197
Rosenthal, J. 15
Rouen 118, 126, 131, 146

Sacramentum Gelasianum 139
St Jean Pied de Port 30, 90, 128, 150
St John of the Cross (S. Juan de la Cruz) 18
St Pierre de la Cour 147, 157, 161, 164; under interdict 164-8; 169; *Cartulaire* of 162, 218 n. 32, 219 n. 52
St Vincent, abbey 160, 176
Saladin 95-6, 99, 100, 102, 103-4
Salerno 77
Salomón Alfaquí of Tudela 42
Sancho VI, El Sabio, king of Navarre 31-35, 37, 46-7, 75, 118, 128, 150, 204 n. 28, 208 n. 15
Sancho VII, El Fuerte, king of Navarre 21, 30, 31, 34, 35, 46, 49-50, 111, 118, 127, 145, 146, 168, 178-9, 181, 205 n. 41
Sanguesa 41
Saumur 9, 118, 134, 142
Scolastica, widow of Le Mans 167
Scott, Sir W. 14
Sicily 48, 71, 76, 77
Simon, cleric 149, 153
Song of Roland 40, 73, 100, 209 n. 27
Song of Songs 17
Stephen Langton, archbishop 152
Stephen Longchamp 99
Stephen of Turnham 111, 143, 158

Stow, K. 174, 205 n. 36, 219 n. 58

Stothard, C. 188

Stubbs, Bishop W. 193, 207 n. 1, 221 n. 19

Strickland, Agnes 26, 126, 188, 196, 201 n. 23

Taillebourg 128

Talmont sur Jard 69, 70, 160

Tancred of Lecce 78

Templars 104

Tenencias, in Navarre 54, 128, 206 n. 60

Thibaut III, count of Champagne 34, 49, 96, 135

Thibaut IV of Champagne, king of Navarre 21, 31, 34, 35, 42, 179, 180, 183

Thomas a Beckett 43, 60, 80

Thomas Beaumont 185

Thorée 90, 126, 167, 168-9, 218 n. 45

Tillières 124

Tristan legend 25, 69, 149, 211 n. 51

Tristan of Béroul 122

Tristan of Thomas 89-90, 211 n. 49

Troubadours 24-5, 61, 109, 211 n. 50; in Spain 43; relations with the Angevins 65; on Crusade 103

Tudela 34, 37, 38-9, 41, 50, 54, 118, 146, 177, 179, 180, 204 n. 27, 219 n. 72

Tulebras, abbey 45, 55, 56, 180

Turner, Ralph 192

Ultrapuertos 30, 112, 128, 212 n. 53

Ubieto Arteta, A. 54, 206 n. 60

Venice 108

Vexin (Normandy) 73, 74

Vie Mancelle 188

Wace 24, 113, 200 n. 15

Walter of Guiseborough 22, 132-3, 215 n. 45

Walter (Gautier) of Perseigne 149, 153, 184-5

Widows, in Middle Ages 137-41

William (Guillermo) chaplain of the queen 152, 180

William of Newburgh 83, 201-2 n. 28, 210 n. 38

William of Tomebu 111

William of Tyre 32, 33, 96, 207 n. 5

William the Conqueror 60, 157

William 'The Bad' king of Sicily 48

William 'The Good' king of Sicily 48, 78, 82

William the Marshal (Guillaume le Maréchal) 24, 66, 112, 117, 130, 132, 200 n. 16, 212 n. 62, 213 n. 16

William IX, count of Aquitaine 25, 61, 117, 201 n. 19

Winchester 112

Wood, M.A.E 153, *see also* Green